*Millie-Christine's signature on
the previous page was taken
from the back of the photograph
on page 189. It is dated 1873.*

MILLIE-CHRISTINE

John F. Blair, Publisher

Winston-Salem, North Carolina

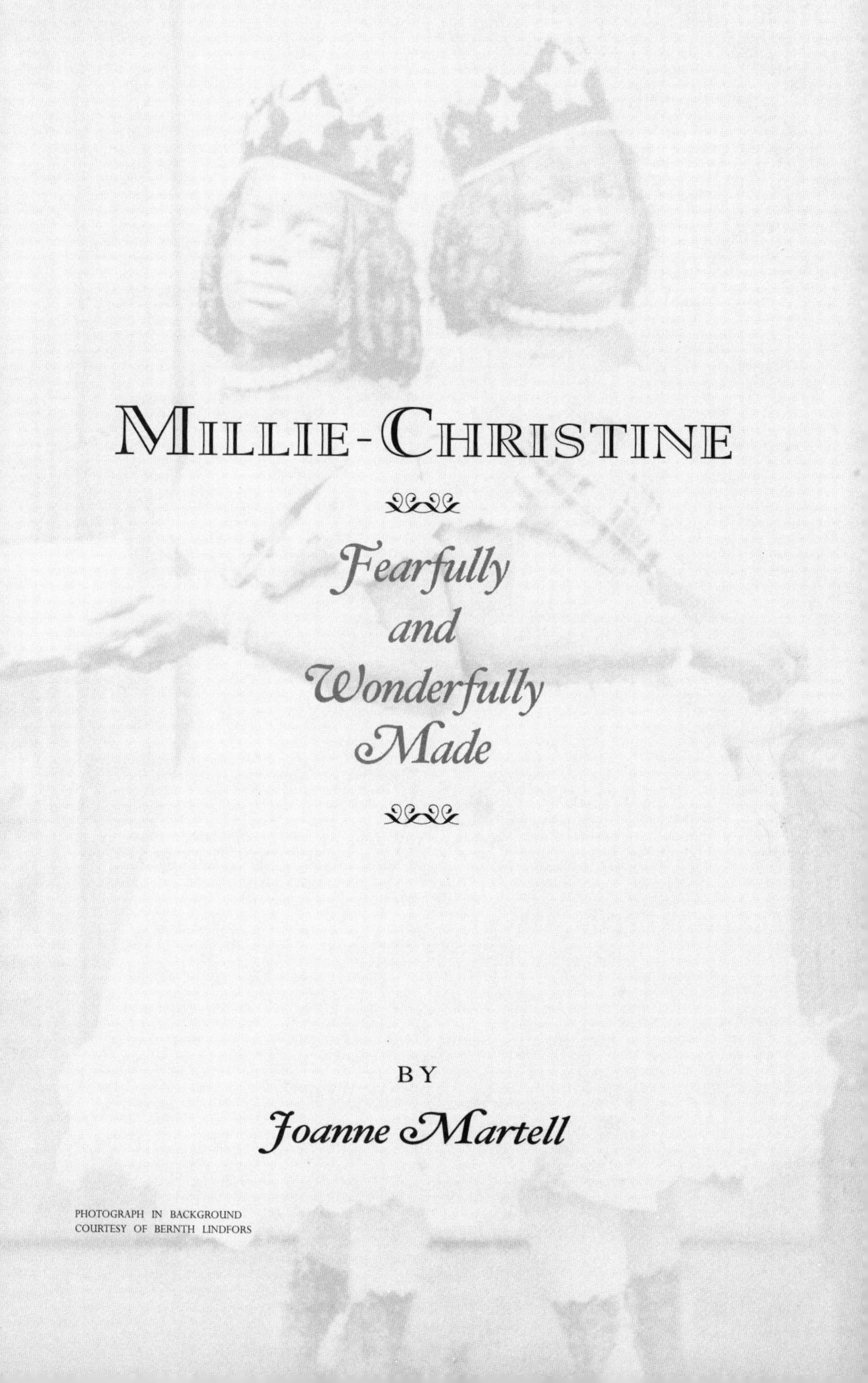

MILLIE-CHRISTINE

Fearfully and Wonderfully Made

BY

Joanne Martell

PHOTOGRAPH IN BACKGROUND
COURTESY OF BERNTH LINDFORS

DESIGN BY DEBRA LONG HAMPTON
PRINTED AND BOUND BY MCNAUGHTON & GUNN

The paper in this book meets the guidelines
for permanence and durability
of the Committee on Production Guidelines
for Book Longevity of the Council on Library Resources.

Library of Congress Cataloging-in-Publication Data

Martell, Joanne, 1926–
Millie-Christine: fearfully and wonderfully made /
by Joanne Martell.
p.   cm.
ISBN 0-89587-194-7 (hardcover : alk. paper)—
ISBN 0-89587-188-2 (pbk. : alk. paper)
1. Millie-Christine, b. 1851.
2. Siamese twins—Biography. I. Title.

QM691.M55 M37 2000
306.875—dc21
[B]
99-052515

Author's Note

Whether to speak of Millie-Christine as "she" or "they" posed a problem. Monemia McKoy said "my baby" or "my child." Family members called her "Sister." But most people outside the family looked at Millie-Christine and saw twins. "They had the nicest personalities," a neighbor recalled. Millie-Christine herself was ambiguous on the subject. "Although we speak of ourselves in the plural, we feel as *one person*," she wrote.

I handled the problem the same way Millie-Christine and people who knew her did—by using either form, as seemed appropriate to the context.

I have preserved the spellings and emphases in quoted material regardless of errors and inconsistencies, including variations in the names of Millie-Christine; and the McKoys; and Jabez

McKay, whose name altered over the years to McCoy. I have also preserved the writers' emphasis.

Finally, a word about the main biographical sources on Millie-Christine. What I refer to as the *History* (*History and Medical Description of the Two-Headed Girl*) dates to 1869. The *Two-Headed Nightingale* (*Biographical Sketch of Millie Christine, the Two-Headed Nightingale*) was written in 1871. The *Description* (*Description and Songs of Miss Millie Christine, the Two-Headed Nightingale*) appeared in 1882. Updated show biographies were later printed. The "Songs of Miss Millie-Christine" excerpts are from the music sections of these booklets.

*For thou hast possessed my reins;
thou hast covered me in my mother's womb.
I will praise thee; for I am fearfully and
wonderfully made. Marvelous are thy works,
and that my soul knoweth right well.*

Psalm 139, verses 13 and 14
Millie-Christine's favorite scripture

Chapter 1

Two heads, four arms, four feet,
All in one perfect body meet.

Millie-Christine's poem

onemia McKoy's amazing babies were born in 1851, the year Topsy came alive under Harriet Beecher Stowe's pen. Had Millie and Christine begun life as ordinary slave children, they would have "growed" like Topsy, rough and tumble, ignorant as puppies. Instead, they were extraordinary twins destined for an extraordinary life.

Aunt Hannah, a slave midwife, delivered Christine, then saw Millie's legs and coaxed her out, tiny feet first. "The larger twin was born first by a stomach presentation, and the second came by the breech," a doctor later reported.

The midwife roused both babies to noisy life but could not pull the slippery, joined bodies apart. One big girl and on her back a smaller twin. The upper bodies faced away from each other, merged at the coccyx into a single pelvis. Two sets of arms and legs. They weighed in at seventeen pounds. Aunt Hannah estimated the larger baby accounted for about twelve pounds and the little one about five. Millie was so frail, her mother said, that if it hadn't been for the legs and arms, she'd have thought it was only a knot on Chrissie's back, instead of a second child.

Jabez McKay, a North Carolina blacksmith, owned the whole family—father Jacob, mother Monemia, and all the offspring they begat. McKay had summoned Aunt Hannah on a July morning to help Monemia deliver her latest baby. The mother was thirty-two years old and stout, with a large frame and pelvis. She'd already borne seven normal children, five boys and two girls. Her labor with Millie-Christine was as brief and easy as any of the others, she said.

Though the summer countryside simmered with mosquitoes and killer fever, the joined sisters not only lived, they flourished. They survived against all odds, as had the Siamese Twins forty years earlier. That famous pair now lived in northwestern North Carolina, up near Mount Airy. Chang and Eng had left the show-business circuit a dozen years ago, rich enough to retire by the time they were twenty-eight years old. Choosing Bunker as a family name, they married sisters and kept them busy raising children. They bought good Surry County land and all the slaves they needed to work two profitable plantations.

Jabez McKay's farm, where Millie-Christine was born, lay in southeastern North Carolina, in Columbus County, ten miles from

Whiteville, the county seat. Marshland spread on all sides—Soule's Swamp to the south, Brown Marsh to the north and west, White Marsh to the east. During the Revolutionary War, General Francis Marion had earned his nickname—the "Swamp Fox"—sloshing through White Marsh, where he and his band of patriots took refuge after Charleston fell to the British.

Word about McKay's newborn marvel spread through the county like wildfire. "'Have you seen the girl?' was the first question asked of every one by every one, and pilgrimages to visit her became all the rage in the country side," says a circus biography of Millie-Christine.

Fascinated visitors discovered that if they pinched the arm of one, only she fussed. But if they tickled the toes of either, both babies giggled. Strangers saw them as twins, but to Monemia, Millie-Christine was her baby, her child. Singular. The family called her "Sister."

Little Millie gradually caught up with her robust sister, although she would always remain slightly smaller. "Remarkably healthy and spritely," Dr. P. C. Gooch reported in an 1852 medical journal. When he saw them, "the older one was in a tranquil sleep, but it was awakened by the action of the bowels of the younger and smaller sister, who was then suffering from diarrhoea."

The circus booklet credits Millie-Christine's good health to tender care by the McKays. "The master himself and his amiable lady," it says, "without stopping to question the designs of Providence, immediately surrounded the extraordinary infant with such care and attention as enabled it to thrive and grow. The dual-headed child was taken from the cabin to the mansion, and Mr. McCoy's family commenced then a course of care and attention to her health and welfare."

More likely, Monemia tended her own remarkable baby. The 1840 census had recorded Jabez McKay and wife—no names for anyone but heads of households were listed on that census—as being between the ages of twenty and thirty. It also tallied one free white girl, plus eleven adult slaves and five slave children. According to Columbus County census records, by the time Millie-Christine was born in 1851, Jabez had lost his amiable lady. Age thirty-eight, occupation blacksmith, he raised four young children in the McKay "mansion." They were Ann, eight; Lucy, seven; John Lloyd, five; and James, three.

Before Millie-Christine was a year old, according to the circus biography, McKay, "being a man in very moderate circumstances, a plain farmer, thinking the girl would become a burden to him and annoyed with the frequent visits of strangers to see her, determined to dispose of her." He was looking for a buyer who understood the tricks of the exhibition business.

The ideal promoter would have been Phineas T. Barnum, the king of showmen. He'd have been delighted with curious strangers flocking to see Millie-Christine—the more the better. As P. T. once said, "Every crowd has a silver lining!" A month before Millie-Christine's birth, Barnum had concluded a wildly successful American tour with Jenny Lind, the "Swedish Nightingale." Wealthy beyond most men's dreams, he was currently back running his fabulous American Museum in New York City.

Although Millie-Christine's path would eventually cross Barnum's, McKay found her first manager closer to home, a man who understood southern ways. When she was ten months old, he made a deal with a South Carolinian by the name of John C. Pervis. On a Tuesday in May, McKay, Pervis, lawyer John Maultsby, and second witness Thomas Memory from the Memory Company store on Courthouse

Square gathered at the county clerk's office in the new courthouse in Whiteville. A bill of sale was what they wanted, with a couple of special provisions. The clerk dipped his pen and set to work recording the bargain.

"Know all men by these presents," the document began, and went on to record that on May 18, 1852, Jabez McKay of the county of Columbus in the state of North Carolina and John C. Pervis of the Chesterfield district in the state of South Carolina entered into an agreement whereby McKay "doth . . . bargain sell and deliver," for the sum of one thousand dollars, "certain twin negro girls about ten months old, and united from their birth."

Pervis was to exhibit the twin girls for pay and give one-fourth of the net proceeds to McKay. He was also to pay McKay one-fourth of the proceeds should he find someone else eager to buy the sisters. McKay agreed to let Monemia accompany the twins without charge for as long as Pervis kept them. In case they were sold to anyone else or died, the mother was to be returned to McKay.

The bill of sale was thus duly signed, sealed, and delivered.

Traces of Millie-Christine's and Monemia's life with Pervis have disappeared, lost to time. The final mention of Pervis's name turned up in another contract with McKay, dated September 30, 1853, fourteen months after the original sale. This time, Pervis paid a final two hundred dollars to McKay, apparently to broker a deal between McKay and a new buyer. He then bowed out of Millie-Christine's story. Maybe Pervis tired of show business. Or perhaps he'd been out scouting for a high-stakes buyer all along and left satisfied with his cut of the final sale price.

The successful new bidder was a Mr. Brower. As for the exact amount, take your choice. The 1882 circus *Description* of the twins' life reported ten thousand dollars. Their 1869 *History* said that Brower "gave for us, two strange lumps of humanity, the sum of thirty thousand dollars." A 1912 *New York Times* story upped the figure to forty thousand.

Whatever the price, there was one major hitch. "This Brower was not possessed of the requisite cash to back his faith, and only offered to give a note of hand for the purchase money," said the *Description*. Blacksmith McKay, showing good business sense, "naturally desired some responsible person to whom to look for the money in case of the non-payment of the note when due."

Brower found such a backer in Joseph Pearson Smith, a respectable and well-to-do merchant from Wadesboro, North Carolina. With Smith as cosigner of the promissory note, Jabez McKay handed over his odd little twins.

Manager Brower began brilliantly with the sisters. A week after the sale, he announced in the *Raleigh Register* that the public would have a chance to see the two-year-old twins at North Carolina's first official state fair.

"GREAT ATTRACTION!" ran the headline. "THE CELEBRATED CAROLINA TWINS will be exhibited at Raleigh during the Agricultural Fair. These children have been pronounced by Physicians the most interesting specimen of Humanity ever seen, . . . healthy, active, and for their age, unusually intelligent. They are joined together at the back by the union of the two spines in one, making the connection much more intimate than that of the Siamese Twins. Many Physicians have examined them, and all agree in their being the greatest curiosity ever seen or heard of—some of their organs being in common, while others are perfectly distinct."

The piece went on to say that, often, one child was playful and active while the other was fast asleep. "Visitors have expressed surprise to find them so PERT and CUNNING, with such intelligent, happy faces, where they had not expected to see such interesting children. Call at once if you would not miss the opportunity of seeing the greatest wonder of the Age, as you may ne'er look upon their like again. Doors open from 9 o'clock A.M. till 12 P.M. for Ladies only; and from 2 P.M. till 4, for gentlemen alone."

Directly beneath the item about the Carolina Twins was an ad for a runaway slave from Orange County: "$100 REWARD. Ran away from the subscriber, . . . a negro Boy named William Henry. . . . The above reward will be given if caught out of the State, or Fifty Dollars if taken in this State, and delivered to me . . . or in any jail so that I can get him." This routine ad in an 1850s southern newspaper had nothing to do with the twins—except for the final, prophetic sentence: "The subscriber has a suspicion that the boy has been taken off by some unprincipled white man, who may undertake to pass him off as his property." If the tiny sisters had somehow wandered into a fortuneteller's tent at the fair, a Gypsy might have foretold exactly such a future for them.

But in those golden days of October 1853, the twins were safe at the fair. "It was a grand spectacle, to see those extensive grounds gay with banners and lively with music," the paper said. "Our streets are thronged with immense and eager crowds, and all the avenues leading to the Fair Grounds blockaded with vehicles of every description. Nothing like the number of persons present has been seen here since the great Whig Convention of 1840."

The fair turned out to be the roaring success that boosters had hoped for. One hundred fifty-seven exhibits sat on display in the new buildings. There were farm implements—smut machine, corn sheller, one-, two-, and four-horse ploughs. There was prizewinning livestock. There were curiosities like "a saw fish sword and a pearl shell from the Dead Sea carved by Jews in Jerusalem," according to the

Register. There were homemade cakes and candy and blackberry wine. There were flowers, prize tomatoes, a box of "Segars," and a magnificent display of North Carolina buggies and carriages "which might fear no rivalry with the best work of the North, either in beauty of design or excellence of workmanship."

Outside the exhibit halls, Siva's Troupe of Chinese Jugglers and Acrobats, forty-two in number, performed amazing tricks at a special side show.

The daily entrance fee was twenty-five cents for a person, fifty cents for a buggy, and a dollar for a carriage. Spend another fifty cents and you could watch the celebrated Carolina Twins at play— "pert and cunning," as the ads promised. Millie and Chrissie were already used to being stared at. They chatted away to each other and to visitors in the manner of all two-year-olds.

A physician who saw them about this time noted that "their intellectual operations are as distinct as though no union existed; they amuse themselves together as do other children—sometimes become angry and resort to blows, and even at their early age are very ready each to accuse the other of faults committed between them."

Walking was a problem. Mostly, Chrissie set out for wherever she wanted to go, while Millie helplessly back-stepped along until they both fell down. As the doctor explained, "They are still too young to determine what will be for them the easiest mode of progression." He predicted that they would ultimately adopt a kind of side step.

Four to six thousand visitors roamed the fairgrounds daily. If half of them handed over fifty cents to see the sisters—twenty-five hundred customers a day for four days—then Brower's take would have added up to roughly five thousand dollars for his first venture with the twins.

It's possible that Monemia accompanied them to the fair. McKay may have let her go with Brower as far as Raleigh. If he did, the twins still had their mother for a few final days. But even if that was the case, Monemia had to give up her special children when the fair shut down on Friday, October 18. The closing gates marked the twins' last sight and scent and feel of their mother for what would seem forever. The saving grace was that they would never have to face the world alone. Millie had Chrissie and Chrissie had Millie, so long as they both should live.

Brower's grand success with Millie-Christine inspired him to venture farther from home. New Orleans doctors encouraged him to bring her down so they could have a look. The worldly old city was a showman's paradise, Brower knew. Millie-Christine was strong and healthy. It was time to take to the road.

Monemia with her amazing babies,
from 1857 "African Twins" poster on page 66.
NORTH CAROLINA DIVISION OF ARCHIVES AND HISTORY

Brower's contact promised to set up medical examinations and invite the press. Promoters with extraordinary living curiosities to exhibit followed such procedures in each new town. Before opening the doors to the general public, they invited local medical men to come satisfy their scientific curiosity. For Millie-Christine, physical examinations were a routine part of life. Physicians probed and pinched above and below, measured the sacral union, inspected the curiously merged genitalia. The doctors then signed a paper certifying that Millie-Christine was the genuine article. The next step was to send copies, press releases, and publicity for the show to local newspapers.

Brower intended to keep Millie-Christine out of the public eye until opening day. The circus biography says that Brower's New Orleans agent advised him to keep her presence in the city as quiet as possible, "as the desire to see her would undoubtedly be very great and might interfere with the examination."

This impossible plan meant that Brower had to smuggle his incredible toddlers into French Quarter lodgings, then wait discreetly without fanfare or fuss until the doctors gathered to examine them. His success depended upon mule-carriage drivers, landladies, maids, cooks, and newspaper reporters all keeping the secret.

Needless to say, "this precaution was not strictly regarded, and soon the rooms and the passages . . . were literally besieged with anxious crowds of people eager to get a sight of her," says the biography. At last, the New Orleans medical-school faculty filed in, conducted examinations, and unanimously endorsed Millie-Christine as "Nature's greatest wonder." By then, of course, half of New Orleans had already seen her free of charge.

On opening day, the show "succeeded but indifferently," and prospects showed no sign of improving. The biography blames Brower, who, "being quite ignorant of the business he had undertaken, despaired of success after a few more efforts."

Then, unexpectedly, like sunlight glinting off the river, Lady Luck seemed to flash a dazzling smile his way. Brower would not be the last of Millie-Christine's managers to mistake the lady's mischievous wink for a smile. He met a smooth-talking adventurer from Texas who boasted of his immense tracts of western land. He might be able to help Brower out, the fellow said. He offered an irresistible deal. "This swindler proposed to purchase the girl by giving for her lands, at a fair market valuation, to the amount of forty-five thousand dollars," according to the *Description*.

Forty-five thousand dollars! Brower accepted the offer, packed up Millie-Christine, and handed her over to "the would-be millionaire." He was to receive the land deeds the following day.

But when neither the Texan nor the deeds were forthcoming, the unpleasant fact broke upon Brower that he had been duped— that his Millie-Christine had vanished as utterly as his Texas millionaire. Indeed, the kidnapper had covered his tracks so adroitly that Brower found "no clue to her, or even the direction she had been carried," says the biography.

After weeks of useless searching, he made his gloomy way back to North Carolina to break the news to Joseph Pearson Smith. Without the sisters, Brower confessed, he was bankrupt. Smith, left holding the promissory note, was now the lucky owner of the celebrated (although missing) Carolina Twins.

The two men grimly set off for Jabez McKay's farm to relate the shocking story. With Monemia's screams ringing in his ears, Brower then dropped out of Millie-Christine's life.

"Words are inadequate to describe the anguish of the parent on learning the fate of her child," the biography says. "For a time she was perfectly frantic, during six days refusing food, and for the same number of nights her eyes did not close in sleep. Her excellent character, uniform kindness and amiable disposition had made her a general favorite, so that everything that could be was cheerfully done to comfort and soothe her mind. She was promised that no amount of money should be spared, no effort left untried to procure her much-cherished child."

Smith paid off the note he'd guaranteed and received from Jabez McKay "a deed which made him the exclusive owner, under then existing laws, of the person of Millie Christine"—when and if he found her.

Thirty-eight-year-old Joseph Pearson Smith managed his father's successful general store, Smith & Sons of Wadesboro. Determined to recover his investment, he approached his dilemma with a businessman's straightforward, practical question: Where was Millie-Christine, and if found, how was she to be recovered? For the answer, he hired private investigator T. A. Vestal, of Selma, Alabama, said to be one of the shrewdest detectives in the country.

Vestal immediately commenced operations, although the trail was cold. He ran down rumors, followed leads. Millie-Christine had not gone the way of ordinary runaway slaves. She was traveling a very different route, moving within a show-business world Vestal didn't know much about and would be a long time learning.

Chapter 2

$\mathcal{W}$hen they were seventeen, the twins wrote a brief history of their early misadventures.

"The man who took us away," they said, "could not, or rather *did not dare* to publicly exhibit us, but gave private exhibitions to scientific bodies, thus reaping quite a handsome income off of 'two little black girls' whom he had stolen away. Finally, when we had been thus dragged over the country for nearly two years . . . our custodian disposed of us to another speculator. . . . He took us to

Philadelphia and placed us in a small Museum in Chestnut street, near Sixth, then under the management of Col. Wood, who is, we believe, somewhat known as a showman."

In later years, one of the twins' managers swore in a custody hearing that he'd found them in Philadelphia with a drunkard who was taking miserable care of them.

In August 1854, just turned three years old, the children showed up at P. T. Barnum's famous American Museum in New York City, where they were billed as "the Celebrated African United Twins."

Barnum's gaudy palace stood on lower Broadway opposite St. Paul's Church and the fashionable Astor House hotel. The five-story corner building had its main entrance on Broadway. It angled at the corner, formed a second facade, then made another shallow angle for a third face on Ann Street.

The "Prince of Advertising" decorated all three sides with full-color oval paintings of animals. Such creatures as a giraffe, an ostrich, and a python filled the spaces between the windows of the upper four stories. Gigantic letters spelled out BARNUM'S AMERICAN MUSEUM. Along the roof edge, foreign flags snapped in the wind. An enormous Stars and Stripes waved over all. From across the street, the museum resembled a three-sided, five-story circus billboard.

"Advertising is like learning—a little is a dangerous thing," Barnum once said.

He would try anything and buy anything to make his museum irresistible to any person with twenty-five cents to spend. "Although I can make more money with General Thumb in two months than I can in the American Museum in a year," he said, "yet my whole pride lies centered in the museum." He was referring to Charlie Stratton, a twenty-five-inch midget Barnum had transformed into the impish

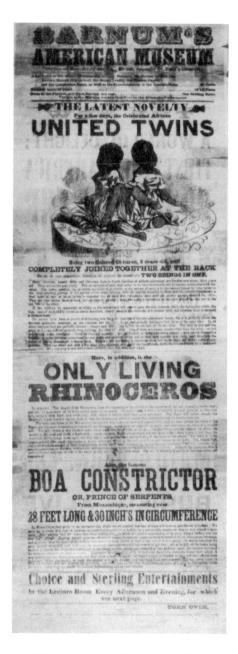

The earliest image of Millie-Christine, from P.T. Barnum's 1854 American Museum poster

General Tom Thumb. Tom had been five years old when Barnum signed him up.

The summer Millie-Christine came to the museum, Tom was sixteen, as popular as ever, and a regular performer there between road shows. If General Thumb was in town when Millie-Christine arrived, she'd have seen his tiny carriage parked conspicuously in front of the museum. Visitors swooned over Tom's adorable carriage. It "will kill the public," Barnum had predicted when he ordered it. "It will be the greatest hit in the universe, see if it ain't!"

All day and far into the evening, a band played from the balcony over the museum's main entrance. As anyone passing by could hear, the musicians were not chosen for talent. A fellow was picked for Barnum's outdoor band because he could blast his trombone or tuba or trumpet loud enough to drown out Broadway's hurly-burly.

Barnum called himself "a caterer of amusements," and he served all tastes. His collection was a kaleidoscope of treasures and horrors. A grand staircase led to the main exhibition rooms one flight up. Upstairs, the Celebrated African United Twins made friends with a multitude of out-of-the-ordinary folks—grownups like Tom Thumb, as small as the twins; lofty giants; a lady twice as fat as the twins' mama; a man as skinny as the bare bones in the Grand Skeleton Chamber.

If one had to stay in New York City during August's dog days, the museum was a delightful place to pass the time. There was a rooftop garden where one might catch a breeze and view the city. Barnum supplied free ice water on every floor. Waiters served ice cream and lemonade from the refreshment stand near the Lecture Room stage. Mr. B. was a reformed drinker. He'd long since signed a Temperance Society pledge, and his museum was a teetotaling establishment. If a customer slipped away from the Lecture Room between the acts of a play and hurried down the street for a quick drink, he had to buy a new ticket before he could return to his seat.

Millie-Christine didn't see much of the great man that August. Ordinarily, he was at the museum daily, shaking hands with thrilled visitors, leading new performers like Millie-Christine onto the theatre stage between play acts, overseeing day-to-day business. That particular summer, he came into the city only once or twice a month. He spent most days at his Connecticut estate, working on *The Life of P. T. Barnum, Written by Himself*, a frank account of his outrageous professional life. His publisher had begged him to finish it in time for Christmas sales.

If the twins had landed at the American Museum another season, when Barnum wasn't so busy, he might have focused his promotional genius on them. If Detective Vestal had spotted the resulting publicity, he might have marched up the museum's grand staircase and reclaimed the stolen girls. As it was, if Vestal ever saw the advertising posters heralding the twins' appearance at Barnum's, it was too late to help him find Mr. Smith's kidnapped children.

The museum advertised Millie-Christine on a long, narrow poster. The "herald," as such announcements of coming attractions were called, measured twenty-four inches long by eight inches wide. Astonishing facts and compelling pictures were printed on both sides.

An eye-catching woodcut of Millie-Christine shows two dark-skinned youngsters sitting back to back, heads cocked toward the person sketching them. They are wearing a pretty dress with matching tops joined to a single skirt full enough to cover their lower bodies and short enough to show their striped stockings and neat little shoes. The artist posed them on a round table, presumably to keep them in one place for the picture.

Large letters in a flamboyant variety of type styles flashed the essential information. "BARNUM'S AMERICAN MUSEUM." "UNITED TWINS." "FRIDAY, August 4th, 1854." Smaller letters under the picture described the twins as "two Colored Children, 3 years old, and COMPLETELY JOINED TOGETHER AT THE BACK So as, in one important function of nature, to constitute TWO BEINGS IN ONE."

Twenty lines of small type gave further details. Doctors reading the poster might have recognized the description as a condensed version of an article in the July issue of the *American Journal of the Medical Science*. The article presented the findings of a southern physician who'd examined "Milly and Christian," as he called them, at age two. Laymen might have stumbled over some of the terminology: "The os coccygis of each child seems to . . . become continuous with the other. . . . The lower portion, to probably one-third of . . . the sacrum of each is in like manner joined by bony union to the corresponding portion of the sacrum of the other, forming, with the muscles attached to them and the general integument, a firm band of two or three inches in diameter, but so short that the nates of each child are pressed against those of the other."

The picture of little Millie-Christine would pull in the customers. The text gave the exhibit a scientific tone.

What a tremendous bargain the old museum was! Twenty-five cents (twelve and a half cents for children under ten) bought a look at the latest novelties (such as Millie-Christine) and a multitude of permanent wonders crammed into seven exhibition halls—the "Seven Saloons," as in Seven Wonders of the World. You could wander all day through the Hall of Statuary, which featured authentic, naked Italian and Greek classical figures; the Picture Gallery; the Natural History Department; and the Chinese Saloon.

The Happy Family exhibit on the top floor was a Barnum tradition. The "family" was a renewable assortment of live owls, mice, wildcats, birds, monkeys—predators and prey all dwelling together in one spacious cage. A full-time attendant stayed close by to lecture and stand guard. A vital part of his job was keeping each creature well supplied with its favorite food, the objective being to make sure the predators never grew hungry. The Happy Family and Barnum's other animals lived beneath the roof garden. The birds and beasts gained sunshine from skylights and were soothed by a bubbling fountain installed as part of their habitat.

Barnum displayed wild creatures many Americans had never even heard about, like a rhinoceros, or "unicorn," as he sometimes called his specimen, which he claimed was the only such animal in America. Another fascinating creature the twins may have seen was Barnum's "famous BOA CONSTRICTOR, OR PRINCE OF SERPENTS, From Mozambique, measuring over 28 FEET LONG & 30 INCH'S IN CIR-CUMFERENCE." Visitors shivered in fascinated horror, listening to the keeper's lecture and reading the spiel from the same herald that announced the African Twins.

Two flights down from the animal dens was the Lecture Room, the most up-to-date theatre in New York City. The hall could seat three thousand people and was decorated with glittering chandeliers, gold-leaf trim, and giant wall mirrors. Barnum promised entertainment fit for women and children, with never a word "offensive to morals or religion" nor "calculated to bring a blush upon the cheek of modesty." Straight-laced people who wouldn't be caught dead in a regular theatre attended Barnum's Lecture Room with almost-clear consciences. To further encourage family trade, he hired sharp-eyed house detectives to collar "every person of either sex whose actions indicated loose habits" and to quick-step them out of the building.

Barnum employed a full orchestra for his theatre. The pianist played a thousand-dollar grand piano. The staff included a full-time repertory ensemble of thirty-six actors and actresses. A comic drama, *From Village to Court*, was playing matinees during Millie-Christine's run. "NEW and exceedingly chaste, as well as most laughable . . . just received from London," the promotion went. Millie-Christine, stationed backstage with some of the museum's other wonders, made brief appearances between the acts. Barnum himself, if he happened to be in town, led her onstage. Standing in front of the new drop curtain, which featured a grand view of Washington, D.C., as it would look if the congressional wings of the Capitol were ever completed, he introduced her to the audience.

Resident actors had to keep their wits about them, for they took on new roles in each of the three daily plays on the August program. Mr. J. L. Monroe, for example, starred as the comical Baron Von Grosonbach in the afternoon play. Evenings at eight o'clock, the troupe put on new faces and accents for the "pleasing Comedy of the MAID OF MUNSTER." This time, Monroe played Sir Lawrence Paragon. The instant the curtain closed on the last line, while the prop crew switched scenery, he and the other actors magically transformed themselves into new characters. Monroe was now King Aboulifar, ready to appear in the concluding play of the evening, "the laughable Extravaganza in 2 acts of BURIED ALIVE OR, THE COCKNEY IN CHINA."

Millie-Christine had missed Barnum's version of *Uncle Tom's Cabin* a year earlier. His script was a happy-ending distortion of the passionate book. Harriet Beecher Stowe was so distressed when she saw a Boston company perform the same upbeat script that she left the theatre in protest.

Barnum's interpretation buried the antislavery message beneath sensational scenery and ingenious stage effects. White actors rubbed on burnt-cork makeup and played the story's black characters as standard comical minstrel types. Audiences loved the show for the special effects. The second act opened with a panorama of the Mississippi River by moonlight, the steamboat *Belle Rivière* gliding across the scene, black smoke—real smoke—rolling from the stack.

Barnum called his *Uncle Tom* the "sumptuous version." A rival theatre called it the "humbug version." *New York Tribune* editor Horace Greeley, though he was Barnum's chum, said it was "mere burlesque." Ticket sales were phenomenal.

✿❀✿

After her August engagement at Barnum's American Museum, the kidnapped Millie-Christine again slipped out of sight.

All the while, and all in vain, Detective Vestal had been trying to catch up with her. A year and a half after Joseph Pearson Smith hired him, rumor led Vestal to Philadelphia. There, says the circus biography, a Negro barber told him that about a year ago, a child answering her description had been in the city and for a time had been secreted in a cellar on Pine Street. Vestal found the place and knocked on the door. A wary face peered out. Vestal asked his questions and "through the influence of bribes . . . an old woman still living in a portion of the house" told him that the child had been carried to New York. The old woman pocketed Vestal's coins. He caught the morning train.

For five frustrating weeks, he crisscrossed New York City, wasting his time and Smith's money. "Every effort was made, but no further intelligence of her could be learned," Vestal told Smith later. "If any one knew of or had seen her there, their mouths were sealed to the influence of money or persuasion."

Though discouraged, Vestal was determined to continue the search. Detective work is a combination of luck, bribery, deductive reasoning, and patience. Luck and bribes having failed, he tried logic. He had every reason to believe Millie-Christine was still alive. When taken from New Orleans, she'd been in excellent health. He'd watched the papers closely and found "no account of the death of any one answering her description, which certainly would have been the case had she died," says the biography.

Patient as a bloodhound, he persevered. Abandoning New York, he braved Boston—abolitionist territory. When a stranger with an Alabama drawl came asking questions about a lost slave child, Bostonians accepted his money. And like informants in Philadelphia and New York, they simply directed him elsewhere. From Boston, he returned to Philadelphia. A hot tip sent him to Newark, New Jersey. There, the biography reports, he "learned from a man then keeping a drinking house that at one time, when engaged as a cabman in the City of New York, he had been hired to convey a girl answering her description to a sailing vessel, the name of which he did not remember, bound for and ready to sail for Liverpool; that he had seen the vessel depart, and knew the child was aboard of her when she sailed."

Stymied at last, Vestal returned to North Carolina to deliver his unwelcome report to Joseph Pearson Smith. He had failed to recover Millie-Christine. Worse yet, as both men realized, whoever held her had evidently carried her beyond the reach of American fugitive slave laws.

Chapter 3

Fanned by the breezes, rocked by the tide,
In our nautilus barque we glide, we glide. . . .
Cast by the winds from shore to shore,
A moment you view us, and then no more.

Songs of Miss Millie-Christine

Millie-Christine passed her fourth birthday aboard the sailing ship *Arab* halfway to England. She'd sailed from Quebec, instead of New York, as Vestal's informant had told him. The vessel was bound for Liverpool, that much was true.

The twins now traveled with two enterprising showmen, William Thompson and William Millar, known professionally as Professor W. J. L. Millar.

The Guardians of these LITTLE WONDERS respectfully announce that, in compliance with the general desire expressed for their stay in Liverpool, they have made arrangements to give a

Professor Millar was a cheerful man, judging from a daguerreo-type portrait of him; the ends of his mustache twirl upward, echo-ing the smile lines beside his mouth. Though he was no Barnum, he was a clever, go-ahead fellow. Like Barnum, he had tried other lines of work but found the lure of show business irresistible. Fortunately, he preserved press clippings about his tumultuous couple of years with Millie-Christine, as well as a memoir entitled "Two-Headed Nightingale, How I Found and Lost Her."

"In April 1855," he began, "I was conducting the Iron City Com-mercial College at Pittsburg, Pennsylvania—an institution which I had founded, and as I was getting rather tired of remaining in one place I concluded to return to my former profession of manager and performer of various kinds of shows and entertainments, so I sold out the College."

He headed to Philadelphia. Unlike Detective Vestal, Professor Millar had valuable show-business connections. Asking around for a likely act to manage, he soon "heard through a friend that there was a strange and curious freak of nature which would secure a fortune to the proprietor, and be just the very thing to take to Europe," he wrote. "Being anxious to see the old world, I concluded to take hold of this wonderful natural freak, which turned out to be two negro children (girls) . . . united by nature at their backbones."

According to Millar's account, he located the twins in Boston, and to put it bluntly, he bought them cheap. He "found them in charge of a spotted woman, who told me she was their mother, of which I was rather doubtful, and soon found out that she was not really the Twins' mother. I told her I would pay her a certain amount of money if she would leave the children altogether, which she, without a moment's hesitation, accepted."

Professor W. J. L. Millar

The twins' version of the abduction differed. Since they were only three years old when Millar and Thompson carried them off, this "memory" was likely suggested by Thompson's later courtroom testimony in a custody battle. As the twins relate the episode in their *History*, they were on exhibition at Colonel Wood's Chestnut Street museum in Philadelphia. "While there, a party saw us, and hearing that we were born South, came to the conclusion to get possession of us. He went to the authorities and said we were slaves, brought into a free State, where we were unjustly deprived of our liberty." That individual asked the court to exercise its jurisdiction and "take us away from the party who held us, and to appoint a guardian for us. This dodge did not work well, for the man who had us spirited us away before the necessary papers could be served."

Whatever really happened, Professor Millar insisted he found Millie-Christine in Boston and was able to "take hold of this wonderful natural freak" by his own efforts. He made no mention of partner Thompson, although in fact they worked together. By the time the professor wrote his piece about how he found and lost the Two-Headed Nightingale, he was trying to forget Thompson had ever existed. They'd had a violent split-up, all because of Millie-Christine.

The partnership began well enough. Once Millar and Thompson managed to get their hands on the twins, they hired a nursemaid, "a lady long resident in Cuba and the slave states of America." Besides caring for the sisters, she'd be part of the show. Visitors would ask questions about the children. The woman was knowledgeable about southern ways, and the partners could coach her on what to say about the twins' past.

Public exhibition of the little twins posed a touchy problem. President Franklin Pierce was strictly enforcing the Fugitive Slave Act throughout the northern states. United States marshals chased down runaways who made their way to freedom, and federal commissioners swiftly returned them on a one-way passage south. Obviously, no one was going to accuse the joined youngsters of running away from home on their own four feet. Yet at any moment, a legal owner might turn up to claim them. Even if that did not happen, picture the awkwardness if, during a performance, someone in the audience asked what right the showmen had to the children. Millar certainly could not explain how he'd paid off a mysterious "spotted woman" in Boston and simply taken the twins.

Prudence pointed the little troupe farther north, across the border, where fugitive slave questions would not interfere with the show. "As I had never been to Canada," Millar said, "I concluded to go to Montreal." He bought one-way tickets for the party, since he was not planning to return to the United States anytime soon.

Across the border at Rouse's Point, the twins became legally free, although it made no difference at all in their daily life. Only the scenery changed.

Henry David Thoreau had journeyed to Canada by train a few years before the twins. It's easy to visualize what they saw from his account of the trip. North of the border, the steam-train passenger car rolled past shop signs decorated with fierce British lions. Soldiers in red coats and white kid gloves drilled at every important point on the way. Country folk speaking French boarded the cars dressed in gray homespun much like the twins' people wore back in Columbus County, North Carolina. The cars joggled on past Mount Royal. The St. Lawrence River widened to a lake. "*La prairie!*" shouted the conductor. "*Montréal!*" The train ground to a stop opposite the island city, whose tin roofs glittered across the water. "Their reflections fell on the eye like a clash of cymbals on the ear," wrote Thoreau upon catching sight of Montreal.

The twins' party detrained and caught a ferry across the great harbor. The wharf swarmed with cabs and carriages for hire. Millar and Thompson likely hailed a *calèche* with an accordion-fold top to shield the twins from public view as the driver urged his horse up the slope of the quay.

The showmen rented Mechanics' Hall for the twins' Canadian debut. They exhibited there for two weeks. At the close of the run, they caught a St. Lawrence steamer downriver to Quebec City's enormous freshwater harbor. Visitors like Thoreau, more agile than the sisters, could trudge up to *la Ville Québec* along a narrow street, climb wooden steps called the "Break-neck Stairs," navigate another steep street blasted through rock, and at last glimpse the town through a massive stone gate. The twins entered by carriage and clattered into the city past the cannon guarding the gateway, a uniformed sentinel at his post. "I rubbed my eyes to be sure that I was in the nineteenth century," Thoreau wrote upon entering the walled fortress-city.

Millie-Christine's little company settled into Russell's Hotel at 22 rue des Jardins. A cannon boomed at Cape Diamond three times a day. On the streets, soldiers were everywhere, dressed in splendid uniforms. Kilted Highlanders and Royal Irish strode by. Esquimaux dogs trotted along harnessed to little carts, delivering milk and groceries and pulling firewood up and down hilly lanes.

"I soon made arrangements to give our levees in one of the large parlours of the hotel," said Millar, "and my curious charge caused amazement and wonder in the old-fashioned, picturesque stronghold of Canada." Visitors spoke to Millie-Christine in amusing French Canadian, English, and Scottish accents and fresh-off-the-boat Irish brogue.

One aspect of a manager's job was coming up with a colorful

background story to captivate the press and the public. Millar and Thompson's history of the twins—part counterfeit and perhaps part true—appeared in the *Quebec Mercury* on June 23. "They were born in Africa," the partners told the *Mercury* reporter, "and when only a year old were dragged off together with both their parents, and three brothers and two sisters, and sold into slavery at Cuba."

During the winter of 1853, the story continued, a Dr. Maginley of North Carolina, visiting a friend in Cuba, purchased them as interesting natural curiosities and took them to the United States. Unfortunately, the doctor, who was very kind, died early the following year. At that point, the twins were sold with the remainder of his estate and thrown upon the world.

The sisters' next purchaser paid four hundred dollars and took them to Philadelphia. "Pennsylvania being a free state, and the little slaves not being runaway negroes, the government, by a judgment of the court, declared them free, and appointed Professor Millar and Mr. Thompson their guardians; and they annually, for five years, pay a certain sum to the state for the purpose of purchasing the freedom of their parents and brothers and sisters, to whom they will be united when manumitted."

This Canadian version clashed badly with Millar's tale of how he had found the twins in Boston. Nevertheless, the partners' story was artful and appealing, designed to satisfy everyone. The children's supposed African birth protected Millar and Thompson. Importing African slaves to the States had been illegal for forty-odd years, so any previous owner would hesitate to step forward to claim the twins. Second, the ward-guardian relationship pacified abolitionists. Canadians would be unlikely to argue Pennsylvania law or to check court records in faraway Philadelphia. Finally, most people would agree that the children were "entitled to the sympathies of the benevo-lent," as the *Mercury* suggested, since the poor little things were work-ing to free their captive family. That claim alone must have sent many a kind soul rushing to Russell's Hotel for tickets.

The newspaper article also spotlighted a macabre fact that sooner or later struck everyone who saw the sisters. "They are inseparably united . . . and their existence is doubly hazardous, as the death of the one would inevitably involve the destruction of the other."

The *Mercury* reporter (possibly prompted by Millar and Thomp-son) championed Millie-Christine over Chang and Eng, who had toured lower Canada twenty years earlier. "The Siamese twins, on the other hand," he scoffed, "whose accidental union has excited so much wonder and curiosity in all parts of the world, could be sepa-rated without the slightest risk to either; they, however, prefer to perpetuate a disgusting union from mercenary motives, that would not have lasted a single hour had their birth occurred in a civilised or scientific community."

Chang and Eng were born in 1811 in exotic Siam, a kingdom as disdainful of the civilized communities of the outside world as the western "barbarians" were of Siam. The brothers, born face to face and connected by a ligament growing between their rib cages, were sons of a Chinese fisherman and a mother who encouraged them to live as active and normal a life as possible. They grew up in a thatched-roof bamboo house set on an anchored river raft. The boys fished, swam, rowed the family boat, and wrestled with brothers and play-mates. Their strenuous life gradually stretched the connecting liga-ment from four inches to five and a half, until they could walk and run nearly side by side, arms around each other's shoulders.

The brothers often longed to be separated, but doctors from Siam, Europe, and the best medical colleges in the United States

Chang and Eng Bunker
NORTH CAROLINA DIVISION OF ARCHIVES AND HISTORY

advised against the operation. No matter what the *Mercury* said, there was enormous risk. Medical literature had recorded occasional failed attempts to separate joined twins. In 1689, a remarkable Dr. Fatio had set a Swiss pair free by severing their short connecting ligament with surgical wire. Chang and Eng's larger band seemed to be mostly cartilage, but there was a strong possibility that they shared the peritoneal cavity. If so, the tiniest slip of the wire or knife could expose their stomachs, intestines, and livers to hemorrhage or fatal infection. Only if one brother died before the other, surgeons agreed, would cutting them apart be worth the risk. Even then, the attempt would need to be immediate and swift.

Meanwhile, still very much alive, the Siamese Twins were busy farming their two North Carolina plantations, dealing with their two wives, raising their many children, and trying to avoid going back on the road.

❦❦❦

After two successful weeks in Quebec, Millie-Christine's handlers felt ready to tackle Great Britain. Before they sailed, they pondered a tempting promotional stunt. "Captain Allan, of the now famous firm of Allan Brothers, offered to call a large ship he was then building *The African Twins* and give our party a free passage to Liverpool," said Millar, "but the ship would not be finished for two months, so I decided to go with Captain Graham, and set sail for England's greatest seaport on the 1st of July 1855."

Captain Graham's *Arab* was a New Brunswick–built, 933-ton, three-masted, square-rigged sailing ship. Her figurehead was a carved and painted dark-skinned man whose eyes kept perpetual watch for approaching squalls and waterspouts. On deck, the twins' Cuban caretaker kept similar watch over them. For three and a half weeks, she managed to keep the lively four-year-olds from washing off the deck in high seas and climbing overboard during fine weather. The *Arab* was 153 feet long and 31 feet broad. There was only one deck, though she had beams below for another. The below-deck space was 22½ feet deep. If a careless sailor left a hatchway open and the twins plunged into the hold, they'd likely not live to see England.

When sixteen-year-old Chang and Eng sailed from Siam, they had one such close call. The "Chinese boys," as the Siamese called them, were great favorites with their ship's crew. One day while they were racing a sailor, all of them laughing and tearing along the deck, the twins spotted an open hatch. Chang and Eng leaped together, without any apparent signal between them or flicker of hesitation, and soared over the gaping hole like a great double-bodied seabird.

Captain Graham's *Arab* made the crossing in twenty-four days. She slid into her Liverpool berth on July 25, and Millie-Christine's party checked into the Waterloo Hotel on Ranelagh Street. Eleven years earlier, Barnum and the seven-year-old Tom Thumb had also stopped at the Waterloo. On that occasion, Tom's mother, Cynthia Stratton, had smuggled him past curious onlookers disguised as a babe in arms.

The twins arrived in Liverpool without advance publicity, so there were no crowds to avoid. "The first thing I did after a short rest," Millar said, "was to send out circulars inviting prominent medical men and members of the press to a private view of the Twins, which was given in the drawing-room of the hotel, and was crowded by the learned and scientific, all of whom were amazed."

A *Liverpool Daily Post* reporter came expecting humbug. Barnum's recently published autobiography, which confessed to occasional fake exhibits, had made cynics of the public. But in spite of himself, the *Post* reporter was charmed by the twins. "A few minutes . . . spent with these interesting little creatures served to dissipate all doubts as to the genuineness of the accounts given of them; and to excite . . . a feeling of awe at the inscrutable ways of Him who had, in these 'little ones,' left . . . human intellect and science so far behind."

Seven Liverpool physicians, including Dr. Thomas Inman, "minutely examined" the twins. These gentlemen all expressed astonishment, the reporter wrote, "and stated that though in 'the books' there were some few instances of similar conformation at birth," in no case had any others lived to such an age or been so perfectly developed.

The doctors signed a medical endorsement: "We have examined carefully to-day the African twins. They are completely united below the body. . . . They are interesting, lively, and intelligent little people, and have nothing of monstrosity in their appearance. It is impossible to see them without being pleased with their manners and lively chattering."

Fate was kind in choosing Dr. Inman as one of the seven examiners. Very soon, he would play hero to the twins.

The sisters had passed British medical scrutiny, but would they catch the fancy of high society? If they did, the hoi polloi would follow. The *Post* predicted the twins would be a hit: "Altogether, there is everything to interest in their appearance, and nothing to scare . . . the most delicate minded or fastidious. Soon as convenient rooms can be had, public exhibitions will take place, which we have no doubt will be extensively and fashionably patronised."

The twins opened for a six-day exhibition at Queen's Hall in Bold Street. Reviewers loved them. Millar couldn't have written better copy himself:

> "In the presence of strangers the twins are exceedingly lively, and exhibit the usual aptitude for chattering peculiar to children of their years." (*Liverpool Mail*)

"A natural wonder, a study alike for the pathologist and the physiologist, which far exceeds in interest and curiosity the celebrated Siamese twins." (*Liverpool Chronicle*)

"Little phenomenas, . . . natives of some country up the river Congo." (*Albion*)

"It only remains for us to add that the twins are lively and intelligent, . . . and that, already showing a consciousness of freedom, they pertinaciously, if called 'niggers,' assert that they are 'coloured individuals.'" (*Liverpool Daily Post*)

Queen's Hall could not hold all the people who were dying to see the twins, so the partners worked out a contract with a Mr. Copeland, who managed two large theatres. They ordered heralds with an etching of the back-to-back sisters in matching pinafores: "THEATRE ROYAL MORNING LEVEES! From eleven till five. For Two Days only, Friday & Saturday, August 10th & 11th, THE UNITED AFRICAN TWINS." The "morning levees," which lasted all afternoon, were soon expanded to include evening performances at Mr. Copeland's larger theatre.

Evening shows brought out a rowdier audience than morning levees. "On our first night," Millar said, "we came very near having a serious disturbance." He and Millie-Christine were stationed in the wings watching a Shakespearean production while awaiting their turn to go on next. The actors took their bows and exited. On cue, Millie-Christine crossed to stage center with her peculiar, perfectly coordinated side-stepping walk. Professor Millar followed, ready to launch

A herald from the Theatre Royal in Liverpool, August 1855

his regular "lecture" before Millie-Christine sang a few childishly sweet duets.

At that instant, he heard the sound every exhibitor dreaded—a boisterous heckler up in the cheap seats. "No sooner had I appeared on the stage with the children than a fellow called out from the gallery—'Humbug, look, don't you see the leather strap binding the children together? I see it; look! look!' For an instant, the commotion was frightful. Not one word would they let me say; nothing but wild hooting and hissing could be heard."

Suddenly, like an avenging angel in evening clothes, a gentleman in one of the stage-side boxes sprang to his feet. In full view of the startled crowd, he clambered over the balustrade and dropped onto the stage. It was Dr. Inman. Standing beside the flustered twins, he announced in a voice that reached the topmost gallery that he himself had examined them and found them actually and unquestionably joined by nature.

"And as the doctor was well known in Liverpool," noted Millar, "the tables were soon turned, and many of the audience, feeling rather ashamed of themselves, cheered us to the very echo, calling us out twice."

Fortified by success, the partners moved on to London, bearing letters of introduction to several famous gentlemen. Among them were eminent doctors, the editor of *Punch*, the manager of Haymarket Theatre, and E. T. Smith, the manager of Drury Lane Theatre. Smith was an expert on the London show scene, and he and Thompson hit it off splendidly.

Did Millar suspect that Thompson was preparing to ease him out? That might explain why, on the brink of success in the largest city in the western world, he pulled a most astonishing trick. On Tuesday evening, August 14, Professor Millar simply vanished, the twins and the Cuban nanny with him. As he ever so casually put it in his memoir, "After remaining in London some ten days I concluded to go north, and took a steamer for Dundee."

Outraged, Thompson immediately set about hunting down his missing cohort and the twins. He published a notice in the *London Sun*: "William Millar, a person in the employment of Mr. William Thompson, the proprietor of the African twins, absconded on Tuesday night and carried off those interesting specimens of Nature's freaks from the Bedford Hotel, Covent-garden, where Mr. Thompson and his charge were staying. Information has been given to the police, and the offender fully described as being about 43 years old, 5 feet 10 inches high, dark moustache and whiskers. The twins are five years old, joined at the back. A reward has been offered for the apprehension of Miller and recovery of the twins."

Chapter 4

What cheers us when we are far away
From home and all we love:
When storm and danger hedge us round,
And all is dark above?

Songs of Miss Millie-Christine

*O*ff in Dundee, Millar prepared to handle the show on his own. He'd be router, advance man, agent, ticket taker, and lecturer. He invited the local press and permitted eleven of Dundee's principal medical men to examine the sisters. They found them "interesting and extraordinary." Millar papered the town with heralds and window cards. Anyone willing to pay a shilling (children half price) could visit the African Twins at Thistle Hall from twelve till four and from seven till ten. For two days, customers crowded the exhibition room.

But sure as the silvery Tay flowed to the sea, Millar's luck was running out. On the third day, a traveling fair set up a short distance from town. By midafternoon, all of Dundee was there. Business at Thistle Hall dropped off entirely by three o'clock, so Millar left the twins with their nursemaid and slipped out to run a few errands. As he left the building, he noticed a cab pull up.

"At that moment I was going into a shop near the hall," he said, "and I had just entered the shop when I heard a fearful scream." He raced back to Thistle Hall and dodged past three rough-looking characters in the passageway. "At the top of the stairs I met a man with the Twins crying wildly in his arms." Millar engaged in a brief tug of war. "I took hold of them, but the man held them firmly, and fearing they might be injured, I instantly let them go, and at once felled the fellow to the floor with my fist, which made him relax his hold. I then got the Twins in my arms." Then the three toughs rushed him, and the man he'd knocked down stumbled to his feet. The gang piled onto Millar and the sisters. "In the hands of four powerful men I found myself helpless. These men turned out to be prize-fighters, hired in London by Manager E. T. Smith for the purpose of taking the Twins away from me." The men forced the sobbing children into the waiting cab, while Millar watched in frenzied helplessness. "I did my utmost to get a policeman, or other assistance, but none could be found, as everybody was at the fair."

"KIDNAPPING EXTRAORDINARY," the *Dundee, Perth and Cupar Advertiser* headlined. "On Wednesday afternoon about three o'clock considerable excitement prevailed in the neighbourhood of Union Street, in consequence of the abstraction of the African twin children."

The newspaper disclosed a troubling detail: "It appears that the children are claimed by more than one party." And local police on duty during the commotion had made themselves scarce. "While the struggle was going on, cries of 'murder' and 'robbery' were heard, and the police were called, but the officers declined to interfere. This was the cause of some surprise." Frantic eyewitnesses rushed to police headquarters for help, where, to their greater surprise, they found that "the officers on duty had been instructed not to interfere between the claimants of the children."

The *Dundee and Perth Saturday Post* compared the abduction to a scene from *Uncle Tom's Cabin* and blamed the police: "Of course they could not be expected to decide to whom the children belonged, but they were bound to preserve the public peace which was unquestionably outraged. . . . The men who carried away the children were at least guilty of a breach of the peace, and ought to have been arrested."

It was a disgraceful affair, the *Advertiser* agreed. "The lives of the children are in imminent danger, and we certainly believe that the whole party ought to have been brought before the authorities, and the matter definitely cleared up. Who was or is proprietor of the infants is not the question. . . . They were taken from the arms of the nurse in the most brutal manner, and the nurse herself received bruises and injuries, the children, too, suffering from the rough usage of the contending parties."

Readers learned that Thompson had chased his fugitive partner all the way to Scotland, accompanied by the Drury Lane Theatre manager and four prizefighters. He'd convinced the constabulary that he was Millie-Christine's court-appointed guardian by waving about legal-looking papers—documents from America, he said. Furthermore, he told Dundee police that a London judge had ordered Millie-Chris-tine returned for a hearing. According to Thompson, he was to take her back to England by any steps necessary, including "forcible pos-session."

Millar thus lost the first round, but he wasn't beaten yet. "What to do after being robbed of my precious charge during the hubbub of Dundee Fair?" he wondered. "I concluded to consult a lawyer, so I laid my case before Messrs Robertson, of Reform Street."

The lawyer asked if the twins had living parents.

"This I did not know," said Millar.

"Well, have they a legally appointed guardian?" Robertson asked.

"This I could not answer," Millar admitted. Could not, would not, or knew very well they did not.

"Ah, then," said Robertson, "you must try to find out their mother." In Great Britain, he explained, in the case of children un-der twelve years of age without living parents or law-appointed guard-ians, one person had as good a right to them as another.

"This rather astonished me," Millar later recalled, "and set me to thinking. I left the lawyer's with a firm determination of recovering the children at all hazards."

He thought his brother Kennedy, back in the States, might be able to help. Kennedy Millar served as business agent while the pro-fessor traveled abroad. "That very night I wrote to my brother, who was living at Newark, U.S.A., stating to him my loss, and requesting him to write to an old friend of mine—Mr. Seaton Gales, editor of the *Raleigh Register*." Kennedy was to pass the word that Professor William Millar wanted to contact the twins' mother.

Apparently, Millar somehow knew the Raleigh editor who had covered North Carolina's first state fair, where the baby Carolina

Twins appeared before they were stolen away. Perhaps a friendship had sprung up in Millar's early show-business days. He managed many performers during his long career. One former client was Thomas D. Rice, who first rubbed on blackface and sang "Jim Crow." Another was John Wilkes Booth's father, old Shakespearean actor Junius Brutus Booth. Maybe Millar had swung an occasional show through Raleigh and dropped by the *Register* office to introduce himself and whip up publicity.

However the two had met, Millar knew enough about the twins' North Carolina past to conclude that Gales might put him in touch with their owner.

Millar didn't hope to hear from brother Kennedy anytime soon. It would take two weeks for a steam packet to ferry his letter across the Atlantic, then more time for stateside letters between Kennedy and Gales, then even longer until someone could locate the mother.

To earn a living while he waited for news from the States, Millar signed up an Italian magician, the Great Bosco. They'd nearly completed a successful engagement in Aberdeen when they heard that Queen Victoria had just arrived at her Highland home, Balmoral Castle. So it happened that when Millar pulled the coup of his career, he took along Bosco instead of Millie-Christine. Her chance to visit royalty would have to wait.

"Being anxious to see a real queen," said Millar, "I asked the proprietor of the Hotel Royal to introduce me as I had seen on a sign board that he was a post horseman to her majesty. He looked amazed and informed me that it was not considered court etiquette."

Millar agreed with Ben Franklin that God helps those who help themselves. "I then went to Mr. Adam of *The Herald* and made a similar request, for a letter of introduction. He was likewise amazed, but gave me a line to an old friend of his, Dr. Robertson, who had charge of the Duchess of Kent's estate at Abergeldie." The doctor passed him on to a Colonel Phipps, who presented the letter to Her Majesty. Three days later, a waiter handed Millar a letter embossed with the regal initials, *O.H.M.S.* The letter ordered him to appear with his "wizard."

Millar and Bosco rode out from grubby Aberdeen to the newly renovated castle, set off by acres of artfully laid-out grounds. Once upon a time, Queen Victoria and her Albert had leased Balmoral for the summer season. She loved the small Scottish castle, passing happy weeks enjoying a queen's notion of simple county life. As more Royal children appeared, the cozy place began to feel crowded. Victoria then bought the estate and watched adoringly as Prince Albert drew up architectural plans for a new Balmoral.

"Every year my heart becomes more fixed in this dear Paradise," wrote the queen, "and so much more now, that *all* has become my dear Albert's *own* creation, own work, own building, own laying out."

Queen Victoria was thirty-six when Millar saw her. He was much impressed with her majestic appearance, "her fine, large, expressive eyes, her lovely hair, and the mild benign expression of her countenance." Bosco performed his magical tricks for Her Majesty, the prince consort, a number of the Royal children, the Duchess of Kent, the Crown Prince of Prussia, the princess royal, the Prince of Wales, and the Duke of Argyll. He entertained them for an hour and a half, "giving to all present both pleasure and satisfaction," according to Millar.

The next day, he and Millar started back for Aberdeen, well pleased with their stay at Balmoral Castle. A Royal thank-you note and enclosure greatly increased their satisfaction:

To Professor Millar.
Balmoral Castle, Sept. 25, 1855.

Sir: I have received the commands of Her Majesty the Queen to send you the enclosed cheque for fifty pounds in payment for the performance of Signor Bosco last night. I am, sir, your obedient humble servant, C. B. Phipps.

"And that," said Millar, "is how I got Bosco before the Queen."

Meanwhile, the twins were having their own adventures. A week after the fracas, the *Dundee, Perth and Cupar Advertiser* printed a dispatch from London that must have reassured any Scot still fretting over their well-being. Judging from the story, the girls were thriving.

After Thompson "rescued" them from Millar, said the dispatch, he and E. T. Smith of Drury Lane had fetched the African Twins to the presiding magistrate at Bow Street Police Court for a custody hearing.

"When the magistrate inquired, good humouredly, if they could speak, Mr. Smith requested their attendant to 'set them on,' upon which they began singing . . . 'O, Susannah' with a gusto that induced his worship to require their speedy removal. . . . The little things, who seemed to enjoy the joke amazingly, were not to be stopped until they had finished one verse of the song, upon which they were removed from the court, exclaiming 'Good morning gentlemen,' as they left."

The saucy scene ended with a fine theatrical flourish: "Smith then wrapped the children up in a large carpet to conceal them from the crowd waiting outside, and he and Thompson carried them off."

The next day's *Dundee Courier* focused on the serious side of the case. The "very violent and unseemly" kidnapping raised questions "deeply affecting the rights of humanity," declared a long, thoughtful editorial. "The assailing party succeeded in carrying off the booty; and . . . exhibited, we are told, a paper purporting to be a deed by the State of Pennsylvania constituting him guardian of the children. The document not having been shown to any Magistrate, there was no one present either qualified or entitled to decide as to its authenticity."

Nor was there anyone present to decide what possible weight such a document could exert in Scotland. What right of property, the *Courier* asked, could Thompson or anyone else have in the unfortunate children?

"Within the limits of the British Empire such a document is utterly void and valueless. The law of this country does not recognise the power of Pennsylvania, or of all the States in the Union, to confer a right of property in human beings." As the *Courier* saw the case, neither claimant could establish valid title to the twins before any court in the kingdom. "Liberty, by the English Law, depends not upon the complexion; . . . and as for the Pennsylvania document, it is only so much waste paper in such a question."

Thompson, in London, ignored the Scottish press and proceeded with the sisters' interrupted engagement. Impresario E. T. Smith invited a roster of the city's leading medical men "and those otherwise interested" to examine the twins at Drury Lane Theatre.

One of the physicians, F. H. Ramsbotham, published his findings on the *pygopagus symmetros* (from the Greek *pygo*, meaning rump, and *pagos*, meaning fixed or firmly set). His detailed report in the September 29, 1855, issue of the *Medical Times and Gazette* described two complete sets of internal organs and nearly complete sets of external genitalia. As to the vital *caudae equinae* (the spinal roots that descend from the lower part of the spinal cord), he believed they were for the most part separate, each enclosed in its own protective sheath.

"The children stand not quite back to back, but rather sideways," he noted, "so that they are able to place their arms around each other's neck, and give each other a kiss; but they cannot walk side by side. When lying, one reclines upon her back and the other upon her side.

"They play together with their toys; they seldom have contrary wishes, and although there are at times little tiffs between them, they have never been known to have a downright quarrel. . . . They run about with amazing ease and activity. Their dispositions are both very amiable, though one is milder than the other in temper, the little one having the most 'pluck,' and their intelligence is equal to, if it does not exceed that of most European children of the same age."

This mention of high intelligence for children of their age was familiar by now. Millar, Thompson, and the doctors believed them to be five, though in fact the twins were a precocious four.

"REMARKABLE HUMAN PHENOMENA! THE AFRICAN TWINS (CHRISTINA AND MILLY) . . . will be ON VIEW for a brief period only, at the EGYPTIAN HALL, PICCADILLY," said Thompson and Smith's London handbill. It featured a woodcut of two black-skinned girls in simple frocks, standing side by side. "These INTERESTING CHILDREN have an extremely Pleasing and Attractive appearance. . . . They sing, with wonderful precision, the Native Melodies of their own country." Soon, they'd be en route to the French capital, said the bill, "and will thence return to Philadelphia to complete their filial mission."

Thompson stood firm on his guardianship claim. "They were born in slavery," the London show bill stated, "and their Guardian, appointed by the Orphan Court of Philadelphia, United States, legally apprenticed them to Mr. Thompson of that city who instantly freed them from their degrading Bondage and determined to appropriate the Receipts arising from their Public exhibition to the purpose of Emancipating the parents of the children, who are at this moment Slaves on a North-American Plantation."

At each London performance, Thompson repeated his preachment about how the twins were working to free their mother, father, sisters, and brothers. They had heard this message since they were first exhibited in Canada. It's likely that much of Chrissie's amiability, Millie's courage, and the cheerful, lively way they behaved sprang from the dream that Thompson held out, the promise that they would eventually rescue their dear, almost-forgotten family.

❧

Professor Millar's letter sailed fast and true to America. Kennedy Millar promptly contacted Seaton Gales. Gales forwarded the message to Joseph Pearson Smith in Wadesboro. Smith traveled to Jabez McKay's farm and struck a deal to purchase Monemia, Jacob, and their seven children. Smith, as the twins pointed out later, was an exceptionally good-hearted man. As they put it, he made "more than one heart rejoice in gladness" by the transaction. He also risked a very large sum of money on the uncertain chance that he could recover the kidnapped twins.

Seventeen days after the Dundee hubbub, Smith sat down at his desk to compose a letter:

C F College 16th September 1855.

K Millar Esq. Dear Sir,

I am in receipt of a letter from you in relation to the purchase of the Carolina twins Christian & Milly joined together by the back bone.

This will inform you that I do not wish to sell the parents, neither do they wish me to sell them, but they are very anxious to get the children back and you will confer a special favour on me (and one that will not soon be forgotten) by letting me know as soon as convenient whether or not it can be done and if it can upon what terms.

If it be impossible to get them back again, you shall hear from me again as to the sale of the parents, as I would like for them to be together, but is much more desirable to me to get them back.

Yours very respectfully, Joseph Pearson.

He folded the sheet and addressed the reverse side to "K Millar Esq., Philadelphia," from "C F College, NC."

Calling himself "Joseph Pearson" from "C F College" suggests that Smith was reluctant to reveal his full name and exact address to Millar. "C F College" was Carolina Female College, eighteen miles out of Wadesboro. Sixteen-year-old Bettie, the Smiths' eldest child, attended classes there. Smith had built a second family home in the new community growing up around the college, where he ran a branch of Smith and Son's General Merchandise.

"I found out," Millar said, "that I could get information about the Twins' mother from Mr Joseph Pearson Smith, of Wadesboro, North

Carolina. I wrote him, and received a reply in which, though assuming that the Twins were his property, he yet admits that he only purchased their mother after hearing from me, at a period, of course, considerably after their birth. This letter of Mr Smith's I still hold."

In fact, Professor Millar kept the letter for the rest of his life, preserving it with all the memorabilia of his show days. Ninety-three years after it was written, his grandson Bertram Millar donated it and the professor's clippings about the twins to the North Carolina Archives. The professor apparently carried his scrapbooks wherever his career led him. His grandson noted, "Few letters can have traveled so extensively as this one, and . . . after crossing the Atlantic twenty-four times, visiting almost every part of Great Britain and Ireland, wandering over thousands of miles in the United States and Canada, it finally returned in safety to North Carolina where it was written."

Negotiations between Smith and Professor Millar dragged on for twelve months, then fourteen.

William Thompson and the twins, knowing nothing of Millar's efforts, continued touring Britain. The announced Paris trip was postponed in favor of a lengthy circuit of provincial English towns in the northern counties: Stamford in April 1856, Sheffield in May, Leeds in midsummer. Thompson and the sisters then moved farther north, into Scotland, then south again, to Birmingham.

By now, Thompson's ads pinpointed the African village where the twins were supposedly born. The British were fascinated with all things African, so he chose a name with an exotic ring to it— "Tamboo, Africa." During performances, Thompson still told audiences how he would take the African Twins back to the States after they had earned enough money to buy their family's freedom. The twins were five years old, and their memories of Monemia were fading.

While Professor Millar schemed to get the sisters back, he, too, stayed busy. For a time, he managed the Theatre Royal in Cork, Ireland. By year's end, he was running an educational novelty called a Diorama show. Louis Daguerre had invented the marvelous optical illusion. Audiences sat in a darkened room and watched illuminated transparent paintings shift, pulsate, and seem to move before their eyes. Millar showed a Diorama of India. The public was curious about all heathen lands under English control. The British East India Company, devouring India province by province, had recently acquired unpronounceable Oudh. Millar's Diorama transported spectators as close to India as most of them would ever get.

Joseph Pearson Smith spent the long months preparing an overseas rescue attempt. Monemia would sail with him. Kennedy Millar would join the party in New York City and travel along to England as his brother's agent and strong right arm in case of trouble.

Chapter 5

Mother would comfort me if she were here.
Gently her hand o'er my forehead she'd press,
Trying to free me from pain and distress,
Kindly she'd say to me, "Be of good cheer."

Songs of Miss Millie-Christine

Smith booked passage on the finest American-built liner in service, the SS *Atlantic*. He and Monemia, trunks, valises, and satchels in tow, headed for New York in mid-December 1856. As planned, they met Kennedy Millar and made their way to the Collins Line wharf, where the great steamship waited. The *Atlantic*'s black hull stretched 280 feet. Paddle wheels protected by wooden fenders jutted from each side like massive shoulders. Compared to the elegant clipper ships in the harbor, she looked clumsy, with her stumpy masts, chopped-off bow, and sturdy funnel. She carried furled sails for emergency use. On an earlier trip, she'd ridden the wind back to England after her shaft broke in midocean.

The *Atlantic* may have looked plain, but she and her sister steamers—the *Arctic*, the *Baltic*, and the *Pacific*—could outrace anything afloat. In 1850, Congress had voted to invest taxpayers' money in an American fleet fast enough to beat the British Cunards. E. K. Collins's four new ships combined speed and luxury. The *Atlantic* set records her first season, and *Punch* magazine saluted her with a jingle:

> A steamer of the Collins Line,
> A Yankee Doodle Notion,
> Has also quickest cut the brine
> Across the Atlantic Ocean.

In 1851, the year the twins were born, the *Pacific* made history with the first crossing under ten days. For six years Congress had voted appropriations and encouraged Collins skippers to run full speed and damn the cost of extra coal, breakdowns, and repairs. Tragically, half the fleet was gone. In September 1854, the *Arctic* had smashed against an iron-hulled ship in the fog shrouding the Grand Banks and carried 319 passengers into the depths off Newfoundland. The *Pacific* had vanished in January of this very year, lost in iceberg-strewn waters with 186 souls aboard.

A safe crossing in any season could never be taken for granted, and Smith was sailing in midwinter. He was leaving his wife and their seven children at Christmastime, Monemia her Welches Creek flock. She carried an unborn baby.

The *Atlantic*'s cannon thundered farewell to shore. Neighboring ships sent answering salutes booming across the harbor. Prayerfully— Monemia was a churchgoer and Smith a devout steward of his church—they sailed off to seek and save their lost lamb.

On New Year's Day 1857, the *Atlantic* berthed at Liverpool. No one met Smith's party as it trooped down the gangplank. "At this time," said Millar in his memoir of Millie-Christine, "I was in Leeds exhibiting the diorama of India."

The next day, Kennedy Millar, Smith, and Monemia joined the professor. They learned that Thompson and the twins were currently playing Birmingham.

"Upon being introduced to Mrs M'Cay, who turned out to be a pleasant mulatto woman of enormous size, weighing 240 lbs.," said the professor, "I set to work to get things in order for the purpose of going to Birmingham to get possession of the Twins. On our arrival there I called on Mr. Glossop, Superintendent of Police."

The African Twins were giving their levees at the Exchange Rooms in New Street. Monemia begged to be rushed directly there to confront Thompson, but the others convinced her that extreme caution should be used in order to take him by surprise. She tried to compose herself while Millar and Smith explained the case to Superintendent Glossop.

They next visited the American vice consul, a Mr. Underhill, who immediately took a lively interest in the affair. He advised them to keep their arrival secret until that evening. They would then enter the hall with a protective force of police. If the twins recognized their mother among the paying customers, Smith would have strong prima facie evidence to use in court.

Monemia, vastly pregnant and dangerously agitated, would hardly go unnoticed in any English crowd. The question was whether the twins would recognize her after all this time. They'd been two-year-old babies when last they saw her. By now, they were five and a half.

ꙮꙮꙮ

So far as Thompson and the sisters knew, it would be an evening like any other. After tea, the twins' nanny would help them dress for the performance. As usual, Thompson would tell the audience how the girls would soon return to the States and free their family. The twins would chat with curious strangers. Someone would probably request "Oh! Susanna," and they'd sing while people smiled and clapped.

Instead, it turned into the most thrilling night of their lives.

Professor Millar noted merely, "Mr. Glossop at once went there and took charge of the Twins, removing them to his quarters at the police station."

The circus biography of Millie-Christine's life, on the other hand, describes a flamboyant scene: "The impatience of the mother was restrained until the hour of the gathering of the visitors," it says. As the hour drew near, Monemia and Smith strolled along New Street and approached the box office. Behind and ahead of them, police officers, "selected for the purpose and disguised," joined the queue. They all bought tickets and hurried upstairs, Monemia puffing like an express on the grade. Trying to look like casual visitors, they entered the hall. "No sooner, however, had the keen eye of the mother caught a glimpse of her long-lost child than she uttered a scream of such heart-rendering pathos that the audience simultaneously rose to their feet, wondering and astonished."

Millie-Christine must have been startled out of her wits.

"The mother, overpowered, fell fainting to the floor." Someone uncorked a vial of smelling salts and held it under her nose. "When resuscitated, she wildly threw her arms about, crying in most piteous tones, 'My own child! O! give her to me! Do not take her away again; she needs my care! Where is she? Where is she?'"

Thompson tried to drag Millie-Christine into an adjoining room. "But an honest Scotchman, divining his intentions, placed his back against the door, and bringing himself into a position that would have delighted a pugilist cried out: 'Ye'll nae tak' the bairn ayant the door, maun ye wallop me first, an' I'm nae thinkin' ye'll soon do that.'"

Audience members threw themselves into the drama. Women fainted. The chief of police mounted the stage to explain what was happening. Men in the crowd, "learning the true state of affairs," moved threateningly toward "the sordid villain who had stolen . . . a helpless child."

Thompson abandoned Millie-Christine and jumped from a second-story window, "which hazardous feat alone, for the time, saved him from certain and well-merited punishment."

Monemia came to in a panic. Strong men hauled her to her feet. Joyfully, she gathered her lost child to her ample bosom.

The excited crowd finally dispersed, and Smith's party returned to the hotel. That night, Monemia slept with Millie-Christine in her arms "and dreamed of naught save happiness and pleasure to come."

She should have known better. "Her troubles were not to end here," continues the circus biography. "The prize was too rich to be thus easily given up by interested ones."

Thompson swore out a complaint. The next morning, officers called at Smith's hotel to serve a writ of habeas corpus requiring mother and child to appear before the Court of Admiralty. Thompson was challenging his opponents to show cause why they should deprive him of Millie-Christine.

ᘒᘓᘒ

This time around, the twins' custody would be resolved by a full-bench courtroom hearing, not a police-court farce. A panel of Her Majesty's richly costumed judges filed in. Barristers in black robes and curled wigs rustled papers and bowed to the honorables seated on high.

Vice Consul Underhill sat with Smith's group. Their solicitor rose to plead Monemia's case. The *Birmingham Mercury* reported the highlights of his argument.

Gesturing toward Monemia, the solicitor said that "the instant that coloured female touched the soil of England, she became a free woman and was entitled to protection and to all the advantages of the English laws." She now came into court "to demand that her children be restored to her," and he, for one, "could not see upon what pretence they could be detained from her."

Furthermore, the solicitor said—pointing a warning finger at Thompson—the plaintiff was indictable on felony charges that could earn him a one-way transport to Australia to serve a fourteen-year sentence. He was prepared to show that Thompson had obtained possession of the children by fraud. This he would do, if necessary, "by calling as a witness in court the man who was a co-thief with Mr. Thompson in their abduction."

At this point, Thompson exploded in angry denial. The presiding judge gaveled him down and sternly reprimanded him for the outburst.

The plaintiff's counsel then offered "to show from documents in his [Thompson's] possession that the children were apprenticed to Thompson for the purpose of learning to exhibit themselves." Those documents, he argued, sustained Thompson's version of the affair, that the children had reached Philadelphia after long wanderings and were there publicly exhibited by a drunkard who took miserable care of them. The Orphans' Court had then appointed a legal guardian, and "this person eventually apprenticed them for five years to Mr. Thompson, and this document, officially signed, Mr. Thompson has with him." (In fact, the docket indexes of Philadelphia Orphans' Court from 1853 to 1858 reveal no transactions involving William Thompson, Professor W. J. L. Millar, or the twins.)

Consul Underhill then placed Smith's voluminous offers of proof into evidence. He'd barely launched his testimony when the chief magistrate interrupted. It would be useless to occupy more time, the judge declared, since from the opening of court, the case had been decided by the bench. Chrissie, especially, looked like Monemia, as anyone could plainly see. She should be given into the custody of her lawful mother. He was convinced that if she "was not the child of the defendant, then mother never bore a child." Every spectator in the courtroom, he added, must feel the same certainty in his heart. Those watching gave a long and hearty shout of approval at this decision.

"The documents were only slightly glanced at by the Magistrates," Millar agreed, "as the resemblance between Christina and her mother was convincing. One of the gentlemen on the bench said he did not require any further proof, as he was sure Mrs M'Cay was the mother of at least one of the children, which remark caused considerable amusement in the Court."

After the courtroom attendants restored order, Thompson offered one last desperate plea. According to the circus biography, he declared to the court that "he was ready then and there to settle upon the mother the sum of ten thousand pounds sterling, and deed to her an elegant house in which she could spend the rest of her days in luxury and comfort, if she would remain in England and give him possession of the child until she was eighteen."

He tried "to prevail upon our mother to *hire* us," the twins said later, "offering her a large sum to allow us to travel over the country and to go upon the continent."

Monemia turned a deaf ear to his enticements. She wanted to go home, she told the court, and live "in the land of her birth, with those she had known from infancy, and among her kindred and friends," says the circus biography.

That settled, the queen's magistrates adjourned the court. Thompson berated his attorney and stomped out. Underhill led Smith's jubilant party to his carriage.

Smith and the others caught a glimpse of Thompson on the street, waving his arms and shouting. "Mr. Thompson was very much excited," the *Mercury* reported, "and, when outside the court, harangued a small crowd of persons hanging about the entrances, and endeavoured to persuade them to assist him in taking the children away forcibly, offering them rewards for their assistance. They declined aiding him, but listened to him as long as he liked to talk." As the carriage rumbled away, Thompson was still pacing the courthouse steps, flourishing his dog-eared documents.

A British correspondent sent an item about the trial to the *New York Clipper*. The weekly *Clipper*, the "Oldest American Sporting and Theatrical Journal," as it called itself, covered all the show-business news that was fit to print, and lots that wasn't, which of course made it indispensable to professionals. When editor Frank Queen mentioned your name—whether as part of a complimentary review or as sly gossip—you could count yourself part of the entertainment world. The twins' first appearance in a *Clipper* column came in this mean-spirited English dispatch: "A great hubbub has been made in Birmingham about 'The African Twins' lately exhibited there. Their mother and a Mr. Smith, her owner, from the United States, put in a claim for them, and they were restored to the mother, who will no doubt sell them over again—if she can."

�'⊱⊰'⊰

Safely back at Leeds, Professor Millar began where Thompson had left off, coaxing Smith to form a partnership. Millar proposed they take the girls to Edinburgh. He would serve as their manager, and Monemia would join the show as an added attraction. They'd all "be the recipients of fine receipts," he promised.

The professor was a persuasive man. "Mr. S. then consented to mother's signing a three years' agreement," says Millie-Christine's *History*.

There was, of course, the professor's India Diorama to run. He showed his brother how to operate the lights and apparatus and left him in charge of that venture. The rest of the party then headed directly to Edinburgh, where Millar leased an exhibition hall at the Waterloo Rooms.

The medical examiners Millar gathered as a leadoff for the Edinburgh run were a notable assemblage.

James Syme, surgeon at the Royal Infirmary and professor of clinical surgery at the University of Edinburgh, was present. He was Scotland's most celebrated surgeon, called by some the "Napoleon of Scotch surgery." If Joseph Lister, Syme's young assistant and son-in-law, also attended, no one would have paid much attention to him. Lister, only thirty, had begun theorizing that blood-and-pus-smeared surgeons passed living bacteria from patient to patient. Most doctors ridiculed the idea. By the time Millie-Christine returned to England a dozen years later, however, Lister's carbolic acid spray would be changing hellish, gangrenous hospital wards into places where patients stood a fair chance of recovery.

James Young Simpson was present for the examination. Like Dr. Syme, Simpson taught at the university. A lowly gynecologist, he had barely slipped on to the faculty, elected by a one-vote majority. Surgeon Syme still looked down his distinguished nose at his colleague, calling Simpson a "vulgar male midwife." Dr. Simpson had been called worse. He was short and burly, a Scottish terrier of a man. Scrappy enough to fight his way up from a barefoot baker's boy to the faculty of Edinburgh University, he was "the most kind-hearted gentleman I ever met," in Millar's view.

By this time, Dr. Simpson had popularized chloroform as a substitute for ether. Doctors had used ether in operations since the early 1840s. It was a blessing, but it smelled dreadful and took several minutes to work. Its sickly sweet odor lingered, and patients awoke vomiting and coughing.

Simpson had used ether in his obstetrical practice but kept his eye—his nose, rather—on the alert for an alternate painkiller. In free hours at home, he experimented on himself, sampling powders, sniffing gasses, inhaling vapors. Late one evening, Dr. Simpson, his brother-in-law, his niece, and two young medical assistants sat down to their hazardous work in Dr. Simpson's dining room. They inhaled several substances without much effect. Then Simpson dug out a small bottle of chloroform buried beneath a heap of waste paper. The sniffers filled their tumblers and breathed deeply. "Immediately an unwonted hilarity seized the party," one of Simpson's colleagues reported. "They became bright-eyed, very happy and very loquacious—expatiating on the delicious aroma of the new fluid. The conversation was of unusual intelligence, and quite charmed the listeners."

Suddenly, the experimenters heard sounds like the racket of a cotton mill, louder and louder. A moment more and they slid off their chairs and onto the floor, unconscious. As the niece remembered it, she fell asleep quietly, arms folded across her breast, in the very act of exclaiming, "I'm an angel! Oh I'm an angel!"

Simpson was so delighted with the effect that within two weeks, he administered chloroform to at least fifty women. Outraged sermons thundered from pulpits. Had not God said to Eve, "In sorrow thou shalt bring forth children"? Anesthesia in childbirth was a "decoy of Satan," one minister preached, "apparently offering itself to bless women; but in the end it will harden something and rob God of the deep and earnest cries which arise in time of trouble for help."

Simpson tossed the Bible back at his critics. How about the first operation of all, carried out under divine anesthesia? "And the Lord God caused a deep sleep to fall upon Adam, and he slept: and He took one of his ribs, and closed up the flesh instead thereof." Furthermore, Simpson argued, John Calvin had written in his *Commentaries*, "It ought to be noted that Adam was sunk into a profound sleep in order that he might feel no pain."

All that fuss was behind him by the time Dr. Simpson met the twins. Queen Victoria had settled the chloroform controversy in 1853 when she used it during the delivery of her seventh child. And she intended to use it soon again to ease the arrival of the newest Royal baby.

Another Scottish doctor who examined the twins was anatomist John Lizars, senior operating surgeon at the Royal Infirmary of Edinburgh. He found them "sprightly and intelligent, romping with great freedom, speaking English like native children, and singing very sweetly." Dr. Lizars disagreed with the London doctors who had concluded the sisters had separate spinal cords. In all probability, their sacral nerves and their spinal cords were united, Lizars believed, "so as to constitute one individual, or two girls with one nervous system."

It mattered little which theory was correct. Whether the spinal cords were united or separate, whether Millie-Christine was one girl or two, any attempt to divide her was unthinkable. Anesthesia had become routine. However, Lister's battle against fatal infection had hardly begun. More crucial still, the intricacies of dividing and re-forming two complete systems from one were beyond possibility until the human eye could somehow see inside the human body.

❧❧❧

To publicize the January 19 opening day, Millar ordered eleven-by-sixteen-inch posters with a splendid engraving of the twins and Monemia. The girls posed in ruffled dresses with a bow on each shoulder and a wide sash tied in front. The engraving shows Chrissie grasping a fold of her mother's voluminous hoop skirt. Monemia rises behind them like a stout pyramid, wearing a frilly mobcap and a handsome dress with lace collar, flowing sleeves, and yards of gathered skirt.

To stress the African Twins theme, the Edinburgh artist pictured the little family in a garden with a couple of palm trees and two weird jungle flowers.

Giant letters above and below the picture announced, "The Greatest Wonder of the Age! The AFRICAN TWINS United by Nature, Accompanied by their MOTHER who has recently been LIBERATED FROM SLAVERY, will hold their DRAWING-ROOM LEVEES."

The printer also turned out batches of handbills about the twins. With Monemia to set him straight, Professor Millar dropped the Cuban background but kept a touch of African exotica in his spelling of their last name. The fliers described "Christina and Milley Makoi," five and a half years old, of African descent, born in Columbus County, North Carolina. "Their parents are persons of more than usual intelligence and piety, being both members of the church," said the bill.

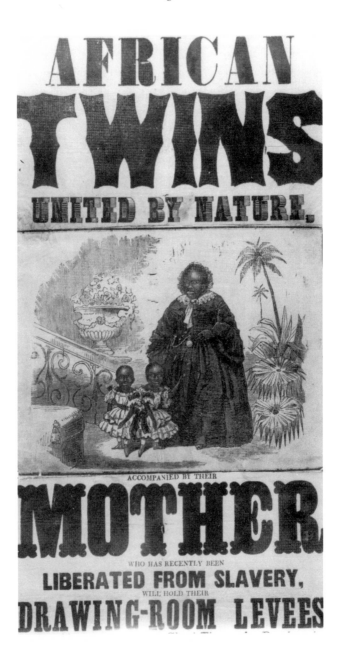

AFRICAN TWINS

UNITED BY NATURE,

ACCOMPANIED BY THEIR

MOTHER

WHO HAS RECENTLY BEEN

LIBERATED FROM SLAVERY,

WILL HOLD THEIR

DRAWING-ROOM LEVEES

Professor Millar's poster for the twins and Monemia in Scotland, January 1857

NORTH CAROLINA DIVISION OF ARCHIVES AND HISTORY

"The proceeds of the exhibition, after paying expenses, will be applied by Mr Millar to assist in rescuing from slavery the Father and the Brothers and Sisters of the United African Twins. . . . At the above Rooms for a Short Time only, previous to their departure for the Continent."

There was even a meditative verse:

> How poor, how rich, how abject, how august,
> How complicate, how wonderful is man; . . .
> I tremble at myself.
> And in myself am lost.

Millie-Christine, before she was seventeen, composed a poem about herself echoing that exalted tone: "I am most wonderfully made," she recited in unison to audiences. "A marvel to myself am I."

The show opened on a Monday. Two days later, Dr. Simpson invited the sisters to a special six o'clock meeting of the Obstetrical Society of Edinburgh, called so colleagues could inspect the marvelous little sisters. Simpson chaired the meeting. According to the minutes, he minutely described and commented on the girls and showed drawings of six or seven other "Pypopaginous Formation" twins from the past.

After the demonstration, the doctors applauded the lecture and chatted with the twins. "Thanks were also awarded to Mr. Millar, the present guardian of the children, who had not only kindly granted the members of the society this opportunity of witnessing his exceedingly interesting and truly wonderful charge, but had, in the most satisfactory and intelligent manner, given every information regarding them," noted the minutes. As for the children, the doctors unanimously agreed that they seemed remarkably happy and very intelligent for their years.

From Millar's viewpoint, life couldn't have been rosier. The Waterloo Rooms were crowded with visitors eager to see the twins and their mother. Editors at the *Scotsman*, the *Witness*, and the *North Briton* were "very interested admirers," Millar said. "Column after column was written about them."

Many of the most prominent ladies and gentlemen of the Scottish capital came to call, "all of whom were astonished and mystified at my wonderful charge." Among the distinguished visitors was the Countess of Camperdown. Anyone who was anyone knew Camperdown House, the pride of Dundee. After the countess marveled at Millie-Christine, she turned her attention to Monemia. She "got into an interesting conversation with the mother, and the quick-witted answers given by Mrs M'Cay to her Ladyship were rather astonishing," according to Millar.

When the countess said, "You surely must feel great relief at being in this happy and free country where you cannot be held in bondage as a slave," Monemia answered, "I guess it's free enough in America for me. I believe I'd rather be back on the old plantation in North Carolina; the eatin' and cookin' don't suit me here."

After a half-hour interview, the countess left "quite astounded that the mother did not realise the happy state she might enjoy in Great Britain," Millar wrote.

Professor Millar was too caught up in travel plans to worry about Monemia's discontent. Visions of Europe danced in his head. After Edinburgh, they'd work their way back through England and cross the channel for a continental tour.

Kennedy Millar shipped the India Diorama to England's North

Country. He set up at Music Hall in the boisterous coal-mining town of Newcastle-on-Tyne, where the others met him in late February after a month-long Edinburgh run. They rented a second Music Hall exhibition room for the twins.

At some point while the show was still on Scottish soil, Monemia presented the sisters with an amazing surprise—their new little sister, Elvy. Mrs. McKoy, however, was growing increasingly unhappy. She hated the way Millar had begun to treat her and the girls. "He tried to vitiate the contract," the twins later wrote, "so as to get things his own way, and thus deprive us of our rights. He abused our mother, and applied the most revolting epithets. He threatened the life of Mr. Smith, and refused to allow us to receive the attention and luxuries which children of tender age require. Our mother got afraid, and begged our good master to assist her and us children to reach the shores of our own beloved America."

With no word to the professor, Smith began studying railroad timetables and steamer schedules.

Millar was focused on the European trip. He intended to head directly for Germany and arrange the details, while Kennedy and Smith carried on in Newcastle. "Just the very thing for Europe," he'd whispered to himself when he first gazed upon the wonderful Carolina Twins. A continent of untapped purses lay ahead.

❦

Professor Millar was nearly to Portsmouth when the Newcastle *Gateshead Observer* hit the streets with a stop-the-presses story about the African Twins. The article started out as a regular press-release description of the sisters, probably supplied by Millar. But then it abruptly changed tone: "Since the foregoing lines were put into type, the twins have disappeared! They were taken on Tuesday night, as usual, to their lodgings in Oxford street by Mr. Smith, who was in attendance upon them, and who paid the cab-hire. Presently, another drove up, into which they were put, with their mother; and then the vehicle drove off to the Central Station, and the fugitives started by rail to Liverpool."

They'd been secretly preparing to make a speedy departure as soon as Millar left town, according to the twins. "Getting a trusty cabman to come to our lodgings, where all our things were in readiness, we were at the depot in London before any one surmised our intentions." They pulled into Liverpool "just half an hour before the steamer *Atlantic* was ready to leave her docks."

Millar, well on his way to Portsmouth, missed the news item. "Next morning I received a telegram from my brother requesting me to return to Newcastle, which I did," he said. "At the lodging I was informed by the landlady that the whole party had gone away in a cab two days previously."

With a sinking heart, he telegraphed the Collins Line agent in Liverpool. He received the following reply: "The children, the negro woman, and, we believe, Smith sailed in *Atlantic* for New York yesterday."

Millar could have wept—and maybe he did, when he calculated the cost of his misadventures with the twins. He had wasted two years chasing a pot of gold at the end of a double rainbow, only to have the sisters slip through his fingers again.

"And here ended all the vast trouble and expense I had gone to with those Twins," he concluded. "To really trace the Twins after their arrival in New York would have been rather difficult and very expensive, so I gave up the idea."

Whatever his faults, Professor Millar remained ever the optimist:

"I turned my attention to other business operations, thinking some day the tide of affairs in the freak of nature line might turn out more favourably."

Chapter 6

Over the billows away and away;
Ours is the freedom that knows no decay.
Braving the tempest, and stemming the tide,
In safety for ever we glide, we glide.

Songs of Miss Millie-Christine

*T*he SS *Atlantic* lay at Liverpool outfitting for the February passage home. Joseph Smith was willing to brave a second wintry crossing to get Millie-Christine away from Millar. He didn't breathe easily until the crew hoisted the gangplank and the ship churned down the Mersey toward the open sea. At last, Liverpool fell behind, drowning in mist.

Millie-Christine's States-bound ship was twice the size of the *Arab*.

The *Atlantic* plowed forward without the billowing, snapping sails the twins had grown used to on the old vessel. Great, wide paddle wheels stirred the water day and night. A thick, black funnel loomed amidships. Painted bright red at the top rim, it trailed smoke and cinders like a giant cigar.

Within the ship, marble-topped tables gleamed and chandeliers shot rainbow sparkles. The first-class passenger areas had steam heat and thick carpets. In fact, the accommodations were so plush that P. T. Barnum had booked a suite on the *Atlantic* in 1850 to impress soprano Jenny Lind when she sailed to the States for her American debut under his management.

Smith's party crossed without mishap. "When we arrived home again at New York," the twins later wrote in their *History*, "Mr. Smith took us under his cloak and carried us on the ferry boat to Jersey City, where he got us on the cars and never stopped until we reached the Monumental City, where we felt safe from pursuit." Nothing but Baltimore's waterfront traffic disturbed their peace. "We rested for a few days under the hospitable roof of Barnum's Hotel, and then left for our own dear home."

Wadesboro, North Carolina. For the first time in their wandering lives, they'd come to a place they could call home. "It was a joyous night when we arrived there and found our 'white ma,' Mrs. Smith, waiting to receive us," they remembered.

The twins had long been each other's only family. Suddenly, they had two mothers, a real father, and their own brothers and sisters, as well as all the youngsters on the Smith place. They'd never spent much time with ordinary children. At Smith's elegant house on the hill, they found a bewilderment of playmates—black, white, and all shades in between. Besides McKoys, there were slave-quarter children named Bill, Jim, Lucy, Sandy, Polly, Louisa, Tinsey, George, Bob,

Violet, and Lilly. At the big house, there were seven Smith children. The twins arrived just in time to celebrate Bettie's eighteenth birthday. Then came John James; Annie; Joseph Pearson Smith, Junior; Carrie; William; and Brightie.

Soon after the twins' homecoming, the *Cheraw* (S.C.) *Gazette* wrote up the rescue. "Mr. J. P. Smith arrived at Cheraw a few weeks ago from Scotland with the African twins, of whom some little talk has been made." The story pointed out that "the mother's claim was respected, even in Abolition England, where the rights of the master are unknown or disregarded."

Baby Elvy raised a provocative legal teaser. "During her stay in Scotland their mother gave birth to another child, whom she brought home with her," said the *Gazette*. "Now the question arises if that child, born on the soil of Scotland, is bond or free? If born free, how can it be held in slavery here? And was not its introduction in this country a violation of the law prohibiting the foreign slave trade? The mother became free when she entered Scotland, but returning here she returns to her owners. The remaining question is, can she enslave her child in her own return to servitude?"

Joseph Smith's main concern, now that he'd finally found the twins, was how to promote them. He'd already seen enough of the girls to realize they were exceptionally bright. The cleverer they were, the more they would appeal to choice audiences. Barnum had polished young Tom Thumb until he sparkled in any company. The twins were eager little creatures. Mary Smith could educate them and smooth any rough edges, just as Barnum had done with Tom. Of course, there was no possibility of the African Twins attending a school in Wadesboro. At home, in the sisters' special case, Mrs. Smith would brush aside the laws against teaching slaves to read and write.

As for exhibiting the twins, Smith's experiences with Brower,

Costumed for a show

Thompson, and Millar had soured him on hired show-business entrepreneurs. Managing the girls himself, on the other hand, would mean leaving the family stores in someone else's care and spending long periods on the road away from his wife and children.

He puzzled over his plans in a March 18 letter to a Georgia cousin: "I have just returned from Her Majesty, Queen Victoria's Dominions, and was successful in recovering the stolen negroes or as they are termed the North Carolina twins. . . . You will no doubt think it strange that I ever had anything to do with them and upon reflection, I am of the same opinion. . . . If they can be put into the right hands for exhibition they are a fortune. They are acknowledged on all hands to be the greatest living Wonder of the age." Now that he'd come to know them, Smith told his cousin, he no longer regarded the twins as curiosities but as "the most sprightly and intelligent children I ever saw of their age." Toward the end of the letter, he confided this: "I am very nearly in the notion of selling out my Negro property." Whether that meant he wanted to be free to travel and manage the twins, Smith didn't say.

One of Joseph Smith's uncles would have shouted amen to the notion of getting rid of Negro property. Uncle Sam and Aunt Peggy Smith belonged to the Primitive Baptist Church and were set against slavery, refusing to own a Negro servant. Samuel Smith cultivated his fertile land on Fall Branch with his own hands, says the *Smith Family Tree* book, "without envying his brothers, who were large owners of the negro, adding tract of land to land and negro to negro." Samuel was an exceptionally powerful man. The "Samson of Anson County," people called him. After weekly militia drills, he'd stroll about the grounds offering to wrestle or fight all comers. But no local man was fool enough to accept the challenge of the acknowledged "King of Prowess."

Millie-Christine must have heard a favorite family story describing the time an outsider took up the gauntlet. One day, Sam was resting peaceably in his own yard under a large white oak tree when along came a bully from Montgomery County riding a little mule. The stranger dismounted, tied his mule to a fence in front of the house, and told Sam he was the Montgomery County athletic champion. He had crossed the Pee Dee River into Anson County to challenge the legendary Sam Smith to a match. "As Mr. Smith arose from the ground," the *Family Tree* book says, "his large proportions, stout legs, long arms and broad chest and giant size struck his visitor with astonishment." As the stranger watched, Smith walked to the mule and, without a word, picked it up and set it on the other side of the fence. The Montgomery County champion, so the story goes, mounted his mule and rode away "fully and perfectly satisfied."

❦

Suddenly, out of the blue, just as the twins were settling into their new life, a ghost from the past turned up in Charlotte, only thirty-odd miles down the road from Wadesboro. Of all the people who might have ventured into Smith's home territory, it was showman William Thompson, last seen waving his alleged court order on the streets of Birmingham, England.

His foolhardy visit rated a long editorial in the *Western Democrat* of Tuesday, March 24. "On Sunday morning last," said the paper, "a man calling himself Thompson, from Philadelphia, arrived in Charlotte and put up at the Mansion House. During the day it was found that he was tampering with the slaves of the place, he having approached a trusty negro man named Elias, belonging to Mr. Sam'l Taylor, on the subject of freedom, that it was wrong for a negro to work for a white man, that the negroes ought to be free, &c. Elias told him that he had a good master and desired none of the kind of freedom offered by abolitionists."

Word spread. A hastily formed citizens' committee gathered at Thompson's hotel to "examine his credentials." The citizens searched his baggage and his pockets but found no incendiary documents. "However, his conduct was better proof against him than anything that could be found on his person," continued the editorial. When the committee demanded to know his business in that part of the country, he said he was pursuing the twin Negroes recently brought from Europe—that he was entitled to them and had come for the purpose of prosecuting his claim.

Thompson's story, the editor scoffed, was obviously manufactured for the occasion, "as he certainly was smart enough to know that he stood no chance of getting the etheopian twins. He could not possibly have any thing like a plausible claim to them. Taking everything into consideration, our citizens became convinced that Thompson was an abolitionist, and that his journey South had better be postponed for the present."

The committee impatiently waited out the Sabbath, but "about day-light Monday morning the fellow was aroused from his slumbers by that appropriate old tune, 'three little pigs and a short-legged sow' (sometimes known as the 'rogues march'), and escorted down to the N.C. Railroad depot where he was invited to take a ticket for Weldon and directed not to show his ugly physiognomy in these parts again."

The committee "did the thing genteely and maintained order," said the editorial. "Monsieur Thompson had reason to congratulate himself that he escaped without a coat of tar and feathers."

Local tempers burned hot for weeks after Thompson was run

out of town. When a female abolitionist lecturer ventured to Charlotte in April, she hunted all over for a place to speak her antislavery piece. Unable to find a hall, church, or public room for rent anywhere in town, she finally gave up and traveled west of the Catawba River to Lincolnton. "Probably she heard of Thompson," the *North Carolina Argus* commented, "and it may have occurred to her that it was far better to 'push along, keep moving.'"

As for William Thompson, the circus *Description*, recalling the episode thirty years later, says he accidentally learned that the locals intended to give him "an admirably fitting suit, composed of good *tar* and excellent *feathers*, and the freedom of the streets for promenading, with the company of a lusty negro to keep time to a *quick-step*." According to this version, Thompson decamped by night, and nothing more was ever heard of him in North Carolina. The only reminder of his visit to the twins' neighborhood was the chorus of a Negro song heard at corn shuckings:

> Massa Tomsin run a race;
> Oh! ho! o-o-o yah!
> He beat de fastest hoss in de place;
> Yah, oh yah! O ha!

The Thompson incident convinced Smith that he had little choice but to manage the twins himself. Clearly, he would need to keep an eye on them if he didn't want to lose them again.

While he settled his business matters, his wife began turning the six-year-olds into polite young ladies. Mrs. Smith wholeheartedly agreed with her husband that they were unpolished gems. First came salvation. "She taught us our first precepts of religion," says the twins' early *History*. "We had heard the Supreme Being alluded to, but not in tones of love and reverence. . . . Now, although we do not wish to speak Pharisaical, we think we can safely call ourselves really Christian children."

Mary Smith, the mother of several young ladies of her own, was a first-class teacher. "Mrs. S. instructed us to read and write," says the *History*, "to sing and dance, and thus while being able to enjoy ourselves and to employ our time usefully, to contribute in no small degree to the amusement of those who called to see us."

According to the *Family Tree* book, Mary Smith insisted that their education also include "the fine art of various kinds of Needlework and other womanly accomplishments." She allowed time for play as well. A later advertisement pictures the twins jumping rope as part of their show, Chrissie holding the handle at one end, Millie the other, the rope skimming under their four feet as they jump together.

Mrs. Smith's child-raising skills were part of a southern lady's training. By contrast, her country gentleman husband seemed ill suited for the show-business world. For one thing, Smith was a Methodist Church steward who called more backsliders up to the mourners' bench than most regular pastors could. For another, he was a teeto-taler in a county where grog shops abounded. Before turning his attention to Millie-Christine, Smith had traveled Anson County cam-paigning for temperance. More than once, he'd paid off a drunkard's debts on the condition that the fellow promise to join a temperance society and take the vow of sobriety—"Touch not! Taste not! Handle not!"

Certainly, he knew plenty of church people who frowned on entertainment of any kind. And yet he finally decided to become an exhibition entrepreneur. He and Mrs. Smith chose a slave woman to travel with and tend Millie-Christine. To be on the safe side, Smith also picked up Detective T. A. Vestal in Alabama.

The party headed for New Orleans, where a silver-tongued Texan had once stolen Millie-Christine from the blundering Mr. Brower. Smith worked the towns along the Gulf of Mexico on the way, learning the exhibition business by trial and error. Little by little, he shaped himself to Barnum's definition of a successful showman: "He must have a decided taste for catering for the public; tact; a thorough knowledge of human nature; great suavity; and plenty of 'soft soap.'"

Toward the end of Smith's first season, the *New York Clipper* began to take notice, although it didn't yet know Millie-Christine by name: "There is a story 'bobbing around,'" said the December 26, 1857, issue, "to the effect that there is exhibiting at Mobile a living negro child with two heads, four arms and four legs. It is six years old, very intelligent, speaks with both mouths, sings well, waltzes and keeps time. . . . The connection is with the spine, and the best physiologists of Europe and this country have pronounced it one individual child. This is certainly a wonderful child, or a wonderful story, we are not prepared to say which."

Chapter 7

Our hearts are light and free;
With a smile we greet every eye we meet,
Two merry hearts are we.

Songs of Miss Millie-Christine

ew Orleans was little changed since Millie-Christine had
landed there under Brower's care. The brown river flowed endlessly
in its wide bend along the waterfront. Steamboats crowded the plank
wharves. Casks and barrels forced pedestrians to detour off the sidewalks. Foul-smelling gutters ran alongside the curbstones.

Place d'Armes was now Jackson Square, although hardly anyone
remembered to use the new name. After dark, long past Millie-
Christine's bedtime, the Quarter sparkled with fashionable gentle-

men and ladies who laughed and chattered and looked down from second-story balconies. One of the men in the drifting crowds below that season was a young apprentice steamboat pilot named Samuel Clemens. In later years, he'd call himself Mark Twain and write about those early days in *Life on the Mississippi*.

Joseph Smith focused his attention on the people behind the wrought-iron balcony grilles—the very ones to spread the word about Millie-Christine. To pave the way, he set up the usual appointments with well-known local doctors. Dr. Josiah Nott examined Millie-Christine and gave his endorsement for Smith to publish: "New Orleans, 10th Feb., 1858. I have this day examined the 'Two-Headed Girl,' and find her to be a very remarkable anatomical curiosity."

Dr. Nott was one of the most interesting men in town. A South Carolinian, he had graduated from the medical college at the University of Pennsylvania and later studied in Paris. Ten years before he met Smith and Millie-Christine, Nott had advanced a controversial yellow-fever theory. Instead of a mysterious "miasma" that poisoned summer nights, he suspected that the deadly fever was of "insect or animalcular origin." Most doctors scoffed at Nott's idea. Prevailing opinion favored a polluted-air theory: toxic gases rose through the earth from fever-infected corpses; invisible miasmas seeped through the marble walls of cemetery vaults and wafted from the miniature Greek Revival and Italianate houses in New Orleans' sprawling cities of the dead.

Since Dr. Nott examined Millie-Christine six days before New Orleans' second grand Mardi Gras parade, Smith had time to use the medical endorsement to coax early visitors into the Two-Headed Girl exhibit.

That year, Mardi Gras revelers celebrated their farewell to pleasures of the flesh on February 16. The parade was a torch-lit extravaganza. The Krewe of Comus unveiled the "Classic Pantheon" as its theme. Chariots and floats carried Jupiter, Minerva, Apollo, Janus, Ceres, and Flora. Fat Bacchus rode a donkey; bare-chested, goat-legged Pan pranced alongside.

"I saw the procession of the Mystic Crew of Comus," Mark Twain recalled, ". . . and in their train all manner of giants, dwarfs, monstrosities, and other diverting grotesquerie—a startling and wonderful sort of show, as it filed solemnly and silently down the street in the light of its smoking and flickering torches."

More than likely, Smith's twins were part of the wonderful show. If so, Mark Twain glimpsed them among the giants, dwarfs, monstrosities, and grotesqueries frolicking behind the Krewe.

❧❧❧

From New Orleans, Smith and Vestal mapped out an extended upriver steamboat tour. They'd stop at river towns along the way, rent exhibition rooms, and catch the next northbound steamboat smoking into sight.

The Mississippi swarmed with two- and three-deck side-wheelers. Steamboat passengers departed New Orleans in high style. The line of steamers stretched two or three miles along the waterfront, sometimes double ranked. Boats pulled out from three o'clock in the afternoon onward. Tall columns of black smoke, pungent with burning rosin and pitch, piled out of the stacks and spread a dark roof over the city.

You didn't need to know how to read to find your boat. Each big paddle box had a brightly painted picture to match the ship's name—the *Princess*, the *Southern Belle*, the *Eclipse*, the *Magnolia*, the *Reindeer*, the *Polar Star*.

Smith and Millie-Christine had already tasted oceangoing luxury aboard the *Atlantic*. Most people, though, had never seen anything to beat the ornate Mississippi steamboats that Mark Twain described. You stepped aboard a roomy deck and gazed up at tall twin stacks with tips cut into the shape of a crown of plumes. Gilt acorns topped the loading derricks; gilt deer horns decorated the big bell. Lavish public rooms—two hundred feet long, some of them—served as social halls and passenger dining rooms, lit by tinted-glass skylights and chandeliers that glittered with rainbow prisms. Soft carpets were everywhere. Millie-Christine could count on a stateroom with a pair of cozy, clean bunks—one for her and one for the woman who watched over her. A pilothouse sat atop every steamboat like a sugary cupola on a tiered wedding cake. Special personages were admitted to the pilothouse up on the high "Texas deck," where they might share a taste of tarts, ices, and coffee carried up to the pilot at midwatch by a white-aproned, black-skinned "texas-tender."

On the dark side, the twins also witnessed scenes that Mark Twain left out of his love song to the Mississippi. Steamboats hauled slaves shackled together in irons. At landings, passengers edged past tethered men, women, and children waiting for the next boat south. Aboard, they stared down on slave gangs camped on the decks. Cheap-fare main-deck passengers shared space with livestock and the boat's furnaces, boilers, and engines.

Steamboat travel mixed danger with delight. Pilots steered a river that changed from one trip to the next. Riverbanks caved in. Currents carved new channels and sand bars overnight. The Mississippi eternally altered shape like a writhing, four-thousand-mile serpent. Riverboats had the life expectancy of alley cats. It was four years, on the average, before owners had to launch a replacement boat under the same old name.

Steamboats running at night cast an orange glow on the shore. Bayou trees draped in Spanish moss reflected the blazing torch baskets hung on each side of the bow, flaming iron cages that extended like outstretched burning hands. In the darkness, a submerged log lying deep in the water might suddenly appear directly below the bow, too close for the pilot to avoid. The best he could do would be to stop the engines and walk one paddle wheel over the log. Befuddled passengers would wake to a thundering racket and hold tight to their tilting bunks or each other.

Smith and the sisters spent three months on and off steamers, covering the stretch of river from New Orleans to St. Louis. Toward the end of May, their boat eased in among all the others at the long St. Louis wharf, and they disembarked for a welcome long stay on land.

A picture of the twins taken about this time shows them on a rustic twig-and-branch settee, wearing neat, plain dresses with long, full sleeves and small aprons. Each girl holds a woven basket full of posies. Their hair is fixed in corkscrew curls. Small, flat pancake hats hang from the settee posts. The sisters sit looking toward the camera, supremely cute and composed as only little girls can be.

Except for one bout of malaria, the children stayed healthy through all their travels. Their sturdy constitutions fought off southern fevers and western waters. St. Louis drinking water, for instance, was so famously muddy that folks claimed a man could grow corn in his stomach by drinking it. If only a fraction of what was said about the awful water was true, river-town doctors spent lots of time treating patients for digestive-tract ailments. You didn't even need a map to know which western river you were on, some said. You could tell from the flavor and texture of the water. Mark Twain told of a

The twins on the twig-and-branch settee

riverboat argument about whether the muddy Mississippi water was "wholesomer" than the clear water of the Ohio. One man maintained that if you let a pint of Mississippi water settle, you'd have a half to three-quarters of an inch of mud at the bottom. What you wanted to do, he said, was keep it stirred up so you could swallow the full "nutritioness."

Four prominent St. Louis physicians examined Millie-Christine on May 28, 1858. "We, the undersigned," they wrote, "having made critical examination of the *lusus naturae* [freak of nature] now being exhibited in our city by Mr. Vestal, would beg leave to state that this wonder, as regards the pelvic arrangements, is in our opinion one, in all other particulars double."

While the twins were in St. Louis, news arrived about the steamboat *Pennsylvania*'s dreadful accident downriver. She'd blown up off Ship Island shortly after the sisters had safely passed that river landmark. Mark Twain had left the doomed boat two days before the disaster. His younger brother was among the victims. Four of the eight boilers exploded with a thunderous crash, and the whole forward third of the boat lifted toward the sky. The main section with the chimneys then dropped onto the boat, and the mountain of wreckage caught fire.

Smith and his party also learned of Abraham Lincoln's bid for Stephen Douglas's seat in the United States Senate. The campaign got off to a red-hot start with Lincoln's remarks at the Illinois Republican Party Convention. "I believe this government cannot endure, permanently half slave and half free," he said in his acceptance speech. "I do not expect the Union to be dissolved—I do not expect the house to fall—but I do expect it will cease to be divided."

St. Louis was filled with show people that June. Two showboats, the *Banjo* and the *Raymond*, were preparing to steam up to St. Paul, Minnesota, with a troupe of trained dogs, goats, and monkeys, plus Billy Birch's Minstrels and a brass band composed of lady musicians. The twins left the Mississippi after their St. Louis run and headed west on the Missouri River to St. Joseph. On July 13, two days past their seventh birthday, they endured another tiresome medical inspection by five local doctors.

Smith saw to it that his party didn't stray beyond the Missouri line. "Bleeding Kansas," just across the river, was risky territory for show folk or anyone else. Vicious hit-and-run warfare raged between proslavery and antislavery settlers. Abolitionist John Brown had recently returned from an arms-gathering trip back east. Out there on the edge of Kansas, Detective Vestal must have daydreamed of collecting the $250 President Buchanan had offered to any man who could capture the elusive Brown. Perhaps he also fumed about the $2.50 Brown had offered in return for the president.

That July, while the twins exhibited in St. Joe, at least one dramatic company was trying to organize a tour in the "wilderness of woe," as the *Clipper* called Kansas. And Billy Birch's Minstrels had already ventured in. "Billy," the *Clipper* warned, "beware of the Border Ruffians; Horace Greeley says they are perfect cannibals. Look out, also, for the Fire-Eaters of the adverse faction."

Millie-Christine followed the western waterways for the rest of 1858. A November *Clipper* reported, "The 'two-headed girl' has just concluded a tour through the principal towns on the Mississippi River. She heads next for the Cumberland river towns."

While Millie-Christine explored western America, P. T. Barnum and General Tom Thumb were touring England. Tom had offered his services for a benefit trip to pull Barnum out of a recent bankruptcy.

"Perhaps I cannot lift as much as some other folks," he wrote when he heard of Barnum's troubles, "but . . . you will see I can draw a tremendous load." The little man with the big heart promised to help his old employer "as long as I, in my small way, can be useful." Sure enough, by the time Barnum's troupe returned to the States in December, it had recouped his lost fortune and then some.

Smith, reading newspaper accounts of Tom Thumb's loyalty to Barnum, couldn't have dreamed that Millie-Christine would one day rescue his own family with the same generous spirit Tom showed Barnum.

Chapter 8

Den hoe it down and scratch your grabble,
To Dixie land I'm bound to trabble.

"Dixie's Land," 1859

$\int$ ince he had Vestal to guard the twins and manage the show, Smith could take occasional breaks from touring. Sometime during 1858, he and Mrs. Smith uprooted their large household and moved from Wadesboro to Spartanburg, South Carolina—ninety miles due west as the crow flies, but a good deal farther bumping along meandering roads in buggies and mule-drawn covered wagons loaded with belongings.

Spartanburg was a thriving upcountry town that offered first-class Methodist schooling for the Smith children. The new young ladies' academy there outshone Carolina Female College. The boys could attend classes at Wofford College. The Smiths' new house on Magnolia Street was only three blocks from Wofford and from Spartanburg Methodist Church. It was a spacious home with tall pillars and wraparound verandas. Lofty ceilings let the summer heat move upward and out cutwork openings. Could the Smiths return to Spartanburg today, they'd find the old house gone from Magnolia Street, moved and reincarnated as the facade and front rooms of the J. F. Floyd Mortuary on North Church.

The 1858 house, like the homes of other well-to-do southerners, had a fireplace faced with pink, green, black-veined, rosy, or golden marble in each room; patterned winter carpets; and cool, bare, polished floors for summer. Out back, handy to the kitchen and the stables, stood the Smiths' seven slave houses. Six of them would have been ordinary little shotgun houses consisting of two rooms on each side of a hallway; they were called "shotgun" because you could shoot straight through the front door and out the back if you had a mind to. Very likely, Millie-Christine's family lived in better quarters.

Spartanburg Methodist Church—ancestor of today's mammoth Central United Methodist—stood near the corner of North Church and St. John. It was a two-story brick building with a short wooden bell tower and four white pillars on a Greek Revival facade. The congregation welcomed the newly arrived Smiths, both white and black.

"The slaves, they went to the white folks' church," recalled a black Carolina woman born about the same time as Millie-Christine. "They had a place separate from the white folks by a railing. We could look at the preacher and hear him preach too. . . . They preached to us to obey our master. . . . The songs that they sung then, they hardly ever sing them now. They were the good old songs. 'Hark from the Tomb, the Doleful Sound.'"

The main house stood near enough to the church that any sick child who had to miss Sunday services could rest by an open window and listen to the congregation sing the good old songs. Often, Mr. Smith's high voice rose above the rest. Smith sang like an angel, according to the family historian, in a clear tenor of great range. If the minister announced an unfamiliar song, others might falter, but Smith would meet the challenge. "In a firm, full sweetly modulated voice he sang the hymn," says the *Smith Family Tree* book, "in clear, distinct words, understood by the whole congregation (a very rare accomplishment)."

Happily, the twins found themselves part of a household where music and religion were regular parts of daily life. In Spartanburg, Mary Smith accompanied them while they worked out harmonies on the popular ballads they sang to paying audiences. One new song they must have practiced was "Dixie's Land." Dan Emmett's popular minstrel song worked its way south in 1859. In New Orleans, forty fetching young ladies dressed in Zouave pantaloons introduced "Dixie" in a march-and-drill routine at the Varieties Theatre.

The five-hundred-dollar pianoforte in the Smiths' parlor was the family's most expensive piece of furniture. Piano lessons posed an obvious problem for the twins. They couldn't share one keyboard because they couldn't sit side by side. Instead, they took turns. For their stage appearances, they had prop men shove two pianos together in a **V**, and the sisters played four-handed pieces to great applause.

Smith and the twins covered a wide southern circuit during their early years on the road. "That 'double-header' of a girl was at Knoxville,

Tenn., on the 16th of June," said an 1859 *Clipper*, "and she is making people see double with wonder around that way." In February 1860, the paper reported that "the two headed girl was last travelling through Mississippi."

While Smith was touring the Gulf Coast circuit, Barnum came back to life in New York City. Dug out of bankruptcy, he took charge of the American Museum again at an official repurchasing ceremony in the Lecture Hall. "Barnum's on his feet again!" his posters announced around town. An enthusiastic crowd welcomed him so warmly that Barnum spoke with tears streaming down his cheeks. "After nearly five years of hard struggle to keep my head above water, I have touched bottom at last, and here, to-night, I am happy to announce that I have waded ashore." Barnum was forty-eight, "scarcely old enough to be embalmed and put in a glass case in the Museum," he said.

The Siamese Twins, Chang and Eng Bunker, had come out of retirement. Barnum booked them for a short stay at the museum. "The ONLY LIVING SIAMESE TWINS," his ads proclaimed. They were there on October 13 when America's first British Royal visitor—Edward, Prince of Wales—called at the museum. He was disappointed to find Barnum out of town. "Ah," said the prince, "we have missed the most interesting feature of the establishment."

As matters turned out, Millie-Christine would never see the old museum again. It survived a Civil War firebombing, only to burn to the ground before the twins left the South and again exhibited in New York City.

Autumn always meant a round of state and county fairs for Smith and Millie-Christine. An ugly incident disturbed the last day of her appearance at the Agricultural Fair in Athens, Alabama. A circus and several side shows—the "Carolina Twins or Two Headed Girl," as well as Carter's Museum of Living Wonders, which included the Santa Fe Indian Giant, a sword swallower, a "Bird Warbler," and a "Bell-ringer"—had pitched their tents during fair week, according to the *Clipper*. As part of the closing-day festivities, local officials sponsored a footrace with a ten-dollar prize. The winner happened to be a black circus performer—a "knight of the spangles and tights"—which was a bitter pill for the locals to swallow.

The crowd found an excuse to turn rowdy when word spread that a black employee with Millie-Christine's show had eyes for a local lady. "One of the attaches of the 'Two Headed Girl' show having got rather thick with a handsome yellow gal," the *Clipper* reported, "the idea got current among the residents that the man intended to steal her away." He made a near-escape, was chased down, and "fortunately for him was only treated to a ride upon a 'rail.'" Hogtied to a split rail, that would mean, paraded through the streets, then dumped outside town into a pond, bog, or briar patch for Millie-Christine's party to rescue.

✥

If Joseph Smith got home to Spartanburg for the highly charged 1860 presidential election, he was entitled to cast a triple vote—his own, plus three-fifths of a vote on behalf of each of his four adult male slaves.

Lincoln's election produced enormous rage in the South. "Let the consequences be what they may," an Atlanta newspaper said, "whether the Potomac is crimsoned in human gore, and Pennsylvania Avenue is paved ten fathoms in depth with mangled bodies . . . the South will never submit to such humiliation and degradation as the inauguration of Abraham Lincoln."

Despite the rumblings of war, Millie-Christine's entertainment world spun on with hardly a wobble, at least for a while. Early signs of trouble came when some theatres replaced "The Star-Spangled Banner" with the "Southern Marseillaise Hymn":

> Sons of the South, awake to Glory! . . .
> Shall hateful tyrants, mischief breeding,
> With mongrel hosts, a thieving band
> Affright and desolate the land,
> While peace—equality—lie bleeding?
> To arms! to arms! ye brave!
> Th' avenging sword unsheath!
> March on! march on! all hearts resolved,
> On victory or death!

In December 1860, South Carolina, Millie-Christine's new home state, withdrew from the Union. Through January 1861, Deep South states Millie-Christine and Smith regularly visited—Louisiana, Mississippi, Florida, Alabama, Georgia—followed suit.

Show business faltered. A worried *Clipper* reader wrote a January 14 letter from Kansas saying, "From all I can learn, there is so much trouble in and out of the Union, it is hard to tell whether next season will pay or not. I look upon it as a lottery." In March 1861, a Kentucky correspondent ascribed the disastrous show-business season to "our black republican disorganizers of the North. Everything is their fault. Lincoln's people are entirely to blame."

The twins spent February and March 1861 in the New Orleans Museum as the most prominent attraction among many "Live Living Wonders," such as Madam Clofullia, the "Swiss Bearded Lady."

They were still in town when word went out that members of

the New Orleans Varieties had organized themselves into a military company "for the defence of the independent republic of Louisiana." Over at the St. Charles Theatre, the orchestra showed its independence by daring to play "Yankee Doodle" and several other old patriotic songs during a performance. "When Key's 'Star Spangled Banner' was struck up," noted the *New Orleans True Delta*, "it was immediately and loudly applauded, and 'Columbia, the Gem of the Ocean,' with its refrain, made the house ring. One enthusiastic individual jumped up and shouted 'hurrah!' and then there was a tumult."

In the aftermath of Fort Sumter, show business suffered further. Attendance in the South fell off completely, "owing to the all absorbing war cry," the *Clipper* reported. "Charleston is a dead cock in the theatrical pit; Mobile no better; . . . Richmond, we hear, has gone up; Montgomery, Ala. company dissolved. . . . New Orleans is trying to keep a stiff upper lip, but it is a sad case, and the end is fast approaching."

As for the twins, their discreet little *History* says only, "We were in New Orleans when the domestic political troubles commenced. Mr. Smith, who had heavy responsibilities resting upon him, was obliged to withdraw us from public life and take us home."

ϨϾϨϾ

Chapter 9

Under the sod and the dew,
Waiting the judgment day;
Under one the Blue,
Under the other, the Gray.

Smith Family Tree

$\mathcal{A}$s the fighting spread, the Smiths marked the war's early battles by their Anson County relatives killed or crippled. A brother-in-law was the first to go, at Shiloh, Tennessee. Next was a nephew in May 1862, mowed down in a muddy rear-guard action near Williamsburg, Virginia, and shipped home to die. Another nephew fell in July at Malvern Hill, Virginia, the victim of a shattered knee. Invalided home to Wadesboro, he hovered between life and death. Yet another nephew caught a bullet at Sharpsburg in September—

the Federals called it Antietam; the two sides couldn't even agree on names for their battles—and went home with a crushed hand and an honorable discharge.

When Joseph Smith decided to pay an autumn visit to Wadesboro, he must have been looking forward to some firsthand war stories from his recuperating nephews. His trip also served a more vital purpose. After a year and a half of war, he was terribly worried about finances. People he'd lent money would not—could not—pay him back. He needed to talk business with his brothers. The family stores were floundering, the shelves half empty, new merchandise cut off by the coastal blockade.

In normal times, Smith might have combined a fall visit home with a profitable Millie-Christine exhibition at the North Carolina State Fair. But as things stood now, North Carolina's October celebration was dead and buried. There'd been half a dozen gaudy fairs since the first one, where baby Millie-Christine had appeared. By 1862, the fairgrounds had been transformed into a year-round army training camp, where marching farmers drilled and about-faced and trampled over the old racetrack. The exhibition buildings served as hospitals and barracks. One rueful private wrote home saying his assigned bunk was in horse stall number 55.

What was even more shocking to the family than the war itself was that Joseph Smith never returned to Spartanburg from that North Carolina trip. His life's journey ended at his eldest brother's elegant home near Carolina Female College.

On Tuesday, November 4, 1862, a cousin and two old friends stood witness to his final wishes. "In the name of God Amen. I Joseph P. Smith a resident of Spartanburg District South Carolina now at my Brother's William G. Smith in the County of Anson State of

North Carolina," the will began. To his beloved wife, he left one-third of his estate, the balance to be equally divided among their seven children. He appointed Mary Smith and his brothers William and Samuel as executors.

He died the next day. That sad Wednesday also marked a special family birthday. His son Joseph Junior turned sixteen.

Smith was laid to rest at God's Acre, the family graveyard five miles east of Wadesboro. Neither the family history nor any of Millie-Christine's biographies reveal what accident or illness carried off the forty-seven-year-old. Millie-Christine's circus *Description* says merely, "The dreadful year which brought so much pain and suffering to the United States of America, brought its own individual sorrow to the home of Millie Christine. Mr. Smith, after a few weeks of suffering, passed quietly away to a better world, mourned by all who knew him, and by none more than those who called him master."

The twins were eleven when he died. They had traveled and lived with him for nearly six years—more than half their lives. He'd reunited them with their own family and made them part of his. "We were old enough then to mourn the loss of our good master, who seemed to us as a father," they say in their *History*, "and we here would render a grateful tribute to his memory by saying that he was urbane, generous, kind, patient-bearing, and beloved by all. We trust, in fact believe, that he has gone to that heaven we have heard him so often describe to us, when he would impress upon our minds the necessity of leading a good life in the hope of gaining a blessed immortality hereafter."

The later circus biography says, "Christine Millie desires particularly that it be inserted in this sketch of her life, that she experienced at his death the affection of one who had lost a beloved father rather than a master." Every person on the Smith estate, the biography says, "while calling the owner and his wife master and mistress, always regarded them in the light of protecting parents." As the *Description* rightly points out, slaves deeply and genuinely mourned the loss of a benevolent master. They dreaded the terrible uncertainties ahead: the unknown next master; the possibility that families might be split up, sold off, separated.

✌❀✌

Midnight church bells rang out the old year and rang in 1863. Frederick Douglass stood on the Music Hall stage in Boston, the town where Professor Millar had purchased Millie-Christine from a "spotted woman." Douglass, swallowing tears, read President Lincoln's Emancipation Proclamation to a jubilant gathering of blacks and whites: "Whereas, . . . on the first day of January, in the year of our Lord one thousand eight hundred and sixty-three, all persons held as slaves within any State . . . in rebellion against the United States shall be then, thenceforward, and forever free." Harriet Beecher Stowe was in the balcony that night. She rose when the crowd called for her and accepted her share of cheers.

In North Carolina, one master called his slaves together to explain exactly what the proclamation meant to them. "Boys," he said, as one of them remembered, "if the North whups, you will be as free a man as I is. If the South whups, you will be a slave all your days."

To Millie-Christine, legal freedom meant no more in her daily life than it ever had. She'd been "free" early on, in Philadelphia and Boston and New York, "free" when she crossed into Canada with Millar and Thompson, "free" in England even after Smith arrived to claim her back. But in 1863 in Spartanburg, she and any of Smith's people could still be traded or sold as readily as a wagon or a horse.

Four months after Joseph Smith's funeral, his cousin William Calvin Smith, a newly elected North Carolina senator, traveled to Spartanburg. He had witnessed Joseph sign his will. One Friday in March, he and Mary Smith crossed the square in Spartanburg to the Court of Ordinary and swore to the district judge that Joseph had been of sound mind and memory. The judge then filled out a form ordering two appraisers, "being first duly sworn on the Holy Evangelist of Almighty God," to "view and appraise all Goods and Chattels" left behind by Joseph Smith, in order to settle the estate.

The appraisal team wasted no time. Mr. Simpson Bobo and Mr. A. H. Kirby showed up the following Monday ready to set a fair market value on the dead man's belongings, from the oldest silver spoon to the newest-born slave baby. They moved through the house itemizing one by one the family furnishings: "1 Hall Stand $10; 1 Piano Forte $500." In the months since Smith's death, there'd been precious little harmonizing around the piano by Millie-Christine or any of the Smith children. The old hymns didn't sound the same without Smith's sweet tenor leading the way, and the crop of mournful new ballads like "The Empty Chair" and "Lorena" would have been unbearable. As for "Weeping, Sad and Lonely," Reb and Union officers alike forbade their troops to sing that song, it made the boys so blue.

The appraisers continued through the front rooms, noting "1 Sett Parlor Furniture $200." The parlor set included two S-shaped "tetetates" designed so a couple could sit facing one another—completely impractical for Millie-Christine, of course. The men listed everything from "Brass And Irons" to "Oil Window Shades," a $30 bookcase, and a $150 set of books.

The sewing room held a "Common Sewing Machine" appraised at $30 and a fancy one at $100, a mirror, a "large firm ironing table," and a set of smoothing irons. It was a room equipped for the never-ending work of stitching and mending and altering clothing for a family with seven growing children and numerous slaves. The twins surely knew all the furniture by heart from hours of standing in that room and slowly turning in a circle, Monemia or a seamstress altering dresses to allow them free movement above the waist, pinning and repinning until the hemline hung straight over their joined lower body and their legs.

The appraisers finished inside the house and proceeded to the outbuildings, where they found three large washtubs, a cookstove with utensils, and so on. The livestock consisted of fourteen cows, one bull, four calves, nine pigs, a large gray horse for the family carriage, a gray pony for the rockaway buggy, three mules, nine sheep, and two lambs. Bobo and Kirby recorded everything from farm wagons to grubbing hoes, sheep shears to a spinning wheel.

Total value of household goods: $5,190.

The team next wrote out "Chattels" and listed the first names, approximate ages, and estimated dollar value of each of the thirty-three men, boys, women, and girls Smith had claimed as property. The figure came to $38,500, plus "1 *Two headed* Negroe Girl Milly-Christina or 'Carolina Twins,' a great natural curiosity, $25,000."

Grand total for household goods and chattels: $68,690.

The rosy picture conjured by the total assets faded when Mary Smith and her brothers-in-law studied the estate's outstanding bills.

Old John Smith, Joseph's father, had been the largest landowner and slaveholder in Anson County. When he died, he had left his widow their spacious home, two thousand acres of land, a year's supply of food, and fifty Negroes of her choice. The remaining slaves and real estate were divided among four sons and two daughters. The difference between his financial circumstances and Joseph's was staggering.

"Master had always been liberal to others," Millie-Christine later explained, "and had, upon frequent occasions, lost heavily in business transactions."

Joseph Smith's business affairs were in great distress. The executors announced the unpleasant news in a March 30 petition to the judge. They stated that the estate was in debt and asked that they "be allowed to sell twenty negroes and such of the perishable property as may be spared."

Over the next three weeks, Mary Smith prepared for the sale.

The auctioneer opened with fifteen lots of household items. He tempted buyers with kerosene lanterns, polished brass andirons, the gray pony's brown colt, and the family carriage. The bids averaged out close to the appraisal values. A corn sheller estimated at $20.00 brought $29.50. The four-horse wagon valued at $100.00 brought only $80.00. In the case of Mrs. Smith's $100.00 sewing machine, the bidding stopped low, and her son Joe bought it back for $70.50. Altogether, after subtracting the redeemed sewing machine, the household goods brought $370.00. Only part of that trifling amount was hard cash. The rules of the sale allowed buyers a choice of paying by cash or by credit to January 1, 1864, with interest.

After disposing of the last household item—a set of old harness to the man who bought the carriage—the auctioneer opened the bidding on the slaves. Mary had selected thirteen of her people for auction. Although the twins were not among them, childhood playmates and friends were. Jim and Letitia went first. They and their two youngest children were expected to bring $1,500, but at the last minute, they got to keep a third child, and Mr. A. P. Turner bought all five for $3,000. Next up was six-year-old Dorthula. Once the bidding started, Mrs. Smith changed her mind and bought the child back for $1,065. Mr. E. M. Cobb was the day's high bidder. He paid $2,350 for twenty-two-year-old James; Cobb also took away Phebe and Mary and her child for $4,000, plus thirteen-year-old Louisa for another $2,000. Nicholas the carpenter, in his fifties, sold for only $695 when his turn came. Eight-year-old Violet went off alone with a buyer who paid $1,770 for her.

The auction netted about $14,000. The three executors worked out a plan to pay some of Mary Smith's current bills and provide a small annual income for her and her remaining people, including Millie-Christine.

ꙮ

The war showed no sign of ending. Two weeks after the auction, General Stonewall Jackson was shot by Confederate "wild fire." The Eighteenth North Carolina Regiment from Millie-Christine's own Columbus County fired the fatal volley. "We heard the firing of musketry in our front, followed by the rapid approach of what we thought was cavalry," said a captain who was present. "The order was given to fire, which was obeyed by the men of that gallant old regiment, little dreaming that they were giving the death wound to their much beloved commander."

As a doctor prepared to saw away Jackson's mangled arm, the wounded general gave thanks for the gift of chloroform from Millie-Christine's old friend Dr. Simpson. "What an infinite blessing . . . blessing . . . blessing," he murmured as he eased into oblivion.

༄༅༄

The *Clipper* continued its lighthearted reporting even in the face of wartime draft rumors. "Enrolling officers are again about, taking names, ages, etcetera," a June 1 column warned. "Actors forget their parts in thinking of the draft; to make them forget that, they take a draught of another and more palatable description; the public are on the 'anxious bench'; hot weather is at hand, and the idea of shouldering a musket, toting along a heavy knapsack, etc., with the thermometer at 90, has induced many of our people to hurry off to the country."

No one joked about the carnage at Gettysburg during the first three days of July. In Spartanburg, Mary Smith's family grieved to hear that one of Uncle Sam Smith's sons had been mowed down in the slaughter. Old "Samson of Anson County," for all his legendary strength, could save neither his boy nor a nephew wounded on the third day of the battle.

A week after Gettysburg—it happened to be Millie-Christine's twelfth birthday—President Lincoln issued a draft call for able-bodied men between the ages of twenty and forty-five. Those who came up with a three-hundred-dollar "commutation fee" or hired someone to join up in their place could stay home. Poor northerners rioted over the "rich man's law," just as poor southerners had raged against Confederate conscription bills. President Lincoln, well over draft age at fifty-four, set a good example by paying a willing substitute. P. T. Barnum, one year younger than Abe, sponsored four recruits.

A funny draft story involving the Siamese Twins came out of the war. In April 1865, as the Confederacy disintegrated, Union general George Stoneman swept into Mount Airy. The general set out to draft new recruits for the Union army from men in the neighborhood where the two Bunker farms were situated. He ordered the names of all males over age eighteen to be placed in a spinning lottery wheel. "Into the fateful wheel went the names of Chang and Eng," reported the *Philadelphia Times*. "But one name, that of Eng, was drawn. The gallant Stoneman was nonplussed. Eng must go, but Chang would not. Stoneman dared not take both. So he resigned his claim to Eng." And rode off with an entertaining story, instead of an aging double recruit.

Mary Smith made sure her own precious twins never came to the attention of the advancing Yankees. General William Tecumseh Sherman and sixty-two thousand men left Savannah on February 1, 1865, and foraged their way toward South Carolina's capital. Seventeen days later, Columbia was in flames. As Sherman and his marauding "bummers" slogged northward, Mrs. Smith packed the twins out of town and into the home of Captain Bivings, a family friend. They spent the remaining days of the war safe in their isolated, majestic hideaway. Today, the bright, roomy structure looks down on a cluster of shabby mill houses and a rusting factory along the Lawson's Creek waterfall, five miles southeast of Spartanburg.

Chapter 10

Children, do you want your freedom?

Tell me, do you want your freedom?

"We Are Climbing Jacob's Ladder"

*A*t war's end, the Smiths and the McKoys found themselves in "straightened circumstances," as they put it. The twins were fourteen. "It was then," according to the circus *Description*, "that the kindness of the past found its fruit."

Millie and Chrissie decided it was up to them to provide for both families. "The only alternative was for us to again go upon exhibition," they say in their *History*. "None can mistake our determination in remaining under the guardianship of Mrs. Smith. Our object is two-fold: We can trust her, and what is more, we feel grateful to her and regard her with true filial affection. We will not go with any one else."

For the first time, Millie-Christine would draw her share of the profits. Her parents would start out with the show, then veer off to resettle the family on the homeplace at Welches Creek in Columbus County, North Carolina. Millie-Christine and her father, Jacob, dreamed of buying the old acreage he had once worked.

Jacob was fifty-two and Monemia and Mary Smith both forty-four when they entered the exhibition business. Mrs. Smith and Joseph Junior would learn how to route the tours and attend to sales. Joe was twenty, ready to follow in his father's footsteps as business manager. The little party would head north. Except for Millie-Christine, all of them were as green as Joseph Smith had been when he first hit the show-business trail.

Millie-Christine insisted on one big change. Now that she was her own mistress and free to set her own rules, there'd be no more intimate examinations by curious doctors in every town. Since her babyhood, male physicians had peered as close as the human eye could see and explored as deep as the human finger could probe. Surely, there was nothing new to see or feel that countless doctors hadn't already reported in graphic detail.

When Millie-Christine opened her Raleigh exhibit in February 1866, William C. Smith, Mary Smith's cousin by marriage, no longer served in the North Carolina Senate. After the war, he'd moved his family west for a fresh start in Texas. Ordinarily, no legislators would have been in Raleigh in February. The current crop should have scattered and gone home, leaving the capital city to nod off for the winter. But the general assembly was back in special session to complete unfinished business.

Senator Leander Gash was there with the rest. A farmer and dry-goods merchant from Hendersonville, he represented a district spread over five counties in the western mountains. Gash wrote newsy letters home, keeping his wife up to date on political happenings as well as his life in Raleigh, which included a visit to see the twins, who, he noted, were about the same size as two of his own daughters. "She is, or they are certainly an anomily," he wrote. "The Siamese Twins are no where when compared to this double negro. They are 14 years old, not far from Julia & Eugenias size.

"I examined the connection at the back it is two or three inches below the shoulder blades and merges together as naturally as the arm to the shoulder. . . . And what is very remarkable . . . you might cut ones arm off and the other would not feel it. But if you cut ones foot it hurts the other just as much as the one you cut. They walk sideways, sing very well and beautiful dancers, exactly suited for it and can dance and swing around more gracefully than anything you ever seen. Out dance anybody. One a grain larger than the other, about the difference there is between Mattie and Addie [his own twins]. They are about the colour of Marth [one of the Gashes' former slaves] and look a good deal like she did at their age.

"They were born in this state," he told his wife, "and was stolen by a yankee and taken to Europe. . . . They can read tolerable well and is beginning to write. They leave this week for the North."

Gash's letter also passed along alarming news from Washington. "There is a bill before Congress to quarter a large standing army on the south and tax the southern states to pay the expense of it, but I have no fears of such a thing passing although it might pass, for there is nothing too rediculous for some people to do and a majority of the present seem to be as crazy as any body, but surely the President [Raleigh-born Andrew Johnson] would veto such a bill as that."

꒰꒱꒰꒱

The sisters left the South to its Reconstruction woes and began gathering regular notices in the *New York Clipper*. "The Freedmen's or some other Bureau in the South has just brought to light a pair of reconstructed twins, on the Siamese twins style of architecture," said the March 3, 1866, *Clipper*, "and the united couple were being exhibited in Raleigh, North Carolina, at last accounts." They were fourteen years of age, the article reported, the offspring of slave parents, and more closely connected than Chang and Eng. "One can engage in a game of whist while the other reads or sings. The lady who has them in charge was their former mistress, and is now commencing a tour with them under a contract with their parents, who are both living."

"THE LATEST SENSATION in the show business in Baltimore is the 'Carolina Twins,'" reported the March 24 *Clipper*. "A New York manager has them in charge and will doubtless be rewarded by a satisfactory influx of stamps." *Stamps* was a breezy way of saying paper money. "We have it from good authority that Barnum offered $50,000 for them for three years, which was refused."

The New York manager was presumably Judge H. P. Ingalls. He'd just concluded a winter tour with the Siamese Twins, who had gone home to Mount Airy to recuperate. The Bunker brothers were back on the road because, in the wake of the war, their outstanding business loans were as worthless as a wheelbarrow load of Confederate scrip. Their thirty-three slaves were either gone or working for wages. Their two wives and numerous children remained. The brothers had bundled themselves off to New England in the winter to compete with other entertainers in Massachusetts, Maine, and New Hampshire. They were "all bobbing around," as the *Clipper* put it, "collecting what few stamps the Yanks have."

In Baltimore, Millie-Christine's show set up in the Temperance Temple. It was a proper setting for what Mrs. Smith liked to call Millie-Christine's "soirees." Nine years had passed since Joseph Smith, Monemia, and her beloved child overnighted at the old Barnum Hotel in Baltimore after fleeing England. Smith had kept Millie-Christine under cover on that stopover. Now, Baltimore doctors, seeing her for the first time, pronounced her the greatest wonder they'd ever heard of or read of in their medical books.

After a month in Baltimore, the show moved on to Washington D.C., the southerners' first visit to the nation's capital. The Capitol dome was finally in place, but the great monument to President Washington was stalled. The Monument Society had run out of money before the war, and the obelisk stood abandoned at 152 feet of its planned 555. Mark Twain thought it looked like a factory chimney with the top broken off.

One of the sisters' Washington callers was Professor Charles A. Lee. "I have just come from visiting a monstrosity that will interest you much," he wrote a doctor friend. Lee enclosed a photograph of the twins, looking gawky and pubescent in an outgrown dress and black clodhopper shoes, their skirt hiked up on Chrissie's side by an off-kilter hoop. Lee also sent a show bill listing the popular tunes they sang. The twins were "quite comely, very intelligent and well educated," the bill said. "They sing finely, dance remarkably well." They skipped rope as part of their show. The bill also promised "experimenting with the twins by a committee selected from the audience."

By choosing a committee, the twins saved themselves a multitude of pinches. Lee was one of the group picked to demonstrate to the rest of the audience what everyone wanted to try. In the letter to his friend, he told of how he had demonstrated that the girls shared sensation below the union, how one of them "could tell, for example, how many times I pinched her sister."

He was intrigued that they had "two hearts, *one on the left side of the one, and one on the right side of the other girl*." They had begun to menstruate seven months ago, he learned. They had been seriously sick only once—fever and ague, taken at the same time. Their appetite was good. The height of one was four feet five and a half inches, the other four feet six inches. "They have both become accustomed to face the same way, so that the outer legs, (one right, the other left,) are larger, better developed and stronger than the inner. The feet, of course, are placed quite obliquely when they walk. The larger one can walk and carry the other. They walk well on the outer legs."

Even though he'd had a chance to examine the twins superficially, Lee felt cheated as he left the exhibition. "The keeper, Mr. Smith, would not allow me to see them naked," he complained, "nor place my hand under their clothes to examine the pelvis."

The twins and their party then moved on to Philadelphia's Assembly Buildings. Philadelphia editors covered their arrival and met the girls. "They chat with each other almost incessantly when not otherwise occupied," the *Daily Evening Bulletin* reported, "and the two talk with different persons upon different subjects at the same moment. They seem perfectly cheerful in their strangely blended condition; declare that they know of no inconvenience resulting from it, and protest that they would be unhappy if they were separated, were such a thing possible."

When the sisters arrived in New York City for a July engagement at Barnum's new American Museum, *Frank Leslie's Illustrated Newspaper* ran a long article on them. "North Carolina," the piece concluded, "which was the birth-place of these twins, seems to enjoy a sort of monopoly of such strange natural productions. It will be remembered that the Siamese Twins have made their home in that State."

Frank Leslie was famous for his excellent engravings. Millie-Christine must have been delighted with the double-column portrait that illustrated the article. The country bumpkin pictured in Professor Lee's May photo has blossomed into a stylish performer wearing a fancy costume dress that fit perfectly and dainty shoes with bows on the toes.

Barnum had located his new museum uptown in the bustling area above Canal Street. His new collection of oddities already overflowed his remodeled building on Broadway between Spring and Prince. Workmen were pounding away next door at 537 Broadway, creating space for a mammoth menagerie. Meanwhile, visitors could shudder at the snakes that had replaced those broiled to death in the 1865 fire and see a living "Ourang Outang" from Borneo, the latest "Happy Family" of caged prey and predators, a tortoiseshell cat nursing a family of squirrels, and an Esquimaux dog from an Arctic exploration.

The new museum had a Photograph Art Gallery. Perhaps it was the museum's photographer who snapped a photo of the twins in the same old dress they had worn in the gawky picture from Washington. This time, happily, someone fixed the hoop so the dress didn't bunch. Best of all, the twins wore up-to-date low white boots with black patent-leather toes and heels, in place of the old clodhoppers.

They exhibited at the American Museum for the entire month of July.

"Thoroughly Ventilated! Deliciously cool!" Barnum's weekly *Clipper* ad boasted of the new museum. In another part of the paper, a smart-aleck columnist said that Barnum's claim was the coolest thing about the place.

FRANK LESLIE'S ILLUSTRATED NEWSPAPER.

THE "CAROLINA TWINS," MILLIE AND CHRISTINA, NOW ON EXHIBITION AT BARNUM'S MUSEUM
BROADWAY, NEW YORK.

Engraving for an article on the Carolina Twins

FRANK LESLIE'S ILLUSTRATED NEWSPAPER, JULY 14, 1866

Giantess Anna Swan and other Barnum regulars lived at the museum in upper-floor apartments. Simple guest rooms housed short-term performers like Millie-Christine and Master Alley Turner, the "Infant Drummer," who made "as much noise on the drum as a whole corps of German drummers just before the paymaster heaves in sight," according to a *Clipper* ad. Museum performers shared a kitchen and living room. The chairs, tables, and sofas had to fit an extraordinary range of shapes and sizes, since Barnum's "Living Curiosities" celebrated the human body's fantastic range of possibilities.

The big people—Anna Swan; Routh Goshen, the "Arabian Giant" from Palestine (who looked and sounded suspiciously African American); and Noah Orr, the "American Giant"—were eight-footers. Each weighed in at about 400 pounds. Miss Rosina D. Richardson, the "Mammoth Fat Woman," weighed 660 pounds. Millie-Christine's 240-pound mama, had she been there, would have looked slender beside her.

As for the little people, the twins towered over the three tiny children who were current Barnum stars. Miss Cora Ballard was said to be ten years old, twenty inches tall, and nineteen pounds. "General Grant Jr." (young Edward Newell) and Master William Wallace, the "Scotch Dwarf," were nearer the twins' age. Of course, it was hard to be sure about that, since management was notoriously nonchalant about ages and measurements. Barnum posters, for instance, announced the Carolina Twins as "aged 13 years." By an ordinary calendar, they turned fifteen that month. The posters said that Master Wallace was fifteen years old, twenty-one inches high, and a robust twenty-two pounds. General Grant Jr. was fourteen years old, twenty-seven inches high, and a mere eighteen pounds. By any standard of measurement, General Grant Jr. looked far more dapper in a full-dress Union army uniform than rumpled Ulysses S. Grant ever had.

As a reminder, museum patrons could view the war-weary military hat that the real Grant had donated to his friend Phineas T. Barnum.

The twins spent their working hours on the second floor, greeting visitors and watching the wonderful assortment of folk who came through the museum. "It is a sight to watch the constant flow of persons, of all sizes and color, coming in and going out of this establishment during the day," wrote a *Clipper* reporter.

The sisters' fellow employees were even more engaging. A talented troupe of master glassblowers and spinners, Woodruffe's Bohemian Glass Blowers, entertained nearby, creating "an endless variety of parlor ornaments, ships, birds of paradise, baskets of flowers, vases of fruit," said the *Clipper*. Mrs. Woodruffe, "the most beautiful fancy Glass Worker in the world," specialized in making "Ladies' Head Dresses" and ornaments for ladies' hats.

The Bohemian troupe included a machinist-engineer who ran a wondrous glass steam engine called the "Fairy Queen." What a contraption! It was nine feet long and had five-foot wheels. Every single part was glass—boilers, steam gauge, safety valve, whistle, bell. The connecting frame tower, higher than a tall man, was made of glass rods twisted like strands of taffy. "The FAIRY QUEEN brilliant with a hundred colors, in complete working order dazzles the beholder with its inconceivable forms of loveliness and beauty, and as he gazes upon the countless charms he realizes that in the frail structure before him is embodied the grandest mechanism in the power of man," said an ad placed by the Bohemian troupe.

One sizzling July Wednesday, a museum visitor climbed to the second floor expressly to see Millie-Christine. Dr. George J. Fisher was the medical friend Professor Lee had written to after seeing Millie-Christine in Washington.

Dr. Fisher, vice president of the New York State Medical Society and member of the American Medical Association and other associations too numerous to list, was writing about "Compound Human Monsters," and he must have been thrilled at the chance to meet a living example. His publication's magnificent title (with one printer's error to mar the cover page) was *Diploteratology—An Essay on Compound Humam Monsters, comprising the History, Literature, Classification, Description and Embryology of Double and Triple Formation; including Parasitic Monsters, Foetus in Foetu, and Supernumerary Development.* Medically speaking, diploteratology was defined as "the sum of what is known regarding joined twin monstrosities."

For the section dealing with *Pygopagus symmetros*, he'd already completed case number 1, on Hungarian sisters Helen and Judith. The Hungarian sisters, born in 1701, had been joined at the lower back. Like the Carolina Twins, they were intelligent girls and fine singers. They'd been exhibited in Europe for a few years, then placed under the care of nuns at Presburg, Hungary, at age nine.

Dr. Fisher's essay included three burning questions debated by doctors and theologians during Helen and Judith's lifetime.

First: Was a separation attempt proper? Such an attempt would be extremely hazardous and unjustifiable, said one Eccardus (German professor Johann von Eckhert). However, he added that "should one die before the other, I would advise immediate separation, which should be done through the lifeless parts."

Second: Would their condition admit of or justify the solemn rite of matrimony? Physically, there were no serious objections, Eccardus reasoned, "but morally there are insuperable ones, more particularly on account of the extreme liability of propagating monsters!"

Third: Would the sisters, on the last day, rise joined as in life or appear separated? Because they were united by accident, Eccardus decided, "we are indeed firmly persuaded that the sisters will rise again, and will appear with bodies separated, or rent asunder."

They died when they were only twenty-one. Judith, the second-born and always the weaker sister, went first, diagnosed with "disease of the brain and lungs." Helen, who'd been in excellent health, promptly collapsed, and the sisters expired almost at the same instant.

Dr. Fisher translated a curious poem from the Latin. Composed by a Hungarian physician as an inscription for a bronze statuette of the "Wonderful Sisters, Helen and Judith," it could have been written for the Carolina Twins:

> Two sisters wonderful behold, who thus have grown as one,
> That nought their bodies can divide, no pow'r beneath the
> sun.
> One urine-passage serves for both, one anus, so they tell;
> The other parts their numbers keep, and serve their owners
> well.
> Their parents poor did send them forth, the world to travel
> through
> That this great wonder of the age should not be hid from
> view.
> The inner parts concealed do lie, hid from our eyes, alas,
> But all the body here you view, erect in solid brass.

Fisher had already written up the "United African Twins" as case number 2 for his publication, based on Dr. Ramsbotham's 1855 description of them at Egyptian Hall in Picadilly. His entire diploteratology manuscript had actually gone off to the printer. Type was already set and the proofs returned for corrections when he learned that the sisters were in New York City. He suspected that the United African Twins and the Carolina Twins were the same conjoined pair and set out for Barnum's museum to make sure.

"The day that I examined the twins was very hot, the mercury was above 90° of Fahrenheit's scale," he wrote. "I counted the pulse of each, while they were standing, and found Christina's to be 68 per minute, and Millie's to be 80. . . . The 'twins' are now in their fifteenth year; they are in excellent health; their combined weight is one hundred and fifty-nine and a half pounds. They are well formed; and resemble each other very much; their complexion is that of the fair mulatto; their features and expression are rather pleasing; they are very cheerful and intelligent; fond of reading; sing very sweetly, and converse modestly and fluently." He also noted that they danced a graceful schottische (a sort of slow-tempo polka) and ran with remarkable speed.

"Christina lifts Millie when she stoops," he noted, "and even walks or runs with her with great ease, no pain or strain is experienced at the seat of junction. Millie being weaker cannot perform the same feat with her sister." Dr. Fisher must have observed this with startled recognition, for he knew from his research on the Hungarian sisters that when Helen had stooped to pick up anything, she "raised her sister quite from the ground, and carried her on her back."

To his chagrin, he "was not permitted to examine the genito-urinary organs." He did examine the joined backs. Moving his stethoscope over both chests, he thought he heard Millie's heart on the right-hand side, as had his friend Lee.

Mary Smith assured Dr. Fisher that the United African Twins and the Carolina Twins were two names for the one and only Millie-

Christine. He left Barnum's museum disappointed that he couldn't examine them more thoroughly but certain that they were indeed the 1855 London case.

Dr. Fisher returned home to revise and update his article with a firsthand report on "this living pygopagus symmetros." He concluded his case study of the twins with an encouraging prognosis: "They present every indication of attaining advanced life."

❧❧❧

For the autumn fair season, Judge Ingalls put together a new "Combination Troupe," teaming Millie-Christine with the Siamese Twins. Two Bunker youngsters would also join the show. Ingalls suggested Chang's son Albert and one of Eng's children. He wanted them along partly to help care for Chang and Eng and partly as an extra drawing card—a reminder to visitors of the Siamese Twins' intriguing married life.

Millie-Christine was fifteen, and Chang and Eng were fifty-five. In their younger days, the brothers had performed amazing gymnastic feats on the stage. Now, they merely wandered about, weary old men answering questions they'd heard a thousand times. The way they walked side by side, each with an arm around the other's shoulder, looked comradely and casual. In fact, Chang was tipsy much of the time, and Eng had to hold him steady.

The Combination Troupe appeared at a mid-September fair at Saratoga, New York. "The Fair," wrote a *Clipper* correspondent. "brought thousands of farmers, thieves, gamblers, side showmen, Yankee peddlers and other folks." One swindler pitched a large tent covered with paintings of exotic animals. Believe it or not, the fellow told the crowd, every animal pictured on the outside of the tent could be seen alive inside. To illustrate, he brought a large bear onto the platform and shook hands with it. "This, of course, caused crowds to rush in, when lo! all that was to be seen was the aforesaid bruin, one snake, gently handled by a lady, and a jewelry case," according to the *Clipper*. When customers complained, the showman warned them that the bear was much attached to him and had once torn to pieces a man who had struck him.

In mid-October, Millie-Christine and the Bunkers played a fair in Hamilton, Ohio. P. T. Barnum showed up in Ohio that same month, giving his popular lecture on "The Art of Money Getting," an amusing and frank story he had told to overflow English audiences when he toured with Tom Thumb. It was a decidedly American tale of how a poor boy amassed a fortune with a combination of hard work and humbug, how he lost it all, and how he gained it back. Barnum spoke at Mozart Hall in Cincinnati a few days before Ingalls booked his double set of double twins there for a week's run.

"We have been travelling with the Carolina Twins since we left Xenia but I dont know how long they will be with us," one of the Bunker children wrote home on Halloween. The main reason for the letter was to check on affairs at home. Like all good farmers, Chang and Eng worried about how the work was going without their supervision. "Pappa says he hope you are done sowing grain by this time," the letter continued, "and have commenced to pull corn put the corn in the loft not the crib it will not be safe Pappa says get the hogs in good order before you kill them. . . . You say corn will be one dollar per bu. Pappa thinks it will be cheaper than that and not to be in a hurry to buy at that price. Let us know when you write again how much corn you have made if as much as last year. and also if the sweet Potatoes are good we think there will be some stealing going on there this fall and winter."

A December 22 *Clipper* item from Indianapolis reported that "the Siamese Twins and the Carolina Twins are traveling through the West." Farther west, Mark Twain was hitting the gold towns on the California circuit. A *Clipper* correspondent who caught his entertaining stage lecture in Sacramento reported, "It seemed to be duly relished by those present and the mirth was frequent and hearty."

Mark Twain evidently read the review, as the correspondent telegraphed back in time for the next issue, "Mark says that since the CLIPPER has noticed him he is entitled to be one of the profession."

TWO HEADED GIRL!

" None like me since the days of Eve,
None such perhaps will ever live,
A wonder to myself am I,
As well to all who pass me by."

This remarkable girl is now 17 years of age, born a slave in Columbus County, North Carolina, is of a bright Mulatto complexion, with

Two Separate, Well Developed Heads

—— AND ——

TWO SEPARATE AND DISTINCT SETS OF ARMS AND SHOULDERS!

All of which blend into One Body,

And actually forms but one person, physically speaking. She TALKS, SINGS, EATS and DRINKS with both mouths, both craving after the same thing at the same time. She has walk upon two of them with ease. Will converse with two persons on different subjects at the same time. Sing and sing together. She is intelligent and pleasing in conversation, and has a fine, happy disposition. about her in the least, but on the contrary is VERY INTERESTING. She has been critically examined, both physically and anatomically, by the leading physicians of Jefferson Medical College, Philadelphia pronounce her the MOST ASTONISHING, REMARKABLE and INTERESTING

FREAK OF NATURE

EVER SEEN ON EARTH

since the creation of our first parents. Far more surprising and wonderful than life time will never be forgotten.

WEEK, at Melonian Hall. Open from 9 A. M. to 9.30 P. M.

Ladies and their children, accompanied by gentlemen,

50 CENTS

Chapter 11

We are indeed a strange freak of Nature, and
upon the success of our exhibition does our
happiness and the well-doing of others depend.

History and Medical Description of the Two-Headed Girl

By 1869, the show was in the doldrums. Judge Ingalls was in England on a Barnum-sponsored tour that did not include Millie-Christine, and Joe lacked a true promoter's flair. "THE DOUBLE-HEADED GIRL—as the gentlemanly blower in front of the house calls 'it'—is on exhibition," an embarrassing review from Philadelphia began. "Judging by the attendance outside, the man who 'talks up' the show is a greater curiosity than the double-headed party inside." Assuming Joe was the "gentlemanly blower" the piece made fun of, even his fond mother must have realized the show needed professional help.

The Smiths hired a new agent who could coax an audience in-side to see the show. Probably at his suggestion, Millie-Christine, age seventeen, wrote the story of her life. It was titled *History and Medical Description of the Two-Headed Girl*. This first show-business autobi-ography was published as a 4½-by-7-inch, thirty-two-page booklet that sold for a quarter at performances.

The artist who drew the cover picture must never have seen the twins. The bottom half is accurate. It shows a hoop skirt short enough to reveal two sets of legs in pretty tasseled boots and two sets of feet angled away from each other. But the top half is all wrong. A tightly corseted waist swells into modest bosoms; two attractive side-by-side heads turn to face one another, as Millie and Chrissie never could. Each girl on the cover has only a single outside shoulder and arm.

"Told in 'her own peculiar way' by 'one of them,'" it says on the title page. Joseph Smith's great-granddaughter, Dicksie Cribb, once passed along a family memory about the way the twins shared writ-ing chores: "My aunt told me Christine did all the writing; she was the correspondent. The other, Millie, crocheted and dictated to Chris-tine what to write."

Like other well-brought-up young ladies of the day, the twins favored inserting an elegant foreign word every so often. "We made our *entree* into this breathing world in 1852," the *History* begins, though July 11, 1851, is the settled-upon date in later booklets.

"Our coming in such 'questionable shape' created as great a *furore* in the cabin as our appearance has since wherever we have been. 'Old Aunt Hannah,' a faithful nurse, whose specialty was to be around and to discharge the first hospitalities to new comers of our com-plexion, couldn't for 'de life or soul of her' tell whether we was a 'young nigger' or 'something else.' But the 'something else' soon gave unmistakable evidences that it could, *viva voce*, intimate a desire for

Cover of the autobiographical History, *printed in 1869*

maternal comforts, just as well as the best developed young African on the premises. So our mother and the rest of the family came to the conclusion that 'a child was born.'"

The twins skimmed lightly over their early adventures as wandering, kidnapped children and their rescue by Joseph Smith. "We might . . . tell many anecdotes of our travels," they said, "but we think a simple narrative of ourselves is all that at present those of our patrons who buy our little book will require." The booklet wasn't meant to tell all. It was written to tease visitors into buying tickets and coming inside to find out more.

One anecdote the sisters did include revealed a secret rendezvous with Queen Victoria! Was it true? The Royal Archives at Windsor Castle did not record such a visit, though it did record a later one for the grown-up twins.

"Our visit to the Queen and the Royal Family at Osborne House, we shall never forget," they wrote. "Her Majesty had 'signified her pleasure' to have us brought before her. Our good mother wrapped us up in real southern style to shield us from the heavy fogs of London. We nor she did not comprehend the glory of the errand we were bent upon, only she knew that a grand and good lady wanted to see us. When we arrived, the pomp and circumstance of the surroundings dazzled our young eyes, and we wondered what was to be done with us. But we can say that 'Victoria was a woman,' for she talked tenderly to us, and to our mother, and when we left we bore away abundant tokens of her good feeling and queenly liberality. A great many artists boast of having been before the Queen. Perhaps they have, and employed great diplomacy to get there. But with us the case was different. Poor little monstrosities, and black babies at that; we were sent for, and that without any influence at court to

Advertising flier for Tremont Temple exhibition, Boston, 1869

DICKSIE CRIBB COLLECTION

gain for us a Royal summons."

The autobiographical booklet included two kind reviews from recent tours.

"The exhibition of these remarkable twins is characterized by the peculiar delicacy, modesty and ingenuousness of these *young girls* themselves," said the editor of the *Louisville Journal*. Returning the compliment, the twins wrote, "Mr. Prentice, we have always heard, could say pleasant as well as very witty and cunning things. We thank him for the handsome manner in which he has seen proper to speak of us."

There was also a nice quote from Brick Pomeroy of the *La Crosse Democrat*, who'd come to one of the twins' Wisconsin levees the past winter. He was pleased, he said, "particularly with the manner in which they conversed. They are not impudent, but they are not foolishly retiring. They sing well, in fact excellent, and dance divinely, considering the manner in which their limbs and body are constructed. They know they are a curiosity, and feel anxious that the public should appreciate their attractiveness. We have no hesitation in declaring them to be the most extraordinary exhibition of a peculiar and 'indissoluble union' we have ever witnessed. The Siamese Twins, in the way of strange formation, cannot bear any comparison to them." The sisters responded warmly to Pomeroy's empathy: "That editor fully knows how we feel in regard to the public. We wish to be viewed as something entirely void of humbug—a living curiosity—not a sham gotten up to impose upon and deceive the people. . . . We have been examined most scrutinizingly by too many medical men to be regarded as humbugs by any one. Still, there are many persons who will not believe anything."

As to the perennial question of whether they were one person or two, the twins said firmly, "Although we speak of ourselves in the plural, we feel as but *one person*."

They closed the first portion of the booklet with a verse they'd composed. "The song we sing, we have so often been requested to give copies of, that we have concluded to insert it in our book," they wrote. "We must admit that, as a literary production, it has not much merit, but it conveys a good idea of our feelings."

> It's not modest of one's self to speak,
> But daily scanned from head to feet
> I freely talk of everything—
> Sometimes to people wondering.
>
> Some persons say I must be two;
> The doctors say this is not true;
> Some cry out "Humbug" till they see,
> Then they say, "Great mystery!"
>
> Two heads, four arms, four feet,
> All in one perfect body meet;
> I am most wonderfully made,
> All scientific men have said.
>
> None like me since the days of Eve—
> None such perhaps will ever live;
> A marvel to myself am I,
> As well to all who passes by.
>
> I'm happy, quite, because I'm good;
> I love my Saviour and my God;
> I love all things that God has done,
> Whether I'm created *two* or *one*.

A medical description filled the second half of the booklet. It was a complete reprint of Dr. George Fisher's account of Millie-Christine, his *Pygopagus symmetros* case number 2.

Doctors from the Harvard Medical School faculty tried in vain to persuade the girls to undergo a full physical exam when they appeared at the Boston Tremont Temple during 1869. Millie refused. No matter how the physicians pleaded in the name of science, she defended her right to personal privacy.

Dr. John Barnard Swett Jackson, professor of morbid anatomy at Harvard, was gathering material for a *Boston Medical and Surgical Journal* article on the "Carolina Sisters." He thought he could get around Millie by interviewing the twins' maid, who said she'd been Joseph Smith's slave when he bought the little girls and the rest of the family. Much of what she told him was already familiar. Monemia had borne fifteen or sixteen children, depending on whether Millie-Christine counted as one or two; her labor with the joined twins had been as easy as with any of the others. The maid verified that the twins' general health had always been good, except for one severe struggle with ague and fever. She said Millie was somewhat smaller than Chrissie. The doctor could see that for himself. Together, they tipped the scales at 170 pounds. "M., however, wears a boot that is one size smaller than C's," he noted.

"They not merely walk rapidly about the room, but they waltz together, and rather gracefully," the doctor wrote. "They seem to have very little difficulty in the sitting position. I saw them touch their lips, but they cannot do it as easily, they say, as in former years. At one of my visits I found them at work, and M. was sewing with her left hand; her habit, formerly, having been to use this hand much more than she does at present."

Jackson was allowed a superficial examination, during which the twins' dress was "so arranged that the union could be seen as well as felt." But he failed to change their minds about a close inspection. "Having seen the girls several times, and finding that it would be entirely out of the question to get a vaginal examination, I requested the attendant to make one, with instructions; but, intimate as she is with them, she had no better success than myself."

Dr. Jackson also wanted to solve the mystery of how Millie's heart was positioned. When he moved his stethoscope across her clothed chest, it seemed to him that her heart was not really on the right side, but only a bit displaced because of the way the girls had twisted their upper bodies during their growing years.

To settle the question, he asked Dr. Henry Bowditch, Harvard's eminent chest specialist, to visit the sisters. Dr. Bowditch reported as follows: "Millie was unwilling to remove her dress. As far as I could examine her heart it seemed about in the usual place, perhaps a little more towards the centre than usual, but I thought undoubt-edly at the left of the sternum."

⁂

Millie-Christine spent the late summer and fall exhibiting in a series of New England towns. She was in Lawrence, Massachusetts, the first week of August, then in Rhode Island in September. "D. K. Prescott, who is traveling east with the two headed girl, reports busi-ness as good," said a *Clipper* notice.

The 1869 New England tour was memorable for both the fall foliage and a bit of unpleasantness in Portland, Maine. Millie-Chris-tine had just appeared on the stage when a boisterous visitor sud-denly shouted that she was a great humbug. The heckler turned out to be a Dr. Gardner, who was upset because he hadn't been allowed to carry out an examination. After a brief tussle, a town constable arrested him for creating a disturbance.

Aside from that minor incident, Millie-Christine and her party found the postwar northern states hospitable and profitable. A southern tour was hardly worth the trouble, *Clipper* stories advised them, not to mention the possible danger. In March 1870, a showman traveling through the South sent a long letter to the paper giving a picture of show-business conditions and expenses. His show followed the same southern routes Millie-Christine and Joseph Smith used to cover, visiting both cities and villages—Louisville to Paducah; Nashville to Chattanooga to Knoxville; the Georgia towns.

"We are moving along quietly and successfully and enduring the curse of high prices," he wrote, "as everybody does who comes into the south." Halls in the South cost 25 to 50 percent more to rent than those in the North, he said, "and half the time you get nothing furnished. In Savannah, for instance, we paid $250 per week for the theatre and we got the bare building. We had to deposit $50 before the gas could be turned on, hire a man to clean and light the theatre, others to work stage, ushers, police." Then there were the miscellaneous fees: "State license, $25; county license $1.50 per day; U.S. license, 2 per ct tax; over $100 for from forty to fifty lines of advertisement in the dailies one week; $40 for bill boards . . . $2.50 per day for thirteen people at a second rate hotel one week, with fires, etc., extra, and baggage hauling, omnibus, van and wagon, etc., at double the rates prevalent in the eastern and middle states."

High prices might be endured, but not violence. On the courthouse square at Dalton, Georgia, was a sight so grisly that it convinced the seasoned troupers to skip the performance and the town.

"On a tree in front of the hall hung the body of a nigger who had been taken from an adjoining jail on the previous night and thus summarily disposed of, because he had attempted to ravish the daughter of some southern," the showman said. The body remained there "for about 30 hours, until, at last, somebody cut the poor devil down. About the time they were doing so, we concluded it would be only a waste of time and strength to play there."

With no incentive to head south again, the twins and the Smiths began to dream of an English tour. "Perhaps now that we are 'grown up girls,'" the *History* says, "we may go across the water once more. A gentleman who called to see us when we were on exhibition in Baltimore told us that the 'double-headed girl' was often inquired after, and that he thought we would prove a 'good card' there."

The gentleman who thought they'd be a good drawing card was probably Judge Ingalls, the agent who'd engineered the tour combining the Carolina Twins and the Siamese Twins. Ingalls was back in the sisters' lives after his British tour with Chang and Eng and one of Barnum's favorite big stars, Anna Swan, the "Nova Scotia Giantess."

Chang and Eng, accompanied by two daughters, had agreed to visit England in the hope of learning about any new European surgical techniques that might offer them hope for successful separation. One of the first physicians they saw was James Simpson, who had once introduced Millie-Christine and Monemia to his fellow obstetricians. He was Sir James Simpson now, personal physician to the queen during her holidays in Scotland. Simpson called on the Siamese Twins on a rainy, disagreeable day. "We have the honor of a visit from *Sir James Simpson* at our evening levee," Nannie Bunker wrote in her diary. Although Simpson was only fifty-seven, a month younger than her father and uncle, Nannie found him a "venerable man, far advanced in the downward course of life . . . an aged man of a mild heavenly aspect."

Chang and Eng saw him in a harsher light, once he gave his opinion about the operation. Dr. Simpson examined their connecting band as thoroughly as possible. Guessing that an interior canal ran between the brothers' abdominal cavities, he used the latest medical trick of trying to see inside the band without actually slicing into it. "You are well aware," he later reported to colleagues in a *British Medical Journal* article "that various attempts have been made of late years by electric and other strong lights to make portions of the body more or less translucent. By placing a powerful light behind the connecting band in Eng and Chang, I tried to make its thinner portions transparent, with a view of possibly tracing its contents better than by touch; but I failed entirely in getting any advantage from this mode of examination."

Any capable surgeon could do the basic operation, he told the brothers. The unacceptable peril would come in closing up the incisions after severing the band. He said that neither he nor any other doctor would attempt the operation unless it were a question of life or death.

If Millie and Christine sometimes regretted their joined bodies and considered an operation, they never admitted it publicly. Indeed, what they wrote in their *History* may be the simple truth: "One thing is certain; we would not wish to be severed, even if science could effect a separation. We are contented with our lot, and are happy as the day is long."

They were also of a single mind with regard to finances. "We have but one heart, one feeling in common, one desire, one purpose," they said in the *History*. "We are interested pecuniarily in the show and are daily receiving and putting away our share of the proceeds."

Their driving purpose was to buy land for the family. The 1870 federal census—the first after slavery—showed that they had already made a good beginning. It listed the twins' father as a landowner in Welches Creek Township, county of Columbus, state of North Carolina, as enumerated on June 9, 1870, by W. L. Maultsby, a relative of lawyer John Maultsby, one of the witnesses to the original sale of the sisters.

The census taker recorded the twins' father as Jacob McKay, age fifty-six, black, occupation farmer, value of real estate owned, $250, value of personal estate, $150. Their mother, "Menenah," age forty, was listed as a housekeeper. The children at home were Amy, Murphy, Hutson, Clarah, Elvy, Coleman, and Preston, who ranged in age from twenty-six to six. Milley Green, age seventy, also lived with the family.

Millie-Christine missed a place on his list. If she'd been home for the occasion, W. L. Maultsby would have faced the dilemma of whether to count her as one person or two.

Her dream of an English tour temporarily on hold, she was traveling with Judge Ingalls at that time. They worked west from New York City, across Pennsylvania and Ohio. Millie-Christine was playing Indiana when African American hero Frederick Douglass arrived in Evansville to give one of his popular lectures. "One remarkable thing," the *Clipper* noted, "was that every seat, without exception, had been reserved in the parquet and dress circle."

Ingalls and Millie-Christine steamed down the Mississippi River, exhibiting in the valley towns Millie-Christine had visited with Joseph Smith in the old days. On this trip, the party headed into Kansas. The bloody skirmishes that had kept Smith and Vestal out had been settled the hard way, once and for all.

The *Fort Scott Daily Monitor* of July 13, 1870, found the double-headed girl "one of those puzzles which philosophers and physicians cannot explain," a wondrous example of "the remarkable and unaccountable freaks sometimes indulged in by usually methodical and precise Dame Nature."

When Millie-Christine exhibited at the Odd Fellows Hall in Iola, Kansas, she was acknowledged to be the most marvelous freak of nature ever known. "All declare that it is no humbug, but a living reality," said the *Neosho Valley Register*.

Traveling shows paid local business-license fees wherever they stopped for a performance. The city of Topeka, for instance, charged H. P. Ingalls ten dollars for license number 191. With tickets costing fifty cents per adult and twenty-five cents per child, the first dozen families through the door made up that cost.

Millie-Christine had a saving sense of humor. While she was touring the western states, a newspaperman wrote a comical essay about her that she clipped, saved, and reprinted in later biographical booklets. "LAUGHABLE ACCOUNT OF THE TWO-HEADED GIRL BY A WESTERN EDITOR," it was titled.

"Girls in this city are divided into two classes—single-headed girls and double-headed ditto," it began. "The single headed ones are certainly the most numerous, but the double-headed ones appear to be the most attractive. This is evident from the fact that while we can see a single headed girl almost any time, we have to pay in order to be introduced to the maid with the duplex cranium. We say 'maid,' because the last double-headed girl we saw was not married. There was one man who courted her successfully, as he thought, for a time, but before popping the question he kissed one face first, and could never get the consent of the other head. She is now waiting till a two headed man comes along, and is gay with hope."

This "duplex" girl would be a good match for anyone, according to the newspaperman. The fact that she ate with both heads counted against her, but she bought dresses for only one person, which was an advantage. "The same way with her talking. The two-headed girl must be extremely circumspect, not only in her walk, but in her conversation. As she can never have a secret, she can have no opportunity to go around telling it. Neither will any one ever tell a secret to one head for fear that the other would split upon it.

"The fact of having two tongues should not militate against her, as, if she had only one, she would probably keep it going all the time, while, if she uses two, the one deadens the sound of the other. Which-ever way we look at the two-headed girl we see her to advantage, though we don't mean to say the least that should be understood to disparage a girl because she happens to be born with only one head."

The twins marked their nineteenth birthday in Kansas but looked young enough to fool a reporter for the *Leavenworth Daily Commercial*. "They are now 17 years old," he wrote. He caught their show at the Opera House, where they were booked for three days. They gave two exhibitions daily—one in the afternoon for ladies and children and one in the evening. "The opportunity should not be lost of seeing this great wonder," the reporter urged. "The children are well mannered and there is nothing in the exhibition to displease even the most sensitive. . . . They strike one at first as being Indians, they having an admixture of African and Indian blood." As most reporters did, he compared them with Chang and Eng: "There can be no doubt but that these girls are the most surprising specimen of humanity ever witnessed, altogether surpassing the Siamese twins."

The sisters were still in Kansas when Chang and Eng staggered home to Mount Airy, North Carolina, for good. The brothers most desperately needed the comforts of home in August 1870. Their European tour had been cut short by war between France and Prussia. Then personal catastrophe struck on their homeward voyage. They were one week out to sea, passing the time playing checkers. The last king crowned, Eng attempted to stand. Unexpectedly, Chang held him anchored to the bench. Chang, in fact, could scarcely move at all. A silent stroke had paralyzed his right side—the side next to Eng. For the remainder of the trip to New York, Chang lay helpless in their bunk while Eng fretted beside him.

Once they were home, a local doctor contrived a way for them to stay on their feet, Chang propped on a crutch under his left arm, his right foot supported by a leather strap that his brother held up as Chang hobbled along.

In November, the *Clipper* passed along the latest word on their physical and mental health: "A letter from one of Chang's daughters says that her father is low spirited, can scarcely move without assistance, and that his whole right side is perfectly useless. 'Uncle tries to cheer him up, but he has nothing to say.'"

Chapter 12

*I have heard there are some nude
photos of the twins. I would like very
much to see them.*

Letter to the author

ow that the Siamese Twins were permanently retired,
Judge Ingalls put together another novel team for Millie-Christine.
The "Two-Headed Girl Combination" brought in New Year's Day 1871
at Baltimore's new Masonic Temple. "During the past week," a Baltimore correspondent wrote, "audiences composed of the more intelligent and scientific portion of our community have been attracted
to see the following curiosities, viz.:—The two-headed girl; Miss
Anna Swan, the Nova Scotia Giantess, said to be the tallest person

on earth; Madame Hallean, the world renowned bearded lady, and Capt. M. V. Bates, the Kentucky Giant, who stands over 8 feet high and weighs 478 lbs." Captain Martin Van Buren Bates, that would be. "The promenades of the giant and giantess elicit the greatest wonderment." The *Baltimore Sun* said of Millie-Christine, "As she moves about she looks like two bright young copper-colored girls tied together in the middle."

A week later, the troupe exhibited in the nation's capital. A Washington paper gave the show a mixed review. "Capt. Bates is really a great curiosity. He is a powerfully built man and is said to measure eight feet in height. Anna Swan, the Nova Scotian giantess . . . is still announced as twenty-one years of age and looks precisely as she did when on exhibition at Barnum's old museum." Indeed, Anna radiated a special glow as she strolled about the hall, her hand tucked in the crook of Captain Bates's mighty arm. Human oddities faced more than the ordinary share of loneliness. Millie-Christine, understanding this all too well, must have smiled to see the giant couple's happiness.

Madam Hallean, the other member of the troupe, had already found herself a husband who could love a bearded lady. Doc Clarke traveled with the show and made himself useful on the business side of things. "Madam Hallean is a prominent feature of the combination," wrote the Washington reporter. Although some bearded ladies cheated with false whiskers, Hallean wore "a handsome growth of beard which is said to be a natural production." A front-page *Clipper* portrait from around that time shows her as a pretty woman with dangling earrings and long, curly hair fastened back with a flowery decoration. Her beard extends from mid-ear down the edge of her cheeks and her chin; the short, dark hair framing her face brings to mind an Amish farmer.

Millie-Christine was the only member of the new troupe who disappointed the Washington critic: "And now of the two-headed girl. There is no such thing. There are two mulatto girls about sixteen years of age, who are naturally joined together . . . at the small of the back. They cannot be called one any more than the Siamese twins, whom many in this city consider more of a curiosity."

Although the reporter couldn't have known, the twins were not at their best the day he visited the show. In fact, they needed to see a doctor.

The troupe moved on to Philadelphia for a January 23 opening at the Assembly Buildings, which stood at Tenth and Chestnut, midway between Independence Hall and the enormous excavation for the new city hall, which boosters said would be the tallest structure in the world.

An unusual seminude photo of the twins was taken soon after their arrival in Philadelphia, a photo ordered by one of the city's most reputable doctors. The photographer positioned his camera behind the girls. From that angle, he viewed Christine on the left and Millie on the right. They bend away from each other, fronts discreetly draped with cloth panels, leaving their backs exposed. The photo reveals Chrissie's humped back, Millie's pronounced spinal curvature, and the startling juncture of their bodies. It also shows bare hips and thighs, white stockings rolled below their knees, shiny black boots firmly laced. They wear the jewelry they'd put on that day— simple drop earrings, necklaces, bracelets. Chrissie hangs her head, a stoic expression on her face. Millie glares at the camera.

The eminent person who coaxed them into posing was Dr. William Pancoast, one of the team of Philadelphia doctors who'd examined them five years earlier. Since then, he had advanced to

Posed for Dr. Pancoast's Photographic Review of Medicine and Surgery.
Christine is on the left, Millie on the right.

demonstrator of anatomy at Jefferson Medical College and surgeon at Philadelphia Hospital and Charity Hospital. He wanted the photo to illustrate a chapter on the twins for an upcoming book, *Photographic Review of Medicine and Surgery*.

"After great persuasion . . . (owing to the modesty of the twins and the natural reluctance of Mrs. Smith)," he wrote, "the accompanying photograph of them was taken. They clung to their raiment closely, as may be seen, and it was only by earnest entreaty that they were willing to compromise by retaining the drapery as photographed. The expression of their countenances shows their displeasure, as their features ordinarily express great amiability of character."

The picture became plate number 17 in his book and the property of Mrs. Smith. "Double headed Girl," the caption said, "entered according to act of Congress in the year 1871 by Mistress Joseph P. Smith, in the office of the Librarian of Congress at Washington."

Dr. Pancoast had been summoned by Mrs. Smith to treat the twins. She wanted his advice about a bothersome physical problem Millie was experiencing. He made his first call a few days before the Philadelphia show opened. His office at Jefferson Medical College was handy to the Assembly Buildings. Struggling, no doubt, with extreme embarrassment, Mary Smith described the ailment to the doctor as best she could.

"This case of pygopagus symmetros came under my professional care January 18, 1871," Pancoast noted, "in consequence of an abscess forming near the genitals, as stated by Mrs. Smith, who is the guardian of the twins."

Dr. Pancoast was delighted with his new patients. "When I was called to see the twins, I found them very intelligent and agreeable, standing about four feet six inches in height, and so closely united that they were clothed in one dress large enough for them both, with sleeves for the four arms and a silken sash tied around their common waist. The frontal development of each was remarkably good." Their complexion was dusky brown, he said, their facial expressions so amiable and intelligent and their manners so well bred that they made a most pleasing impression.

As for the "abscess," he discovered a fistulous opening—an abnormal passage from an internal organ to the body surface—located in a depression that he judged to be an abortive effort of nature to make a second anus and rectum. In his writings, Pancoast did not mention his remedy; some fistulas close spontaneously, but most need to be cut and repaired surgically.

During the course of treatment, whatever it was, Dr. Pancoast returned often, sometimes with other doctors. Early on, he brought his father and Professor Samuel Gross "to establish the accuracy of my examination."

Joseph Pancoast, William's father, was professor of surgery and anatomy at Jefferson Medical College. The elder Pancoast had originated some delicate surgical techniques. Years earlier, using ether to anesthetize his patient, he had cut and repaired a vaginal fistula.

Samuel Gross, regarded as the greatest American surgeon of his time, was the younger Pancoast's professor at Jefferson and a specialist in pathological anatomy. A few years later, Philadelphia artist Thomas Eakins would shock the city with a gruesomely true-to-life painting of Dr. Gross's operating theatre.

The twins were in for another kind of shock from Dr. Pancoast. On one of his visits, he brought along Dr. William Pepper and Dr. R. M. Townsend to join him in a tingly experiment.

"We placed the pole of a Faradaic current in the hand of Millie," Pancoast wrote, "another on the outside of the outer limb of Chrissie. They both felt it." He repeated the experiment. This time, Chrissie held one pole and the doctors pressed the other end against Millie's leg. The electrical charge produced powerful contractions of the peroneal muscle on the outside of Millie's leg. "The sensation was recognized from the points of application down to the ends of each one's toes," noted Dr. Pancoast.

When he asked about their family history, he found out that their parents were both alive and had fourteen children, the twins having arrived ninth in order. Pancoast shared the general public's curiosity as to how such unusual babies developed. Chang and Eng had once been banned from exhibiting in France, for fear that unborn babies might be "marked" if pregnant mothers caught sight of the Siamese Twins. Monemia could "assign no cause" in her case, Pancoast said, "nor did she ever see the Siamese twins."

Everything about the sisters fascinated their physician. "Their movements are very graceful," he wrote, "and all the curves of their bodies yield harmoniously to their gliding step as they walk to and fro, run with swiftness, or dance. . . . Chrissie can now, as she has always been able to do, bend over and lift up Millie by the bond of union. This she was in the habit of doing as a part of the exhibition, but as Millie is now so strong and well developed, I advised them to avoid it as a practice, so as not to injure Chrissie's health.

"Millie, though the weaker physically, has the stronger will, and is the dominating spirit, usually controlling their joint movements, though from long habit one instinctively yields to the other's movements, thus preserving the necessary harmony. Mrs. Smith tells me that when they were little it was somewhat difficult for them to understand this, and individual desires sometimes led to little struggles and quarrels for supremacy."

They ate together from a single plate, he noted. "They are usually hungry at the same time, and generally desire the same food and drink, both drinking a great deal of water. . . . They generally sleep and wake at nearly the same moment, and sometimes one turns over the other one in bed without awaking her."

Pancoast had studied records of the conjoined twins Helen and Judith in his anatomy classes. "It is an interesting feature in this case," he wrote, "that it presents many points of similarity to that of the Hungarian sisters, born October 26, 1701, and that there is no similar case reported reaching adult life for one hundred and seventy years." Now, here in Philadelphia in 1871, he found his golden opportunity, his anatomist's dream come true, his chance to observe a living counterpart to the Hungarian sisters.

Their births were much the same, he noted. "Helen, the stronger twin, was first delivered as far as the navel, Judith following in a reverse order." So, too, "the larger child of the Carolina twins (Chrissie) was born first by a stomach presentation, and the smaller (Millie) came by the breech."

In each case, one sister was robust and the other delicate. Judith was struck by paralysis in her sixth year. Although she recovered, she remained much weaker than Helen. In the case of the Carolina Twins, "Chrissie is larger and more developed than Millie, who was quite weakly as a child, but is now strong and hearty, owing to the support she has received from her connection with her more robust sister." Pancoast learned from Mrs. Smith that both girls had suffered fever and ague at the same time but that only Millie had caught diphtheria.

Both pairs menstruated regularly. Both pairs were intelligent. In both cases, one sister might sleep while the other was awake. Anatomically, the unions were similar, from the sacra to the end of the coccyges. The Hungarians, however, had never learned to walk side by side. When one went forward, the other went backward. By contrast, Millie and Christine had gradually twisted toward each other until their spines yielded into the wide **V** shape that allowed them to move in the surprisingly graceful way Pancoast admired.

As for the Carolina Twins' marrying, he partly agreed with what old Eccardus had said about Helen and Judith. "Physically there are no serious objections," Pancoast wrote, "but morally there are insuperable ones; but I do not believe with him that such marital union would necessarily produce monsters."

As for the prospect of separating conjoined twins, Pancoast had this to say: "The Hungarians lived to the age of twenty-one years, and as in their case it was considered impossible to separate them with safety, so I believe it to be with these; and as the Carolina twins are united in life, so I believe they will be in death, and that the analogy to the Hungarian sisters will be carried out to the last. The union, arterial and nervous, is so intimate that if either Millie or Chrissie shall die first, the other will succumb almost at the same moment."

He later published his findings and his clinical photograph in a chapter called "The Carolina Twins" in *Photographic Review of Medicine and Surgery*. He included a woodcut illustration for the benefit of students, a startlingly explicit rendering by a medical artist following Pancoast's description. It shows the twins lying back upon a bed, ready to submit to a gynecological examination.

Under Dr. Pancoast's care, Millie-Christine became her vibrant self again, and the Philadelphia run was a grand success. The engagement stretched to a month, then two. Everyone wanted to see her. "The Judge has 'worked up' the city until the girl has become the talk of the town," said a March *Clipper*.

One way Judge Ingalls worked up enthusiasm was to talk Millie-Christine into letting Dr. Pancoast exhibit her for a teaching clinic at Jefferson Medical College before the show opened to the general public. Pancoast's demonstration was a curious blend of show business and science. Faculty and students could shake hands and chat with Millie-Christine, enjoy a close-up look, and recommend her to their friends. Pancoast invited newspaper editors to watch and interview and publicize.

His father and Dr. Gross attended the clinic, as did a roomful of other doctors. There was a general feeling of astonishment, *Forney's Press* reported, when Pancoast introduced Millie-Christine. "Instead of a monstrosity, there was exhibited to the professional talent assembled a well-educated, intelligent, quick-witted girl, . . . a wonder and a source of scientific information to those learned in anatomy."

Pancoast demonstrated how Millie, looking away, could feel a touch upon Christine's foot but was unaware of pressure upon her sister's shoulder. Two doctors timed the twins' pulses. Millie's, as usual, was about four beats slower than Chrissie's. The twins then put on an impromptu performance. They "walked about with a pleasing undulating motion," according to *Forney's Press*; they also danced and carried on conversations with two doctors at the same time. Although Dr. Pancoast had warned Chrissie against lifting her sister, this was a special occasion. She showed the doctors how she could tilt her body and raise Millie off the floor. "To cap the climax," they sang "Sweet Spirit, Hear My Prayer" in a duet that displayed "musical knowledge, culture, perfect time and tune, one head taking the soprano and the other the alto."

The "Two-Headed Girl Combination" attracted such big houses in Philadelphia that Barnum decided to back it for a British tour. "Judge Ingalls goes to England next month," said the February 25 *Clipper*, "taking with him the two-headed girl, the Nova Scotia giantess Anna Swan, and Captain Bates, the Kentucky giant."

Joe, Mrs. Smith, and two other members of the family would accompany the troupe abroad. A trip to England seemed the perfect chance for Mrs. Smith to show her youngest daughters a bit of the world. It was also a way for her to spend time with them. Brightie was fifteen and Lalla, the baby, twelve. Their mother and their big brother Joe had been five years on the road with Millie-Christine. Leaving the show to finish its Philadelphia run, Mrs. Smith returned to Spartanburg to help the girls pack and to enjoy a good-bye visit with her other children and her grandchildren.

The bearded lady would not be sailing to England with the rest of the troupe. Madam Hallean was throwing in her lot with a circus. In addition to all the regular shows playing Philadelphia while the twins were in town, several wagon circuses in nearby winter quarters were preparing to roll as soon as the roads dried out. The owner of Hallean's circus, John O'Brien, wintered his traveling show in Frankford, seven miles out in the country. Battered, weather-beaten circus wagons lumbered into his mammoth workshop at season's end. In the spring, they emerged like butterflies, painted and gilded and glorious to behold, ready for another season of boggy roads and muddy circus lots.

Traveling circuses encountered worse trouble than getting stuck in the mud. While Millie-Christine's troupe was still in Philadelphia, a Mississippi River steamboat carrying part of Van Amburgh's Menagerie blew its starboard boiler near St. Louis, hurling two camels and their keeper overboard. The camels drowned, but a boat managed to rescue the man. A few days later, a severe storm on the river forced a second Mississippi steamer loaded with Van Amburgh's animals to pull ashore for an emergency landing.

Hallean, like Millie-Christine, was used to the hardships of life on the road. The two circus men who'd signed her up for the coming season were partners George Batcheller and John Doris. Batcheller was a retired acrobat; Doris had been a comic performer called "Hunkey Dory." They'd purchased what circus people called "the privilege"—the privilege to manage the sideshows and run the popcorn and lemonade concessions, that is—for John O'Brien's circus. Doris and Batcheller were ambitious men who would one day parlay their concession profits into their own circus and negotiate a fabulous contract with Millie-Christine.

During the two-month Philadelphia stand, the twins found time to pose for *cartes d'visité*—photos mounted on cardboard that performers passed out for publicity, sold to fans, and exchanged with friends. Advertised in the *Clipper* were naughty "Parisian cartes d'visité" one could send away for: "VERY RICH—VERY GAY—VERY SPICY. New Styles received by every steamer." For the proper sort of portraits the twins wanted, they visited two Arch Street photographic studios, Gihon & Thompson and the Temple of Art. The Temple of Art photograph shows the sisters in an elegantly pensive pose, leaning against a carved chest. "Chrissie Millie" is written on the back of a surviving print, in Chrissie's clear hand. They wear flat little flower-and-ribbon caps. Their dresses, plain in one picture and fancy in the other, have Empire-style high-waisted skirts, à la mode.

Before Millie-Christine and the giants sailed for England, they played a short run of nearby Pennsylvania towns. They performed at Norristown, then gave a series of exhibitions in the Main Street Opera

Temple of Art studio photograph, Philadelphia, autographed "Chrissie Millie" on reverse

MILNER LIBRARY SPECIAL COLLECITONS, ILLINOIS STATE UNIVERSITY

Gihon & Thompson photographic studio, Philadelphia

House at Johnstown beginning on April 1. So they missed the latest act opening in Philadelphia that April Fools' Day, when Wicked Ben trotted onstage at the Coliseum Museum. "The chief attraction is the wonderful performance of the learned pig, 'Wicked Ben,' that spells names, solves examples in arithmetic and concludes by playing a very fair game of 'seven-up' against any opponent who may present himself," the *Clipper* said. A quip printed in the paper when Ben played Washington, D.C., undoubtedly hit the mark in Philadelphia as well: "Ben is not the only educated hog at present in that city."

Chapter 13

*Two distinct smiles are winked at you by
two pairs of sparkling and roguish eyes, and
thrown at you through two different sets of
the purest ivory that ever adorned the
mouth of an Indian Sultana.*

Liverpool Leader

The twins and the Smiths (Mary, Joe, Lalla, and Brightie), accompanied by Anna Swan, Captain Bates, managers, accountants, publicity agents, wardrobe assistants, and a mountain of valises, carpetbags, hatboxes, suitcases, and steamer trunks, sailed from New York on Saturday, April 22, 1871, aboard the *City of Brussels*. According to Ingalls, 150,000 people had visited the troupe during its eight weeks in Philadelphia; some 10,000 had flocked to see it in a single day in New York.

English reporters and editors, well primed by advance publicity, met the ship at Liverpool and trailed the colorful party to the Washington Hotel, where the travelers freshened up for press interviews and chats with Liverpool's upper crust. Ordinary Liverpudlians would have a chance to see Millie-Christine and the giant couple "in due time," the papers promised.

News stories praised Millie-Christine. "Yesterday a private party of ladies and gentlemen had an interview with this extraordinary person," said the *Liverpool Mercury*, "and were both astonished and pleased. She seems remarkably cheerful. . . . In figure, Christine Millie, who is 19 years of age, is rather short. . . . In conversation the countenances brighten with intelligence, and those who have had the opportunity of seeing the girl could not fail to be pleased with the geniality of her manner, and with the store of information which she has at her command."

"Christine Millie is a phenomenon of the Siamese twin order but far more wonderful," claimed the *Liverpool Daily Post*. She possessed an exceedingly amiable and merry disposition, said the *Post*, "and in no way differs in appearance from two animated and engaging young negresses, who for sport have agreed to pass an hour tied together nearly back to back." The *Post* also made appreciative, if slightly confused, mention of Mary Smith: "The lady on whose estate she was born, and by whom she has been most affectionately and successfully educated, accompanies her in her wanderings." The article concluded, "There can be no doubt that the members of this party will make a distinguished figure in London during the Exhibition season; and in due time the Liverpool people may expect these wonders back again amongst them."

Millie-Christine's keenest fan wrote for the *Liverpool Leader*: "Of all the curiosities ever unearthed by the immortal Barnum, none can compare in the most minute degree with Millie Christine, a daughter or daughters . . . of the state of North Carolina." The writer joked that the mother who produced this daughter with one body and two minds was presumably the founder of the American Woman's Rights Association. "All the intelligent men who saw her at the Washington Hotel the other day can bear witness to the marvellous intelligence which predominates in both brains." The *Leader* reporter conceded that a two-headed lady might not be everyone's cup of tea. "There are a lot of people here, as elsewhere, always ready to strain at the smallest gnat and swallow the biggest camel, who will doubtless put this young lady down as outside the pale of ordinary humanity. If this prejudice should carry any one so far as to avoid her they alone will be the losers. We can testify that no person of ordinary intelligence can be in her company for half an hour without yielding to the charm of her manner and the fascination of her double smiles. She has you on both sides. If you remove your head from one position, you are immediately the victim of another pair of eyes, which fix you and, in fact, transfix you."

The *Liverpool Daily Courier* stressed Barnum's behind-the-scenes role. "Amongst the visitors who arrived at Liverpool from New York on Tuesday in the Inman steamer *City of Brussels*, was a party of ladies and gentlemen whom the indefatigable Mr. Barnum, of showman notoriety, has sent over to this country for the edification of the curious." According to the *Courier*, "The most singular and physiologically-interesting member of the party is a young lady, . . . or rather, two young ladies rolled into one, who is certainly a rival to the famous Siamese Twins and very much more attractive in appearance than Messrs Chang and Eng. Those who saw the Siamese Twins during their presence in England will have a vivid recollection of the pained look that their features bore, and the constrained movements of their bodies while walking in any direction." Not so with Miss Millie-Christine, "whose four bright black eyes and dazzling rows of pearly-white teeth light up a fair Creole complexion with an animation that is really attractive." Her costume was styled low on the back so visitors could see the upper portion of the dorsal connection, "and it was done without any infringement of modesty."

The newspapers also welcomed Anna Swan and Captain Bates. Editors already knew Anna, who had recently toured with Chang and Eng. A lady of her proportions was not easily forgotten, the *Post* pointed out, "especially as her deportment and conversation fully entitle her to remembrance." Twenty-three-year-old Captain Bates was a newcomer, but the papers predicted he'd be popular in England. "He is a handsome, well proportioned young fellow, . . . as well set up as any of Her Majesty's Foot Guards," the *Courier* said. He was eight feet tall, measured sixty-two inches around the chest, and was as active and light in his movements as any healthy, well-built ordinary man. Bates also seemed a congenial fellow: "His conversation is that of a self-possessed and highly intelligent American gentleman," said the *Post*. The handsome couple "created some consternation" while taking an afternoon drive through the streets of Liverpool the day after arriving.

✧✧✧

After the Liverpool run, the troupe moved on to London. Judge Ingalls ordered copies of a new booklet about the twins to sell to British audiences. He titled the updated account, *Biographical Sketch of Millie Christine, The Two-Headed Nightingale*. "Two-Headed Nightingale" was an inspired touch. Barnum's beloved Jenny Lind, the Swedish Nightingale, was living quietly in England at the time, tending her family, out of the limelight but still a famous figure.

The updated biography attracted English audiences with a clever slant on American-British history. Millie-Christine was born in the state of North Carolina in the year 1851, it began. The next sentence would have sent Revolutionary War soldiers from the Old North State spinning in their graves: "North Carolina is specially endeared to England from the fact that it was the very last of American Colonies which surrendered its allegiance to the mother country, and even then did not become disloyal, but yielded to the force of circumstances, which rendered the union of the new country necessary to its existence."

A biographical section described the twins. Each girl "has a pair of sparkling black eyes which are constantly lit up by intelligence, and which, at any outburst of fun and humour, seem literally to dance with glee; while each mouth is adorned with such a set of brilliant ivory, as an American dentist observed, that many of his patients would be glad to purchase for twenty-five thousand dollars." The sisters were never lonely, the *Two-Headed Nightingale* said, for each had at all times an intelligent and interesting companion.

One of the appealing things about Millie-Christine was her desire to help her family. Managers Millar and Thompson had capitalized on that from the time she was four years old. After freedom, when she could spend what she earned, she regularly sent money home, and Jacob McKoy continued to buy Welches Creek acreage. The *Two-Headed Nightingale* spotlighted the heartwarming rags-to-riches story: "It may be mentioned as an interesting fact, illustrating the vicissitudes of life and fortune, that the father of Millie Christine was at one time the slave of a planter named McCoy, and that at this moment he is the owner of the plantation upon which he was once a slave."

The second half of the *Two-Headed Nightingale* was a "Musical Entertainment" section that included the words to fifteen popular songs. "Selections from the following, and many other Songs, will be sung as Duets, by Millie Christine, at each reception," the booklet said. The songs were a Victorian medley, from the sugary sweet ("Where the warbling waters flow,/And the zephyrs gently blow,/ The fairies dwell/In grassy dell") to the mournful ("So I bless my lot, though with breaking heart/For that grave enstarred with daisies/The beautiful, beautiful daisies/The snowy, snowy daisies").

One song, "Love Among the Roses," indicated where Millie-Christine was to execute a little dance as she sang her duet:

> Now I hate to tell, but then I must—*Dance*.
> I fell in love with her head first—*Dance*.
> . . . Oh how we met, I'll not forget,
> My love among the roses—*Dance*.

Rave notices from the States were scattered among the songs:

> "As for Millie Chrissy, the two-headed girl, she is a perfect little gem or gems, or a gem and a half, we don't know which. Great care and attention must have been bestowed upon her education." (*New York Times*)

> "Their afternoon levées are the fashionable resort of the elite of the city." (*New York Item*)

> "Their reception at the Masonic Temple has been attended by thousands of our best citizens." (*Baltimore American*)

> "Take the children, and go to Odd Fellows Hall, and see

the wonderful two-headed girl combination while you have an opportunity, and you will thank us for the advice." (*Washington Republican*)

"This wonderful Exhibition is of the most chaste character, and we can safely recommend it to fathers, mothers, sons and daughters." (*Boston Transcript*)

"Every one is wishing to see the double-headed girl. She is, without doubt, the wonder of the age, and we are not surprised to find such a feeling of anxiety to see this living curiosity." (*Forney's Press*)

"Excursions from the country, filled with visitors to see the two-headed girl, arrive every evening." (*Albany Evening Journal*)

"The two-headed girl would be a good juror—she could look at both sides of the case at the same time." (*Cincinnati Enquirer*)

Londoners observing the warm, if lofty, glances between Anna Swan and Captain Bates during carriage drives and showtime promenades were thrilled when the happy couple announced marriage plans at a press conference. Queen Victoria summoned the "Tallest Couple Alive" to Buckingham Palace. Her Majesty gifted the bride-to-be with a cluster diamond ring and a wedding gown and gave the groom an engraved pocket watch that sounded a chime on the hour.

Anna Swan married Martin Van Buren Bates at St. Martin's Church, Trafalgar Square, at eleven o'clock on Saturday morning, June 17. Her splendid gown was said to have been cut from a hundred yards of white satin and trimmed with fifty yards of lace. "The bride and bridegroom were attended each by their friends," said a *Harper's Bazaar* article, "among whom, it may be remarked, were the twin negro girls, Christine and Millie, . . . who usually hold their public levees with the giant and giantess. A number of privileged persons witnessed the ceremony, and there was a crowd of people outside. The proceedings were conducted with perfect order and regularity, and the happy couple withdrew, having duly signed their names on the parish register like any other newly married couple of private folks."

The story included a handsome etching of the wedding party. Captain Bates is shown slipping a ring on to Anna's finger. In their wedding finery, they tower over the Reverend W. Rupert Cochrane, though he stands upon an elevated platform. Behind the giant couple stands Judge Ingalls, who gave the bride away; his face is even with the back of Anna's waist. The smiling Carolina Twins watch from a front-row seat.

Harper's Bazaar supplemented its dignified "Giants' Wedding" story with a second, mocking account of the ceremony, as "described by an English witness." According to this version, Trafalgar Square was jammed with people, a "goodly company of those spectators to whom any kind of wedding is always gratifying, and a monster wedding a joy forever."

The groom arrived at the church at a quarter to the hour "and walked composedly up to the altar. He did not wear the uniform of that corps . . . in which he is understood to hold a captain's commission." Like many Civil War veterans, Martin Van Buren Bates ordinarily dressed in his Union army uniform, much as lame uncle William Alexander Smith back in Wadesboro always wore his

Confederate gray. Indeed, a cousin once remarked about "Uncle General" Smith, "We do not think he now had any other outer garment." This day, Captain Bates wore proper, formal wedding attire, "if we except an exceedingly blue tie," *Harper's Bazaar* said.

At 10:50, "loud whispers, succeeded by a dead silence, announced the approach of the bride, who, pale of face, and clad in a few acres of 'white samite, mystic, wonderful,' and with her veil thrown back, moved as majestically as her peculiar circumstances or circumferences admit of, up the nave, and stood in front of her affianced husband, and looked down upon him from her superior eminence with the ghastly smile proper to the occasion." The reporter was going for effect here. Anna topped Martin by only half an inch. Photos and the magazine drawing show an attractive, well-proportioned, astoundingly large couple.

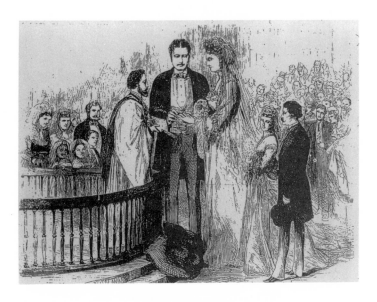

"The Giants' Wedding"
HARPER'S BAZAR, JULY 29, 1871

Millie-Christine also drew the reporter's attention. Anna was preceded up the aisle "by the two-headed nightingale combination, whose misfortune naturally caused a buzz of comment and much hilarity."

The service itself was "read amid a reverential scene of whispering, giggling, and climbing over pews; and when it was over, the usual signing of names appeared to occupy much more than the legitimate time. As the reason could not be the length of the names, which by no means corresponds with that of the owners, one is driven to the conclusion that children of Anakim [biblical giants], like some other great folks, find writing a laborious and difficult operation." In reality, just as Mrs. Smith had educated Millie-Christine, so Barnum had tutored Anna Swan from the time he'd brought her down from Nova Scotia years ago. Both Anna and Martin constantly autographed pictures, booklets, and cards for admiring visitors. They'd have had no trouble signing a church registry.

"At last, however," said the sardonic story, "the pair of Titans emerged from the vestry and strode arm in arm, followed by the sympathizing 'combination,' and accompanied by the strains of the 'Wedding March,' to meet the plaudits of the outside crowd. At a quarter past eleven all was over."

Four days after the wedding, Judge Ingalls arranged a private reception at Masonic Hall, where the Prince of Wales and assorted dignitaries visited the picturesque American troupe. A few days later, on Saturday, June 24, by command of Her Majesty, Millie-Christine gave a special performance for Queen Victoria.

"Directly after breakfast went down with the children to see an extraordinary object, far more extraordinary than the Siamese Twins," says an abridged transcript of Victoria's journal for that date. The journal describes "a 2 headed girl, or rather 2 girls, yet one, joined together by a sort of bar of flesh not far from the region of the heart. The lower part of the body is one, whilst the upper parts are distinct. There are 2 heads with different brains & will power, 2 hearts, arms, & 4 legs, grown together! It is one of the most remarkable phenomena possible. They are very dark coloured, if not exactly negros, & look very merry & happy. Their parents were slaves from South Carolina, & they speak English. They sang duets with clear, fine voices."

Joined near the heart? There is a likely explanation for that incredible description. Queen Victoria began keeping a journal when she was thirteen, and her lifelong habit was to observe accurately and write down exactly what she saw. Regrettably, not all her journals survive intact. In later years, the queen gave her youngest daughter the task of transcribing passages from a stack of old journals and burning the originals as she finished with them. Many passages, to put it kindly, suffered in transcription. Princess Beatrice edited ruthlessly, destroying whole entries she found unsuitable and substantially altering others. Beatrice was twelve years old when Victoria summoned the Siamese Twins to Buckingham Palace in 1869 and fourteen when Millie-Christine sang for the queen and her children. By the time it fell to Beatrice to transcribe the journals, the two sets of joined twins may have merged in her memory, and so she perhaps "corrected" her mother's June 24 entry.

Photos from W. & D. Downey's London studio show how the twins looked that season when they met the queen. For their session, they wore a flattering and frilly white dress. The photos show their hair styled in glossy ringlets on top, with corkscrew curls hanging to their shoulders—the kind of curls other sisters made by winding each other's hair in overnight curlpapers or using sizzling-hot curling tongs. Someone else fixed the twins' hair, for they could never reach to help each other.

One pose from that studio session brightens the cover of a special collection of their favorite songs. The twins stand within an oval frame below elaborate letters spelling the title, *Nightingale Music*. The picture is notable because, due to the reversal characteristic of daguerreotypes, taller Chrissie is on the left for a change.

Every sentimental song in the collection was suitable for the ears of Queen Victoria and her children. The twins' popular duet "Sisters We, Gay and Free" was included, as were "Nightingale Schottische," "Nightingale Mazurka," "The Song of the Whip Poor Will" (with whippoorwill calls indicated at the end of each stanza), "Put Me in My Little Bed," and a song written expressly for the sisters, "The Dear, Dear Friends at Home":

> What cheers us when we are far away
> From home and all we love:
> When storm and danger hedge us round,
> And all is dark above?
> When lightnings flash and thunders roar
> O'er ocean's seething foam?
> It is the thought that heaven hears
> The prayers of friends at home.

The queen gifted the twins with a matched pair of diamond-studded hair clips, and the British tour was off and running.

Princess Alexandra invited them to Marlborough House. "So much pleased was her Royal Highness the Princess of Wales with the 'Two-headed Nightingale,' on her departure for the continent

W. & D. Downey, Photographers to Her Majesty; Newcastle-on-Tyne and London studios.
Anonymous note on reverse reads: "Millie-Christine, Famous Negro Grown-together Siamese Twins."

Cover from a song collection especially written for the twins. The picture shows Christine and Millie in a reversal of their real-life positions, with slightly smaller Millie on the right here.

she left orders that a couple of brooches should be presented to the two-in-one young ladies," said the *Standard*.

His Royal Highness the Prince of Wales took His Imperial Highness the Grand Duke Vladimar of Russia and Prince John of Glucksburg to visit the troupe at Willis's Exhibition Rooms.

The twins and their party later entertained less regal crowds in the grand concert hall at the Crystal Palace, the iron-and-glass showplace left over from England's Great Exhibition of 1851.

On October 13, 1871, a gentleman who had visited the show— Mr. Robert Barclay of Tottenham—presented a copy of the *Two-Headed Nightingale* booklet to the British Museum. The cover shows the same inaccurate picture as the old *History* booklet—a girl with a single upper body and two heads; on his copy, Barclay jotted "quite incorrect & sensational" beside the picture. "Presented . . . to the British Museum," he wrote in an inside note, "with two photographs showing these twins in different positions with their autograph in pencil on back." The photos came from the Temple of Art studio in Philadelphia, each signed "Millie Chrissie" in neat, clear script. In one picture, Chrissie holds a guitar and Millie holds sheet music; they both played a little on the guitar, according to the booklet. The other photo shows them standing, each balanced on one foot. "This is intended to describe walking on 2 legs instead of four," Barclay wrote below the picture. In his cover letter with the donated booklet, he said of the twins, "They are well educated and converse very intelligently. They are in all respects two persons. . . . They appeared to me very happy & thoroughly to enjoy life—being more like girls of 18 or 19 years. I conversed with both sisters or heads. . . . Altogether all painful impression was removed by seeing them."

The troupe moved out from London on a northerly run. By late

November, it was back in Liverpool at Queen's Hall. Audiences "were both astonished and delighted" with Millie-Christine, the *Liverpool Mercury* said. At the receptions, "the necks of the young lady were adorned with handsome brooches, the gift of the Princess of Wales."

Millie-Christine and the giants arrived in Edinburgh for a one-week engagement beginning December 13. Sir James Simpson was dead by that time. He would have been glad to see that Millie-Christine was thriving. He would also have been interested to learn that Anna Swan Bates was four months pregnant.

While Millie-Christine was crisscrossing Britain, so was Tom Thumb. General Thumb and his company of little people had arrived in England a month ahead of Millie-Christine, on the homeward leg of a three-year round-the-world tour. They'd been a hit from Yokohama, Japan, to Colombo, Ceylon; drawn crowds in China and India; amused audiences from Albany, Australia, to Alexandria, Egypt. The robust troupers were Tom, his wife, Lavinia, her sister Minnie Warren, and Commodore Nutt. According to sham publicity, George Washington Morrison Nutt had been an unsuccessful suitor for Lavinia's hand and was now a confirmed bachelor. "Commodore Nutt is the most cunning little cuss in the whole crowd," said a review of Tom's show. "Neither Thumb nor his wife can sing much."

Tom's and Millie-Christine's troupes converged in London in April 1872. Millie-Christine and the Bateses exhibited in Agricultural Hall for a week, and Tom's group moved in the next week. Other top talent was also gathering in London that month for a special benefit performance. A popular showman had died suddenly, leaving his wife and small son unprovided for. The entertainment world rallied in their behalf.

The gala April 17 benefit packed Astley's Amphitheatre to the rafters. London theatre managers went all out to aid the bereaved family. Taking part with Millie-Christine's troupe were equestrian companies with trick riders and performing horses, a forty-man Christy Minstrels troupe, General Tom Thumb and company, and Blondin, the "Hero of Niagara," on the high rope.

Blondin was a sinewy, 140-pound Frenchman who had first crossed Niagara Falls in 1859, when young Millie-Christine and Joseph Smith were playing the Mississippi Valley towns. For his heroic feat, Blondin had cinched a two-inch cable around a giant oak on the American side of the falls and a boulder on the Canadian side. The cable stretched 1,200 feet across the thundering gorge near the suspension bridge. The distance down was 190 feet.

The act that the twins watched Blondin perform at the Astley's Amphitheatre benefit may have been something like the one Mark Twain saw in an outdoor pleasure garden near Paris. Blondin "appeared on a stretched cable, far away above the sea of tossing hats and handkerchiefs, and in the glare of the hundreds of rockets that whizzed heavenward by him he looked like a wee insect," Mark Twain said. Blondin walked the rope with his balance pole, carried a man across on his back, danced a solitary jig, performed gymnastic and balancing feats almost too perilous to watch, and "finished by fastening to his person a thousand Roman candles, Catherine wheels, serpents and rockets of all manner of brilliant colors, setting them on fire all at once and walking and waltzing across his rope again in a blinding blaze of glory that lit up the garden and the people's faces like a great conflagration at midnight."

A month after the benefit show, Anna's baby girl was born. She weighed eighteen pounds and measured twenty-seven inches long. She died at birth.

Anna and Captain Bates arranged to sail back to the States in June with Tom Thumb's company. Still longing for a family, the big couple planned to retire from show business, build a giant-sized house in Seville, Ohio, and live as normal a small-town life as possible. Millie-Christine promised to visit—and eventually, she did find her way to Anna's big house for a happy reunion. But that was years in the future, for at this point, Millie-Christine had more exciting prospects in mind.

She and the Smiths stayed on in England. A July *Clipper* noted that "Christine Milly" was performing at the South London Palace Music Hall. Farther down the column was a tragic item: "A Berlin physician recently tried to dissever the bodies of two twin girls grown together like the Siamese Twins. One of the girls survived the operation one day and the other lingered for three days. This is bad news for the Siamese twins and 'Double Headed Nightingale.'"

Millie-Christine celebrated her twenty-first birthday during an engagement at London's Standard Theatre.

Mrs. Smith and her daughters remained in England long enough to help work out a schedule for Millie-Christine's first big continental tour. After signing a contract with a show-business entrepreneur who knew his way around Europe, Mary Smith packed her trunks.

Before the family members separated, they and Millie-Christine spent a holiday together in Brighton, where they marveled at the fanciful Royal Pavilion and went to Bertin's studio for parting photographs. The camera caught Millie-Christine standing poised and well dressed. "With Millie Chrissie's love" is handwritten on the back of a surviving print. Another Bertin portrait shows Mary Smith, a handsome woman, sitting at the center of her family. Lalla, seated on the floor at her feet, cuddles close, resting one elbow on her mother's knee. Brightie and Joe stand at Mary's shoulders. "Grandmother Smith, Uncle Joe P. Smith, Aunt Brightie Cannon, Aunt

The Smiths at Brighton, England.
Mary Smith sits in the center with Lalla; Brightie and Joe stand behind them.
DICKSIE CRIBB COLLECTION

Joseph Smith, Jr.
DICKSIE CRIBB COLLECTION

Lalla Redhead," someone later wrote on the reverse side. Yet another shot shows Joe posing alone, debonair in a gleaming top hat tilted just so. He sports curly muttonchop whiskers, his mustache joining a pair of sideburns shaped narrow at the top and broad and rounded at the bottom, his clean-shaven chin separating the two "chops."

Mary and her daughters sailed from Liverpool in plenty of time to enjoy a South Carolina Christmas.

Millie-Christine and Joe left London on December 5, 1872, for Vienna, Austria, where she was to commence her public receptions after meeting the Royal family and being seen by members of the medical profession.

Chapter 14

*Her tour abroad was a
continued ovation of success.*

Description and
Songs of Miss Millie Christine,
the Two-Headed Nightingale

$\mathcal{B}$y the early spring of 1873, Millie-Christine was nearly
five thousand miles from home. Hinne's Circus was performing
in St. Petersburg, Russia, said a May *Clipper.* The circus's chief attraction was the "Double-headed Nightingale." Millie-Christine was
also "holding crowded levees at her hotel daily."

In Czar Alexander II's St. Petersburg, she rode in one-horse
droshkies over skull-sized cobblestones, like the Siamese Twins had
done a few years earlier. She saw the painted and gilded domes and

heard music from the city's 626 bells. She undoubtedly entertained the czar's family, as had the Siamese Twins. Monarchs traditionally had the first chance to greet and inspect the latest visiting wonders.

Letters from home—wherever they caught up with Millie-Christine during her first summer abroad—would surely have mentioned the death of blacksmith Jabez McKay. Millie-Christine's original owner left his son John Lloyd what remained of the farm—"all my back woods land, . . . all my stock, . . . all my house hold and kitchen furniture, . . . all my shop tools, and farming tools." To his daughter Ann Eliza Lumsden, he bequeathed the sum of $2.50, to daughter Lucy Jane Smith, the sum of $5.00.

༄༅༄

A chief attraction of the twins' performance was hearing Millie speak to one visitor while Chrissie carried on a conversation with someone else. To make the demonstration all the more fascinating, they worked with tutors across Europe until they'd mastered German, Italian, Spanish, and French.

Thus, they were able to read for themselves an impudent French article that appeared soon after their show hit Paris in November 1874. *Le Trombinoscope par Touchatout* was a lighthearted, gossipy Paris journal. Editor Touchatout—meaning "Busybody"—used a frisky caricature of the smiling, waving sisters doing a skirt-whirling dance for the cover page of the issue that featured them.

"Millie and Christine were born, both of them, in North Carolina," he began. He offered his own tongue-in-cheek theory about how the double phenomenon developed. "All that we know at present is that nine months before their birth, on a hot summer night, their sleepy father dozed off in the middle of a conversation he was having with his wife, woke up two minutes later, and not remembering at

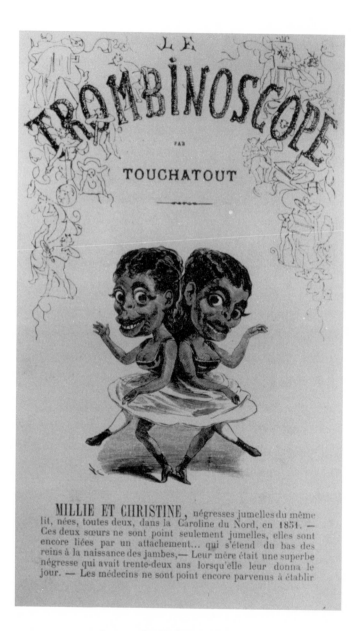

LE
TROMBINOSCOPE

PAR

TOUCHATOUT

MILLIE ET CHRISTINE, négresses jumelles du même lit, nées, toutes deux, dans la Caroline du Nord, en 1851. — Ces deux sœurs ne sont point seulement jumelles, elles sont encore liées par un attachement... qui s'étend du bas des reins à la naissance des jambes, — Leur mère était une superbe négresse qui avait trente-deux ans lorsqu'elle leur donna le jour. — Les médecins ne sont point encore parvenus à établir

Caricature from Touchatout's Paris journal

just what point he had stopped, he began the phrase all over again."

When Millie and Christine came into the world, Touchatout said, perplexities presented themselves. There was only one *layette*, for instance, but that was a minor problem. The first major *conflit* arose when the parents had to register the babies with the civil authorities. Millie was healthy and thriving, according to his account, but Christine was weak, and the doctor said she mustn't leave home. The town clerk, "crotchety like every employee paid by the taxpayers," visited the parents' house and duly recorded Christine's birth but refused to register Millie's, claiming that the doctor had declared her fit to be carried to city hall.

Touchatout further claimed that when Jules Ferry had become mayor of Paris in 1870, his first official act was to telegraph North Carolina to request that he be sent a hundred or so employees of the same caliber as the town clerk to help him organize his administration. Judging from the way the mayor had run the city ever since, "a large cargo of employees from North Carolina must have arrived in time."

Meanwhile, said Touchatout, the two sisters had grown well and developed equally. "When they played at running," for instance, "they almost always arrived at the finish at the same time." But as the girls became young ladies, what had once been childish inconveniences became stumbling blocks. "One dramatic adventure had for them a terrible *dénouement*." As Touchatout told the silly tale, a young Negro of the neighborhood began calling on the family. He fell violently in love with Millie and ended up asking for her hand. Millie was more than agreeable. "But a fatal obstacle was going to come between the two lovers. A malicious little god who had only aimed at one heart, without wishing it had pierced two. Christine also was dying of love for her sister's suitor!" Generous Chrissie proposed that Millie share the adored object. Millie heatedly refused, whereupon Chrissie made a somber resolution.

The next day at lunch, the lover sat beside his *fiancée*, drinking her in as she passed the sandwiches. Christine leaned over to her sister and said to her in a low, feverish voice, "Divide in two! There is still time!"

"*Non!*" Millie responded energetically.

"*Eh bien!*" said Christine in a resolute tone. "You wanted him for yourself! Now he won't be for either of us!"

That night, the desperate Millie arose, dressed herself quietly, so as not to wake her sister, and ran toward the river intending to destroy herself. But the cold water woke Christine, who seized Millie by the hair and dragged her back to shore. Christine then begged her sister's pardon for ruining her marriage, and all was forgiven.

Afterward, Touchatout said, the twins accepted Barnum's offer to exhibit in Paris. Though certain grumpy French scientists doubted that the *phénomène* was genuine, the public could decide for itself by visiting the sisters at the cirque des Champs-Elysées, the story said.

Touchatout then added a whimsical little tag on to his invented romance, predicting that after the sisters made their fortune in Europe, they would marry the Siamese Twins and produce 118 joined offspring, who would "form a human chain without end."

⁂

It was true that several French scientists questioned whether the sisters were a genuine *phénomène*. Paris doctors were immensely frustrated because the twins refused to permit intimate examinations.

Dr. Bertillon, for one, apologized to scientific colleagues in his paper on the twins published in the January 5, 1874, issue of *La*

Nature. He said he regretted that any report about their pelvic structure was secondhand, unreliable information communicated by *le directeur* of the young ladies. They had been much too well brought up to consent to any *indiscrète* examinations, even by France's leading physicians. "Happily," he wrote, as only a doctor would put it, "one of them had several years back a very bad abscess ready to be opened." Dr. Pancoast had at that time examined them and reported his findings.

Bertillon related several fascinating minor facts he had discovered about the twins. First, their mother was a *zambo*—that is, a mixture of black and redskin, *nègre et Peau-Rouge*—while their father was a pure-blooded Negro. The ancestral Native American blood would account for the twins' curly hair, which was more wavy than wooly, and their bronze skin tint. He also noted that the twins used all four legs when they danced, "and they dance more gracefully than one could believe." If one of the sisters sang alone, only her heart accelerated. Both enjoyed good health, although one sometimes suffered migraines; so long as it was a light attack, her sister didn't feel it, but if it was heavy, she, too, had a slight headache. They had crossed the ocean several times and never gotten seasick. "Unfortunately, they were vaccinated at the same time," Bertillon wrote. "It would have been interesting to see if the vaccination of one would have protected the other."

Should this single being composed of two persons be called *mesdemoiselles* or *mademoiselle*? In Bertillon's opinion, the twins should be addressed as *mesdemoiselles*.

He reminded his colleagues that experts offered three theories of how a "double monster" was formed: (1) at some point in development, two individual *germes* somehow joined; (2) two embryos were situated in a single *germe*—like an egg with a double yolk, to cite a familiar example; and (3) double monsters came from a single ova and a single embryo, which improperly divided into joined "scissor-like" twins. Modern doctors go with Bertillon's third theory—that conjoined twins were meant to be identical twins. A fertilized egg begins separating into two individuals, but at some point, complete cleavage fails. At the spot where cleavage fails, they remain connected—at the lower back like the sisters, at the chest like the Siamese Twins, or at the head, shoulder, or abdomen. An American illustrator drew ten possible variations of conjoined "Human Monstrosities." As befit the casual cruelty of the times, the *Clipper* ran the picture on its April Fools' Day cover in 1871, the year the sisters sailed for Europe.

Dr. Bertillon finished by pointing out that when Catholic priests had faced the perplexing question of whether the dying Hungarian twins had one or two souls, they had treated them as two, administering first to one and then the other after Judith was taken gravely ill. On the other hand, he joked, if the decision were left to a Dutch *curé*, he would probably allow a double monster to die unbaptized while he waited for the opinion of a bishop, who in turn would wait to consult his colleagues. And if an English priest found two heads to baptize, he'd promptly claim two converts.

Another French doctor who yearned to examine the twins was an obstetrician, E. Verrier, who suspected they might be a fraud. In fact, he admitted in a *Gazette Obstétricale* article that he had distrusted all American show people ever since the "spiritist" Davenport brothers had fooled the public with their tricks. For years, Ira and William Davenport staged theatrical *séances* during which they sat face to face in an open-topped wooden cabinet. Two volunteers from the

Millie-Christine abroad
NORTH CAROLINA DIVISION OF ARCHIVES AND HISTORY

audience bound them securely in full view of the audience. Assistants placed musical instruments in the cabinet, closed the cabinet doors, and dimmed the lights. Soon came the ghostly tones of trumpets and banjos, while glimmering hands mysteriously floated and waved at the spectators. The trickster brothers had come a cropper in Liverpool when someone tied them up with a special "Tom Fool's knot" that their nimble fingers couldn't untie.

Currently, said Dr. Verrier, all of Paris was running to see the twins—all of Paris, that is, except for learned persons like himself and his fellow obstetricians, who would not give ten *centimes* to see them with their clothes on. He scoffed at the information given out by *le propriétaire*, as it was too suspect to take at face value. "Let me merely say that we have been told that the mother underwent a Cesarean operation when the infants were eleven months old! We give that a double question mark??"

French bureaucrats, like French medical men, took an active interest in the twins' case. The Paris prefect of police, moved by doubts about their authenticity, asked *l'Académie de médecine* to send someone to make sure they were legitimate. The academy contacted Dr. Tardieu, who agreed to examine the sisters and bring back a detailed scientific report, which he expected would prove *très intéressante*.

Tardieu told the academy's January 13 meeting what had happened when he and a Dr. Robin went to examine Millie-Christine: "Last Saturday one of the higher-ups in the administration came begging me to proceed with the examination of the monster, and that very day at one o'clock monsieur Robin and I, accompanied by the bureau chief of theatres, went to the Cirque des Champs-Elysées and presented ourselves to *le directeur* of the establishment and to *l'entrepreneur* of the exhibition of Millie-Christine. The latter received us with quite bad grace."

The reason Joe Smith gave for the cold reception was that Millie-Christine had already been examined by numerous physicians.

The doctors urged that their examination had an official character. They were authorized—and indeed had a duty—to make sure the Parisian public was not made a toy and a dupe by Millie-Christine and her agents.

The insult seems to have stung Joe's pride, for at that point, said Tardieu, "the *propriétaire* of the monster yielded to these observations" and called for Millie-Christine.

Joe knew what the doctors would soon find out—that Christine might give in to French authority, but Millie would stand firm. Her refusal, Tardieu observed, had absolutely no feeling of playfulness about it, not for a single moment. He found it very *piquant*, in fact, to see how the individuality of the sisters emerged as he and Dr. Robin continued pressing for an examination. Millie and Chrissie argued briefly between themselves. It was most interesting, said Tardieu, "to recognize by the sound of the voice and the expressions of the face the difference in the feelings and the wishes in one and in the other." The demand "especially seemed to touch and even shake one of the two sisters when the other manifested her opposition, in a sort of little quarrel between the two."

The parties negotiated. The twins offered to hold up their blouses in back and pull down their skirt band, allowing the men to inspect their joined backs through the gap. The doctors protested that the academy demanded an unrestricted examination. At last, seeing that "despite all of our insistence it was impossible to have shown to us the most secret parts of the body," Tardieu and Robin compromised. They were admitted into a neighboring room, alone with the sisters and "a German lady who served as a governess and who appeared to have some medical knowledge." The twins undressed to the waist.

The doctors examined each body from head to hips and from knees to toes—all but the most secret parts, the very parts Tardieu and Robin had come to see.

When Tardieu reported back to *l'Académie de médecine*, he described the sadly twisted spines, deformed by the twins' early struggles to turn face to face "to embrace each other as they do today." Otherwise, he said, their physical development was truly remarkable. He ended his talk with the horrid thought that struck anyone who spent time with the sisters: "This almost-complete independence of the two beings . . . permits one to foresee as a terrible eventuality the day when one succumbs before the other and the survivor remains attached to the *cadavre* of her sister."

After Tardieu's report, Pierre Paul Broca rose to add a few words. Dr. Broca was a professor of surgical pathology, the founder of the Anthropological Society of Paris, and a brilliant surgeon who had begun to unlock the secrets of the human brain by demonstrating that the center for speech lies in the left frontal lobe. He, too, had looked forward to examining Millie-Christine at a meeting of his Anthropological Society.

"Our examination was unfortunately no more complete than that of Monsieur Tardieu," he admitted. As a surgeon, he was frustrated. As an anthropologist, he offered some fresh data. He had questioned Millie-Christine's entourage about race, he said, and found out that Monemia was "a mulatress of the first blood," whose mother had been born of a white father and Negro mother and whose father was an Indian. Millie-Christine shared, then, "the nature of the *zambos*."

The intricacies of nineteenth-century racial categories preoccupied Broca and his contemporaries on both sides of the Atlantic. They drew elaborate charts illustrating every possible mix, each named according to fractions of "white," "black," and "red" blood. Whatever the exact recipe, Millie-Christine's bloodline apparently reflected that distinctive American blend of European, African, and Native American ancestry.

Four days after the scientific reports to *l'Académie de médecine*, the "terrible eventuality" that Dr. Tardieu foresaw for all conjoined twins struck down Chang and Eng. Millie-Christine was still in Paris when the papers announced that a blood clot to the brain had killed Chang in the early-morning hours. Eng, in a panic, died from fright before dawn. No doctor lived within calling distance, so the great question remained unanswered. Could a skilled surgeon have tied off the connecting band, severed Chang, and saved Eng's life?

❦❦❦

The Paris *préfet de police* was correct to warn the public about show-business trickery, though he was wrong to suspect the Americans. Under the very noses of local *gendarmes*, a lively little cabaret called Les Porcherons advertised that it would feature a woman with two heads, four legs, and four arms. The notice attracted an immense and curious crowd. Corks popped in time to the house orchestra. At last, the marvel appeared, to deafening applause. A moment later, it spun around. Bamboozled customers saw two laughing girls bound together in one bodice, at which time excited chatter turned to angry jeers.

The director of the cirque des Champs-Elysées, where Millie-Christine was appearing, quickly swore out a complaint. Franconi was his name, and like any good circus director, he was happy to seize publicity when it came his way. Barnum would have approved. "The plaintiff now affirms that the defendant had no phenomenon whatever, and so claims 10,000 fr. as compensation for the prejudice raised to his own exhibition of Millie-Christine," said the *Clipper*.

Any entertainer could overlook a bit of dishonest competition. Fire, a perennial hazard for performers and audiences, was a more serious matter. Soon after Millie-Christine arrived in Europe, the Theatre of Ulm suffered a disastrous evening. Twenty-four petroleum-burning lamps attached to a chandelier exploded while a performance was going on, and the flaming liquid fell in a shower on the spectators. In an instant, the dresses of some twenty ladies were afire, producing agonizing burns. One victim died a few hours afterward.

On stages everywhere, ladies in fancy costumes were at constant risk of setting themselves aflame by a careless brush against the kerosene-burning footlight jets. A high-kicking New Orleans dancer once ignited her skirt through contact with a chandelier over her head! Few theatres covered the stage lights with safety guards. An actress or dancer or singer in a gauzy gown who swirled too near the footlights was instantly ablaze. If her stage partners were brave enough and quick enough, they'd smother the flames in time.

The *Clipper* offered one fireproofing recipe:

> There was a young woman, and
> What do you think?
> She soaked her light dresses in
> Caloride of zinc.
> Then fire couldn't hurt her,
> Though close she came by it;
> O, ladies! O, managers! why
> Don't you try it!

Tragically, the traditional zinc chloride method often failed. After the Paris winter season ended, Millie-Christine and her

Bertin photographic studio, Brighton, England
Autographed on reverse, "With Millie Chrissie's love '73"

company traveled on to bookings in the provinces. In late May, they crossed the capricious Loire into Tours. The thriving merchants' town claimed St. Martin as its patron saint—generous Martin, who'd once torn his cloak in two to share with a beggar. Tours was a place of pilgrimages and miracles. It is easy to believe that it was one of St. Martin's miracles that protected Millie-Christine when she finally faced her trial by fire.

"Mlle. Millie-Christine, the 'Two-Headed Nightingale,' has had a narrow escape from being burnt to death," reported the June 6 *Clipper*. "She was performing at a circus in Tours, France, when her dress caught light. Fortunately, one of the company seized hold of her, threw her down, and put out the flames before they had done much harm. The courageous lady phenomenon insisted on finishing her performance, much to the admiration of the audience."

Chapter 15

The wind blows fair, our vessel sails
Right gaily o'er the foam,
And soon again we hope to greet,
The dear old friends at home.

Songs of Miss Millie-Christine

*M*illie-Christine stayed seven years abroad. Her Combination Troupe with Anna Swan and Captain Bates had sailed for England in 1871, when Ulysses S. Grant was president. While she was in Europe, the former general rode out the storms of his first term and survived a second. Rutherford B. Hayes was president by the time Millie-Christine returned.

Her ship docked in New York on October 1, 1878. A *New York*

Herald reporter climbed aboard to greet her, according to the circus *Description* of her life, "and the next morning that journal gave forth to the whole United States the return of one of its children, who had fully established herself to be the greatest curiosity of the greatest country in the world."

She had exhibited in England, France, Germany, Belgium, Italy, Hungary, Austria, Holland, and Russia. "While abroad Millie Christine made herself mistress of the French, German, Italian and Spanish languages," says the *Description*. Her "Grand Tour" of Europe was filled with experiences and friendships beyond the reach of ordinary travelers. She'd met more titled personages than most Americans could dream of glimpsing on their own Grand Tours.

Millie-Christine counted on Americans' boundless enthusiasm for foreign nobility. She and Joe ordered a stack of handbills announcing her triumphs. The handbills bore the Royal seal of England—a lion and unicorn rampant, spinning a crowned globe with their front paws. "ROYAL GUEST," the bills proclaimed. "The Famous TWO-HEADED NIGHTINGALE, Three Times by Command before the Royal Family. Twice before the Prince and Princess of Wales, and also before all the Crowned Heads of Europe."

Millie-Christine brought two diminutive Italians to the States with her—Baron Littlefinger and Count Rosebud, the brothers Magri. Count Rosebud joined her in a program of songs, accompanied by Baron Littlefinger on harmonica and Professor Albert H. Fernald on piano.

The new combination opened for a season's run in Boston's Horticultural Hall. In the old days with Joseph Smith, October's bright blue weather had always meant county fairs and state fairs. For their first season back in the United States, however, Joe and the twins had more ambitious plans. They banked on their fresh-from-Europe appeal and concentrated on profitable big-city audiences in the East.

In Philadelphia, Millie-Christine's physician friend William Pancoast invited her to a another teaching clinic at Jefferson Medical College. Dr. Pancoast was the persuasive man who'd coaxed her to pose for his medical photographer before she left for Europe. While she was abroad, he had managed to convince the distraught Bunker families to let him autopsy Chang and Eng.

Pancoast wanted to show off Millie-Christine to his current crop of medical students. Although he may not have spelled it out, the bald truth was that, at age twenty-seven, Millie-Christine was of increasing interest to the medical community. Fit and healthy, she had already set a record in the pathological anatomy field by outliving her Hungarian predecessor.

Dr. Pancoast's second clinic featuring Millie-Christine was an even more intriguing blend of show business and medical instruction than his earlier one, for this time, the Magri brothers also showed up.

A reporter from the *Philadelphia Evening Telegraph* who came to the operating theatre early, before the sisters arrived, described the scene: "The well-like room was crowded, and Professor Pancoast busy removing a cancer from a patient. During the operation Baron Littlefinger and Count Rosebud, two most intelligent dwarfs—perfect little men in figure—were present, and appeared interested spectators of the operation." Shortly before the sisters were due for their one o'clock appointment, Dr. Pancoast gave a brief lecture. "In introducing Millie and Christine," the reporter noted, "the Professor said that he considered them the most interesting monstrosity of their class that has ever come under the notice of scientific men, far more interesting than the Siamese Twins. In the midst of his discourse the young ladies entered, clad in green silk on their two bodies, pretty little bronze boots on their four feet, white kids on their four hands."

The spectators marveled as Dr. Pancoast ran through the usual demonstrations. While the twins looked away, he tapped Chrissie's shoulder. Millie was unaware. He pinched Millie's leg with tweezers. Chrissie felt a touch.

Pancoast described the sisters' struggles for supremacy as youngsters, and how they had "early concluded that the best way to get along in their novel path through life was to yield to each other." A wise lesson for us all, the *Telegraph* reporter pointed out. "Their present happiness and affection for each other is an example for couples who are yoked together in marital bonds."

Speaking of which, someone at the clinic raised the subject of matrimony. "To the question by Professor Pancoast whether either was engaged to be married," the reporter said, "each denied the soft impeachment with decision, though the Professor explained that physically there are no serious objections to the marriage of Her or Them; but morally there was a most decided one."

Millie-Christine and the Magris exhibited in Philadelphia's Concert Hall for the entire month of January 1879. Midway through the run, tragic news came from Ohio. After a horrendous labor, Anna Swan Bates had borne a second giant baby by a disastrous forceps delivery. Anna's doctor reported that the infant weighed twenty-three and three-quarter pounds, the size of an ordinary six-month-old child. He was thirty inches long, taller than many of the little people Anna and Millie-Christine worked with—taller than General Grant Jr., Commodore Nutt, and Minnie Warren. He lived less than a day. The grieving Anna and Captain Bates laid him to rest beneath a headstone carved with a single word, *Babe*.

At the close of the Philadelphia run, Millie-Christine's troupe headed west. Travel had changed since the early days, when Millie-Christine and Joseph Smith had bounced over muddy country roads. Now, show people relaxed on up-to-date transcontinental trains that offered reduced rates for professional travelers, snappy service by dark-skinned porters, dining-car tables decorated with silverware, white cloths, and fresh posies, and Pullman Palace sleeping cars where one—or two together, in Millie-Christine's case—could stretch out while the cars joggled on through the night.

"Managers and Agents of Combinations Visiting the West," said an ad for the Chicago, Rock Island and Pacific Railroad, "THE ROCK ISLAND ROUTE has more good show towns on its line than any of its competitors. We also run the finest dining and restaurant cars used on a railroad, and serve meals from bill-of-fare at seventy-five cents each."

Fine as the new cars were, no public train could offer accommodations to match Phineas T. Barnum's private railway car. He was back on the road, traveling with the Barnum-London Shows. He'd contracted with the Pullman Company to build an elegant nine-thousand-dollar coach fitted for the exclusive use of his family. It included a drawing room, a reception room, a library, and a refectory for private family dining. His new car outclassed that of every other circus owner on the road and put his main rivals—Adam Forepaugh, for instance—to shame.

For a year and a half, Millie-Christine toured the West from Denver to Portland. Joe announced the troupe's return to the southern states with a boldface *Clipper* ad on New Year's Day 1881.

To Circus Proprietors:

After spending a most enjoyable season of eighteen
months . . . principally on the Pacific Slope, I am again east
of the Rocky Mountains, and take this opportunity of letting
you know that I am still manager for MISS MILLIE CHRIS-
TINE, The Two-headed Nightingale, and should any of you
wish to engage her or them, The Most Wonderful and Interesting Personage to-day in the Known World, for appearances
in Big Show Season of 1881, I would be pleased to negotiate
with you. Letters addressed to me at SCRIVEN HOUSE,
SAVANNAH, GA., will be duly received.

Respectfully,

JOS. P. SMITH
Manager for Two-headed Lady

Before Millie-Christine left Savannah, an ad appeared in the *Clipper* that upset her terribly. Showman Francis Uffner, "Proprietor of
American Midgets," advertised a new attraction from Europe in a
notice spread across two wide columns in giant letters: "THE
DOUBLE-HEADED BOHEMIAN WONDER. . . . A child with two
heads, one body, four legs and four arms; five years of age, highly
intelligent, and a perfect beauty." Then came the devastating part,
for everyone in show business to read: "The Siamese Twins [and] the
Two-headed Nightingale . . . are repulsive in comparison to this beautiful and extraordinary human phenomenon."

Repulsive.

A good portion of Millie-Christine's strength and dignity and
self-confidence flowed from her belief that she was one of God's

special creations. She grew up in a time when most people experienced a sense of wonder upon meeting her—"a feeling of awe," as one English reporter put it, "at the inscrutable ways of Him who had, in these 'little ones' left . . . human intellect and science so far behind."

"I am most wonderfully made," Millie-Christine recited or sang with all sincerity at every performance. "A marvel to myself am I, as well to all who passes by."

Uffner's derisive words cut deep. Who could grow impervious to words like *freak* and *monster* and *repulsive*? Over the years, the sisters had heard all the hurtful words. Even Dr. Pancoast, lecturing his students, had spoken of the twins as "the most interesting monstrosity of their class" ever to come to his attention.

Millie-Christine had learned to practice public forbearance from her earliest days. This time, though, her anger flashed. She fired off a bitterly sarcastic reply, which ran in next Saturday's paper.

TO MR. FRANCIS M. UFFNER, The Midget-Man, Piccadilly Hall, London, Eng.

I have just read of the wonderful Prodigy advertised by you in THE CLIPPER, and cannot refrain from expressing to you my gratitude, after seeing the good taste (something no one else has ever given you credit for) displayed by you, in speaking of repulsive people, in that you do not mention yourself as one of them, for we of education and refinement, Mr. Uffner, would seriously object to having one classed with us who is so devoid of traits by which a gentleman is characterized as yourself.

If people lived to as great an age in these days as some of them did in olden times, OF WHICH I HAVE READ, no doubt you would grow to be a more monstrous monstrosity than you are, but, sir, you would never grow to be a gentleman.

MILLIE CHRISTINE, THE TWO-HEADED NIGHTINGALE

So much for Mr. Uffner. Not only was he a monstrous monstrosity—even worse, he was no gentleman! Millie-Christine thus made it clear that no one was going to disparage her in public and get away with it.

The Double-Headed Bohemian Wonder soon faded from the public eye. Show business indeed makes strange traveling companions. Eventually, Millie-Christine and manager Uffner would call a truce and strike out together on a successful New England tour.

~~~

Millie-Christine put together a new show with a troupe of Bohemian glassblowers and sailed to Cuba for the rest of the winter. She played the Matanzas Exposition, then Havana. Joe sent back word that she was creating a sensation. Leon's Iron Amphitheatre always needed circus and variety specialties—any novelty acts that did not depend on the English language. "Artists with more than one act preferred," one of Leon's ads read. "We pay Salaries in Spanish Gold, 100 cents on a dollar. . . . Board Ten Dollars per Week, first-class." Millie-Christine was a special drawing card in Cuba because she could chat with visitors in Spanish.

Later in the year, she appeared in New York City for a long run at Bunnell's Museum. "REMEMBER OUR ATTRACTIONS!" said Bunnell's ads. "THE EUROPEAN WONDER, MILLIE CHRISTINE, THE TWO-HEADED GIRL, who has no rival."

George B. Bunnell was the new museum king, now that Barnum was caught up with his circus. Bunnell's New York City showplace had opened the previous December at the northwest corner of Broadway and Ninth Street. By August 1881, when Millie-Christine settled in, Bunnell's Museum, "THE ONLY FAMILY MUSEUM," was "crowded with pleased patrons." Cheeky ads claimed that all other museums had closed their doors since Bunnell's had come to town, their interiors desolate and shrouded in loneliness. "HEAT, COLD, STORM AND ALL THE ELEMENTS have no effect upon the business of this THE CROWNING SUCCESS of the AMUSEMENT WORLD. UNAFFECTED BY SCORCHING SUN, TORRID TEMPERATURE, RUSHING RAIN." This was a dig at the great outdoor traveling circuses like Barnum's, as weather mattered a great deal to them.

Millie-Christine had plenty of interesting companions at the museum.

On the lower floor was a gentleman who played a small organ, a violin, and a cello at the same time. Colonel Routh Goshen strolled nearby, a hefty giant Millie-Christine knew from Barnum's old place. A glassblower worked at his delicate art. William Henry Johnson— longtime Barnum favorite "Zip, the What-is-it?"—grinned down from a raised platform. Zulu warriors lounged about when they weren't performing war dances, singing native songs, and exhibiting their skill in throwing their assegais. Since most of the "Zulus" were American-born, they needed considerable practice with the exotic hunting spears.

On the second level were the Seven Wonders, seven sisters with remarkably long hair; midget Nellie Keeler; bearded lady Annie Jones, described as "handsome and a good conversationalist"; fat girl Adah

Briggs; Ibonia, an albino lady; Costentenus, a tattooed Greek; and Antoinette, a young lady whose fine blond hair touched the platform she stood on.

Bunnell's Museum had a hall large enough to accommodate four hundred people. Its stage hosted such acts as the Sutherland Family, who sang quaint songs; Captain Beach and Ida La Selle, who performed subaquatic feats; Professor Ned Smith and his trained dogs; Harry Everett, magician; the Lovenburgs, who played musical glasses and the piano; Master Nelton, a boy juggler; and Professor Abt's Grecian Mystery. Also appearing while Millie-Christine was in residence were a "Hindoo" snake enchantress and Hungarian gypsies.

George Bunnell was constantly on the lookout for clean and novel exhibits. He concluded his ads with a standing invitation: "If you have a curiosity alive or dead, write. If your act is free from vulgarity and pleasing, write. If you have invented anything new, write. If you have anything you think I want, write to G. B. BUNNELL, at the Hub, Broadway, corner Ninth street, New York."

Millie-Christine was still at Bunnell's when President Garfield died, the second American president shot down in her lifetime. Swaths of black cloth swung from the museum windows, as they did from buildings up and down Broadway. "The nation mourns James Abram Garfield. . . . The bullet of the assassin has completed its frightful work," said the obituary that ran in the *Clipper* on September 24, 1881. Garfield had been wounded by a disappointed office seeker on July 2. He lingered for over two months before slipping away in mid-September.

In October, Bunnell expanded to Brooklyn, into the former Waverly Theatre on City Hall Square. "ANOTHER IRON IN THE FIRE," the *Clipper* announced. "The building has been repainted and decorated and presents a very showy appearance." Bunnell called his new place the Annex Museum and promised to make it as healthy as possible.

Brooklyn's waterfront did pose health problems, there was no question about that. A special Joint Committee on Health and Law had just sent Mayor Howell a recommendation about "the great nuisance at the offal and night soil dock in the Wallabout. *Resolved*, That from and after the third of October, 1881, no public wharf or dock in the City of Brooklyn shall be in anywise occupied or used for the purpose of receiving or dumping any dead animal matter or night soil."

Bunnell's Annex Museum, "Featuring Jos. P. Smith's TWO-HEADED NIGHTINGALE," opened on Monday, October 10. The house was packed. The *Brooklyn Eagle* sent a reporter to interview Millie-Christine. He titled his story "What Both Heads Had to Say to an Eagle Reporter Yesterday—Peculiar Conversation of Christine-Millie."

The story began, "They call her the two headed woman. She is at Bunnell's new museum. . . . She can't see herself—that is, they can't see each other—because the backs of their heads almost touch. They sing and dance well. She was talking to herself—that is, the two mouths were engaged in speaking—behind the scenes, when the Eagle reporter entered yesterday, and one of her was gently tapping her foot on the floor."

If he didn't take down every word exactly right—surely, she didn't tell him she was born in Virginia—at least the interview comes as close to a real conversation with Millie-Christine as we're ever likely to recapture. It is reprinted here in all its idiosyncrasies.

"How do you do?"

"I am well," said one head.

"First rate," said the other.

"And what is your name?"

"I'm Millie," muttered one.

"And I'm Christine," murmured the other.

"Could Millie feel well and Christine the opposite?"

"Bet your—"

Millie

Christine

Fie

"You see," said Millie, as she gracefully plied her fan, "we generally feel the same."

Indeed!

"Touch me on the foot a certain number of times," said Millie, "and then Christine will tell you how often you did it."

The reporter touched the foot four times and then Millie, with a ripple of laughter, asked:

"How often, Christine?"

"Four times, Millie, dear," was the reply.

"Below the point where the junction occurs," said Christine, "we both can feel alike. But you could touch me on the cheek a certain number of times and Millie would know nothing about it."

"Do your thoughts run in the same direction?"

"Not always," said Millie. "Now I might think a man was perfectly horrid, and Christine might think he was simply charming."

"And yet," jocosely remarked the reporter, "you couldn't settle the question by a little 'run in,' as it were."

"For a very good reason," said Millie. "Because, if Christine is hurt below the point where we are united, I am hurt also."

"Does Millie do the eating for both?"

"Not at all. We generally eat at the same time."

"And while Millie might relish a beef steak for supper, Christine might fancy a reed bird or a prairie chicken?"

"That might be the case, although, as a rule, we both eat the same things."

"But you order supper for two?"

"Yes."

"And one person eats it?"

"Cert."

Christine

Millie

"Don't say 'cert.'"

"How old are you?"

"We are 30, and we were born in Virginia."

"Since then, I presume, you have traveled around the world?"

"Pretty nearly," was the reply from both, and then she arose from her seats and walked to the stage, where she sang a duet.

Chapter 16

$\mathcal{A}$t this point in her life, Millie-Christine sometimes longed to settle down to a quiet family life. She was thirty, a couple of years past the age when the Siamese Twins had first retired. On the other hand, she'd lived in the show-business world since before she could remember—lived with applause, with the excitement of the unexplored next stop. She'd moved in a special society where extraordinary people were the norm. And of course, she'd grown accustomed to a substantial income.

During her years abroad, American traveling circuses had begun carrying their gaudy glamour to every city and small town along the train lines. For exuberant show business, there was simply nothing to compare with a top-notch railroad circus.

Here's how Millie-Christine happened to join Batcheller and Doris's Great Inter-Ocean Railroad Show, as told in her 1882 circus *Description*. When John Doris first approached her with the idea, she turned him down. She'd come back to America, she told him, to build a retirement house. She vowed that she would appear no more in public. Doris urged her to sign up for just one tenting season, as a featured attraction with Inter-Ocean. Again she refused, but Doris persisted. He asked for her lowest terms. "Seeing no other way out of the difficulty than to demand a salary so exorbitant that it would not nor could not be paid for a single feature in so vast an establishment as the Great Inter-Ocean Show she replied, '$25,000 for the season with traveling expenses for a maid and man servant.'"

Twenty-five thousand dollars was the value set on Millie-Christine when the appraisal team of Bobo and Kirby had combed through Joseph Smith's Spartanburg estate. She had apparently kept that amount in mind all the years since. Imagine her surprise when Doris pulled a contract from his pocket, all filled out except for the salary. He wrote in the requested amount, signed his name, and handed the contract to her for her signature. She signed it.

George H. Batcheller and John B. Doris were the same two Philadelphia showmen who had once hired Madam Hallean. They had assembled their one-ring circus in 1879. "Batcheller of the new circus firm of Batcheller & Doris was in former years a famous leaper," the *Clipper* reminded readers. "Doris is the original and only 'Hunkey Dory.'"

"Our performers represent every nationality under the sun" was

Inter-Ocean's full-color poster, printed by Strobridge Lithograph Company for the 1882 season
CINCINNATI ART MUSEUM, GIFT OF THE STROBRIDGE LITHOGRAPHING COMPANY

Batcheller and Doris's claim for the Great Inter-Ocean Railroad Show.

Despite all their years of touring, the twins were strangers to American circus life. European *cirques* were different, held inside proper buildings, instead of outdoors in tents on muddy fields. On the positive side, American circus folk traveling by rail didn't need to pack into and out of a series of hotels. To the twins, personal space on a sleeper car—an extrawide berth with a window— was a cozy prospect. For once, Millie could decorate to her heart's content.

Inter-Ocean was a thriving little outfit when the sisters came aboard. Like every show on the rails, it claimed more novelties, surprises, and sensations than had ever before been gathered under one management. More rare wild beasts than ever before exhibited under one canvas. The best acrobats, trapezists, bareback riders, leapers, and tumblers in the profession.

Besides the salary, Inter-Ocean appealed to the twins because of its reputation. "The Great Inter-Ocean is a 'high-toned affair' throughout," said an ad. Everybody entering the Midway, it promised, would immediately notice the extreme neatness and discipline pervading the entire establishment.

In circus lingo, it was a "Sunday school show." No gambling was allowed, everything was as advertised, and customers were admitted to all shows for the price of one ticket. Inter-Ocean was a circus where cursing concessionaires and roistering roustabouts were warned to keep their mouths shut and their hands out of people's pockets. Management promised that under no circumstances would it allow any of its "hundreds of attaches" to do or say anything in the slightest degree offensive to the most fastidious.

What's more, the show lived up to its claim. It was "a splendidly equipped establishment," said the *Cleveland Morning Herald*, "and their force of employees are a gentlemanly, well disciplined body of men. There is nothing coarse nor boisterous in their deportment."

The 1882 season would last thirty-five weeks, from April to December. That worked out to seven hundred dollars a week for Millie-Christine, plus expenses for a manservant and her indispensable traveling companion, Englishwoman Blanche Brook. The contract specified that Millie-Christine would appear as a regular performer in the ring, rather than as a sideshow curiosity. She'd have her own neat little curtained roomette on the train, eat meals in the "pie car" and the circus cookhouse tent, and perform two shows a day—at two o'clock and eight o'clock—with Sundays off.

Batcheller and Doris put together a lively forty-page *Description* of the life of Millie-Christine, whom it described as "the Two-Headed

Lady, the Double-Tongued Nightingale, the Puzzle of Science, the Despair of Doctors, the Dual Unity." "Only one living creature is like Millie Christine," said the introduction, "and her name is Christine Millie."

The eye-catching cover shows a perky bird holding the pole of a huge American flag in its beak. Millie-Christine is superimposed against Old Glory's field of stars. The "Eight Wonders of the World" are printed on the stripes—the Seven Wonders of the Ancient World and Millie-Christine added as number eight.

A little poem followed:

> The Pyramids first, which in Egypt are reared;
> Then Babylon's Gardens and Ramparts appeared . . .
> Last—but not least—is MILLIE CHRISTINE,
> The Two-headed Nightingale, alive to be seen.

In retelling her life story, the circus *Description* embellished her earlier booklets and repeated the proud claim about her Columbus County real-estate holdings: "Jacob, the father of this wonderful being, once the slave of the planter McCoy, now owns, with his wife Monemia, the very plantation on which he was once a bondman, and on which Millie Christine first saw the light of day, the same having been purchased by her with the proceeds of her exhibitions as a present to her father and mother." There were a couple of pages of "Certificates of Eminent Medical Men." Hundreds more might have been provided, the booklet correctly stated. There were lyrics to her most popular show songs, from "O'er the Waves We Float" to "Wandering in the May-Time."

Inter-Ocean also ordered up a glamorous full-color picture of its new star attraction, a delicately tinted poster from the Strobridge Lithographing Company. Millie-Christine stands upon a circular carpeted stage chatting with half a dozen well-dressed gentlemen, ladies, and children. "A HUMAN MIRACLE," it proclaims. "Engaged for the SEASON of 1882 at the enormous salary of $25,000." The poster is printed in rich shades, from Millie-Christine's rose-colored gown and cinnamon skin to a young visitor's blue sailor-suit collar.

❧❧❧

Millie-Christine's new circus family was a first-class ensemble. Happily so, for as things turned out, she would spend the next two years living and working with most of them in very close quarters.

Inter-Ocean's posters proudly boasted of the show's constellation of "ONE HUNDRED ARENIC STARS." Shortly before the April 9 opening, all performers under contract for the new season streamed into Philadelphia from winter jobs in New York and Mexico and England. Animal trainers, hostlers, "canvasmen," "blowers" to talk the crowds into the show, lecturers, wagon drivers, and cookhouse workers reported to their bosses. Old pals greeted each other, then fell into serious training for the upcoming season.

Millie-Christine must have felt the vibrancy of her new life from the first rehearsal. The program featured seventeen numbers. Run-throughs timed out at over two hours for the complete show.

Professor Harry Armstrong's Magnificent Military Band blared the overture. In order, each act ran, tumbled, or galloped into the tent as the master of the ring shouted lavish introductions.

The acrobats were circus royalty. First among Inter-Ocean's splendid array of leapers, tumblers, gymnasts, and "equilibrists of matchless merit" came "Prince Satsuma and his Complete Company of the Wonder-Stirring People of the East!" The tent flashed to life as Prince

Satsuma's troupers bounded into the ring. They were a dazzle of jugglers, acrobats, and magicians flourishing ribbons, mock butterflies, fire, and fans. They leaped into precarious four-man columns, dangled by one toe from swaying ladders, danced on barrels balanced on spinning rings balanced on Prince Satsuma's muscular legs and nimble feet.

When the first Japanese athletes had performed in the States fifteen years earlier, a San Francisco reviewer declared that "their truly wonderful feats" had erased all his prejudices. No one could continue to believe in "the effeminacy and weakness of the race," he said, "when we see an undersized Jap, while lying on his back, raise, support and balance by his feet a group of five wooden ladders, weighing in the aggregate three hundred pounds. . . . The contractor who makes his living by houseraising would do well to import a few of these iron legged Asiatics, and dispense with his hydraulic pumps."

As Prince Satsuma's troupe exited, in dashed the Rice Brothers, gymnasts par excellence upon the horizontal bar.

At later points in the show, countless other acrobats appeared. The Royal Russian Athletes, "Undisputed Champions of the World!" The Three Siegrist Brothers, "Graceful Gymnasts Unparalleled in the Annals of Arenic Art!" The Two Sylvester Sisters, "Female Women of Rubber, Startling Contortionists!" Professor H. M. Parker's New Dog-Circus, "Best and Original Troupe of Canine Acrobats and Athletes!"

Thrilling young and old alike were the dazzling young ladies in spangled tights. Mademoiselle La Favre, "performing perilous feats on the Flying Rings!" Millie Tournour, "the Queen of Flight, the Finest Trapeze Artiste in all the World!"

Millie-Christine, "the Renowned Two-Headed Nightingale," entered the tent as the roustabouts swiftly laid a temporary stage floor in the ring. She sang a couple of songs and danced a polka to the lilting music of Monsieur Goulet and his famous French band from the Paris Hippodrome. When she finished, she bowed in two directions and sidestepped out to warm applause.

Then into the arena rode "the Pleasing, the Petite Sallie Marks," fifteen years old and already a star.

If acrobats were circus royalty, equestrians were the aristocrats. In fact, the first full American circus had been an exhibition of horsemanship by a former British Royal Circus star rider, John Ricketts, who introduced his show to Philadelphia in 1793. Ricketts's circus brought out overflow audiences. President George Washington, himself an ardent horseman, occupied a box seat at one performance.

Inter-Ocean's "Superb Selection of Equestrian Stars" was led by William Showles, "the very personification of grace and manly beauty. The Peerless Phenomenon, OUT-CHAMPIONING ALL THE CHAMPIONS—The GREATEST RIDER that ever Stood upon a Horse." His five-thousand-dollar challenge to outperform any other rider in the world "means business," Inter-Ocean ads promised.

Millie-Christine and others may have noticed that little Sallie Marks couldn't keep her eyes off handsome Willie Showles.

Several other gentlemen and ladies on horseback added dash to the show. Señor Don Jose Ramirez, "the Spanish Sensational Somersault Rider," performed airborne flips. Mademoiselle Millie Elizie stood with her right foot on the back of one horse, her left foot on another, galloping the team side by side around the arena. Mademoiselle Rosetta was billed as "the Female Four-Horse Rider!" Ella Stokes, "America's Pride, America's Own Best Known and Favorite," was described as the most daring, dashing, and beautiful bareback rider in Europe or America.

Another band of great bareback riders stirred up the sawdust for Inter-Ocean. Described as a "Genuine Tribe of Sioux Indians, headed by White Cloud, of Sitting Bull's Band," these Native Americans had once galloped across the grassy plains. White Cloud and his tribe were stragglers from a lost world when Millie-Christine met them. "The buffalo is gone, and the red hunters must die of hunger," White Cloud once lamented. After the Civil War, Phineas T. Barnum himself had lent a hand in killing off the buffalo, as part of a western hunting party outfitted by George Custer. White Cloud and other aging warriors now burlesqued old times, performing with traveling circuses like Inter-Ocean and Barnum & London.

When Millie-Christine first saw White Cloud, only six years had passed since he and his brothers shook the country with one final blood-drenched victory, at the Greasy Grass stream—which whites called the Little Bighorn—on June 25, 1876. This season, the sixth anniversary of the battle would fall on a Sunday, a circus day off. On Saturday, they'd be playing Princeton, Illinois. On Monday, they'd be setting up in St. Louis, where, as usual, White Cloud and his band would raise tepees within the big top and whirl their horses around the arena in a pell-mell parody of a battle charge.

Five great clowns "representing all nations" carried out the "inter-ocean" theme. The funny five were "the Irrepressible Italian Clown," Losci Giovanni; "England's Own Jester," Charles Ray; the German-Hebrew "Dialectrician Clown," George Drew, who entertained with Yiddish-flavored skits and stories; "the Great French Grotesque," François Kennebel, who "clowned" the equestrian and acrobatic stars; and the one and only Johnny Patterson, the lead clown. Patterson, "the Famous Irish Humorist, Conversationalist and Rambler from Clare" worked with a talking clown's unpainted face. A photo of him shows him sporting a handlebar mustache and wearing a troubadour's doublet and hose and a small pointed clown hat. Patterson was blessed with a sweet Irish tenor voice and was famous for his spontaneous humor. In fact, he would be witty to the end. Seven years later, when Johnny Patterson lay deathly ill, his doctor cheerfully remarked, "Well, I'll see you in the morning." The great clown found such a setup line irresistible. "I know, doctor," he answered, "but will I see you?"

A spectacular finale by the Great Zazel—"ZAZEL, the HUMAN CANNON BALL!"—closed each performance. Like all great aerialists, Zazel could walk, run, and dance on a braided steel wire not much thicker than one of Millie's crochet hooks. What set her apart—what made her the Great Zazel—was her nerve. A composite Inter-Ocean poster shows Zazel gracefully seated on the high wire, waving from beneath a parasol; Zazel gliding through the air, reaching out to grasp a flying trapeze; Zazel swinging by her feet with the greatest of ease; Zazel diving boldly toward a distant net; and Zazel emerging in a cloud of smoke from a cannon barrel.

For Zazel's spectacular act, Professor Armstrong's band shifted into a suspenseful tune. At the far end of the tent, a circus crew guided a huge wooden siege gun into place. The ringmaster then gave his spiel, and the band switched to a new tune. On cue, the peerless, fearless Zazel swept into the ring. She sighted, adjusted, and readjusted the cannon's aim. Finally satisfied, she turned and flung off her silk wrapper. For a long moment, she posed regally in her pink tights, greeting the audience with outstretched arms. To build suspense, she flashed through her high-wire and trapeze routines. Primed now for her finale, she climbed to the cannon's open mouth. The music suddenly broke off. The tent grew quiet except for a heartbeat throb from one muffled drum. Finally, the cannon exploded, and Zazel shot out in a cloud of smoke and a burst of flame.

Sooner or later, Millie-Christine must have learned the cannon's secret. Once Zazel slid out of sight into the dark muzzle, she stood on a small, circular platform attached to a powerful spring. When she or an assistant pulled a lever, the spring released and propelled her out the muzzle; a light gunpowder charge was set off for extra effect.

As for how she landed, Inter-Ocean publicity says she flew to a trapeze sixty feet away. From there, near the peak of the tent, she threw herself headlong into a breathtaking dive straight downward. Women hid their eyes, children screamed. A few feet above the ground Zazel rebounded from a bone-jarring net landing.

Everyone agreed it was a superlative stunt. Zazel "is simply a marvel," said an eyewitness, "for, explain it how we may, the fact remains that a human, breathing being is propelled from a position of inertia with sufficient force to traverse sixty feet of space to a lodgment in the dome of the tent. Applying the formula to bodies at rest, their weight, the space traversed, and speed attained, the motor that is effective without being fatal, must continue a bewilderment to the excited audience."

Circus visitors could also wander the animal tent to marvel at the "MONSTER MILLIONAIRE MENAGERIE! More rare Wild Beasts than ever before exhibited under one canvas." Batcheller and Doris had a fine little collection. In February, a German steamer had ferried over a shipload of newly captured exotic animals. Inter-Ocean invested in two small elephants, a camel, a dromedary, a stork, a white bear, and fifteen snakes to add to the animals it already owned.

Inter-Ocean bragged that it had three "Exclusive Zoological Features" that couldn't be seen in any other show.

One of them was a "SEVEN-TON, TWO-HORNED, BLACK, HAIRY RHINOCEROS!"

Even more impressive were the "Voracious, Vicious VAMPIRES, the Most Insidious Blood-Sucking Destroyers of Mankind. The first successful attempt to Import and keep Alive these Terrible Man-Killing Monsters. A substitute has been found for their fearful feasts on human blood. The only Live Specimens of this awful Animal Atrocity, half-Beast, half-Bird, ever exhibited in America."

Rarest of all was the "Great Egyptian Bovalapus, The most Curious Beast or Bovine of the Sea." A surviving poster shows what appears to be a rampaging horse crossed with a wild ox lunging from a lake. An unlucky native dangles from its gigantic jaws. Its unusual swept-back horns stretch half the length of its body. According to the poster, the incredible beast was caught in Lake Ujiji—where Stanley and Livingstone had rendezvoused a decade earlier—and was purchased by Batcheller and Doris for twenty thousand dollars.

But did anyone actually see the bizarre Bovalapus from Lake Ujiji? Fifteen years later, this same curious beast (or one exactly like it) appeared (or was supposed to appear) in Kansas with the Lemen Brothers Circus. "The Mighty Bovalapus, the rarest, strangest, awfulest of all the mighty monsters of the deep," said a Lemen Brothers ad in the *Walnut* (Kansas) *Eagle* in August 1897. The illustration was the same one Batcheller and Doris had used. When Lemen Brothers played Osage City in September, a *Free Press* reporter noted wryly, "Then there was the wonderful Bovalapus—But we didn't see the Bovalapus and therefore won't say anything about it." Folks in Kingman were even more skeptical about the elusive creature when

Lemen Brothers pulled into town in October. "The menagerie was a fizzle," said the *Leader-Courier*, "the marvelous 'Bovalapus,' the 'mighty monster of the seas that sweats blood,' was not to be seen. The show people said the animal died while they were in Minnesota."

ๆ๛๛

Inter-Ocean's animals would trot, thud, and clatter down ramps from their cramped train-car stalls at each new stop, happy to feel solid ground under their feet. The lucky ones that didn't have to ride in cages helped off-ramp the circus wagons. Ready at last, they would line up with all the human performers for the grand, free street parade to the circus grounds.

"SEMIRAMIS, the ASSYRIAN QUEEN, . . . the $10,000 PRIZE BEAUTY of the World, the acknowledged Supreme Empress of Loveliness" led the parade. She and her Royal train brought biblical days gloriously to life, "personating Assyria's Queen on her triumphant entry into Babylon from successful conquest." An Inter-Ocean poster shows Semiramis swaying regally into Babylon in a canopied howdah atop a gorgeously draped elephant. Long tassels swing from each side of the elephant's embroidered head cap; a turbaned trainer straddles the beast's neck.

Semiramis was the creation of the circus's press agent, J. V. Strebic. He had placed enticing ads early in January: "$10,000 WILL BE PAID FOR THE FAIREST, HANDSOMEST, AND LOVELIEST LADY IN THE LAND, to appear daily in the Greatest Spectacular Street-Pageant of Modern Times. . . . No personal interviews granted. Applications, inclosing photograph, to be made by mail only, until March 1, 1882, on which day a committee of three well-known citizens of Philadelphia will award the prize."

Actually, Strebic had stolen the idea for a "$10,000 Beauty" from

Philadelphia circus man Adam Forepaugh, who'd pulled the same stunt the year before.

Competing with Forepaugh was a rash and risky thing to do. A rapacious man with a hawk's beak of a nose, he was a dangerous fellow to cross. Forepaugh (or "4 PAW," as Barnum gleefully spelled the name) was born a Philadelphia butcher's boy. He learned his father's bloody trade early and hired out at age twelve for four dollars a month and board. Young Adam scrimped and saved until he could buy a cattle- and horse-supply business. He fell into the circus business by chance in 1864, when he sold John O'Brien forty-four horses on credit. O'Brien defaulted, and Forepaugh took over the show and found the career he'd been born for.

The Great Forepaugh Show had run its well-publicized competition by announcing, "A FORTUNE FOR A FACE. 10,000 Premium for the LOVELIEST LADY IN THE LAND." The lucky winner would star daily in a street pageant entitled "Lalla Rookh's Departure from Delhi," which Forepaugh declared would beat any street parade ever attempted or thought of by any circus manager. Over three thousand hopeful contestants sent photographs, according to Forepaugh's press agent. He showed some of them to *Clipper* editor Frank Queen, who uncharitably said, "To see these pictures, and realize the homeliness of some of the damsels who consider themselves the most beautiful of their sex, is a new and most startling revelation of female vanity."

After Forepaugh wrung the publicity dry, he announced that he'd found the most beautiful woman in the world right in his own backyard. Louise Montague, a well-known Philadelphia variety performer, would star as Lalla Rookh. Inter-Ocean's 1882 street-pageant poster of Semiramis riding her elephant into Babylon wasn't an exact copy of Forepaugh's 1881 poster of Lalla Rookh departing from Delhi, but it came mighty close.

Currently, Miss Montague was on the outs with Forepaugh. She had a number of unsettled court cases against him—one for breach of contract over unpaid salary, another to recover the promised ten thousand dollars, a third to recover damages on a personal-injury claim alleging that during one of the parades, her elephant had become unmanageable "and finally went down on his knees and threw plaintiff out of the basket in which she was sitting, and which was strapped to his back."

Soon, Millie-Christine would become intensely interested in the Montague lawsuits and the dozens of others pending against Forepaugh—especially her own.

Chapter 17

PROCLAMATION! WHAT IS THE INTER-
OCEAN, Who are the proprietors and the
agents they employ. . . . They are SHY-
STERS OF THE FIRST WATER who will
defraud and disappoint the generous public.

Unsigned rat sheet, 1882

Millie-Christine's first circus season opened Saturday, April 8, in Pennsylvania, so she missed seeing the famous Jumbo lumber off the ship onto a New York dock on April 9. Jumbo was Barnum's newest acquisition, a colossal elephant eleven and a half feet tall, some said twelve. Barnum called him "the Towering Monarch of His Mighty Race, Whose Like the World Will Never See Again."

Inter-Ocean's tour schedule was a daunting, yet typical, circus run. From early April through May, the performers would ride the cars westward, pitching their tents across Pennsylvania and into Ohio, then play a three-day stopover in Cleveland, then cross Indiana, then zigzag through Illinois. The last week in June, they'd lay over in St. Louis. They'd set up on Chicago's lakefront the first week in July and give an extra Tuesday-morning performance to celebrate the glorious Fourth. From Chicago, they'd jump to Wisconsin; if the circus stayed on schedule, Millie-Christine would spend her thirty-first birthday in Racine. By late August, after the wheat crop was harvested and the plains farmers had money to spend, the performers would play Nebraska and Kansas. They'd roll into eastern Texas in mid-September. For ten weeks, they'd raise the canvas and pull it down on fairgrounds and weedy lots from Clarksville to San Antonio to Galveston. The last two weeks in November, after the cotton farmers cashed in, the circus would enjoy an end-of-the-season stay in the old queen of show towns, New Orleans.

This was Batcheller and Doris's fourth season with Inter-Ocean. They'd worked their circus into a tightly disciplined, efficient, smooth-running community. The logistics of moving to a new location overnight were simply astounding. In the evening, what amounted to a good-sized town with a menagerie of wild animals went to sleep in Milwaukee, for example. The next morning, they all woke up in Waukesha. And this magic happened nearly every night, a new town sliding into view at dawn.

Inter-Ocean played to good crowds across Pennsylvania. The Saturday-morning parade through Erie's principal streets "was a brilliant one, and delighted the thousands who had come to see it," said the *Observer*. At least six thousand people attended the afternoon performance, the *Herald* estimated. "Those who wish good seats must go early this evening, as a rush is certain," that paper advised. "The menagerie and splendors of the ring are unsurpassed. The audience is wild with delight. The two-headed lady, Mlle. Christine, is on exhibition in the main tent, and is seen by all who enter. She sings sweetly, . . . waltzes finely, and is a brilliant conversationalist, and has a most attractive appearance."

The circus set up for its Cleveland run on marshy Stone's Flats. Although a drenching Lake Erie squall blew in, business was remarkably good. "The Batcheller & Doris Inter-ocean show is most inconveniently located on the flats, and yet thousands of men, women and children waded almost knee-deep in mud, and not a few sat in puddles of rain water charmed by the mysteries of the magic circle," said the *Penny Press*. The evening crowd was enormous. The ticket office sold out and closed up at eight o'clock. "The main attraction was Millie Christine, the two-headed lady, though the display of animals was unusually good, and the circus performance above the average," the paper said.

"There is a novelty and artistic finish to everything presented that is particularly pleasing," echoed the *Cleveland Herald*.

Batcheller and Doris looked forward to a sensational season. For the first six weeks, their dream came true—nothing but crowded tents, applause, and good reviews.

Unfortunately, Inter-Ocean and the Great Forepaugh Show overlapped routes all spring, Inter-Ocean usually one jump ahead. Competition roused Adam Forepaugh's killer instinct. Few men could savage a competitor as viciously as "4 Paw." He began firing off the nastiest "rat sheets" he could concoct, aiming to demolish Batcheller and Doris.

Rat sheets sprouted like weeds when two circuses trouped the same area. "Billing crews" rode a railroad car ahead of the main circus train. At every stop, men would hop off and sweep through the town with paste pots and long brushes, layering every available surface with circus posters. If they spotted a competitor's ads announcing dates ahead of their own, they slapped up malicious rat sheets, ran mean ads, passed handbills door to door, belittled their rival any way they could. The idea was to convince the locals that the incoming circus was a disreputable, seedy outfit and that they should save their money until a first-class show came to town.

Rat-sheet authors disregarded all rules of fair fighting. Their words snarled off the page and went for the jugular. "PROCLAMATION!" said one particularly horrid example. "WHAT IS THE INTER-OCEAN, Who are the proprietors and the agents they employ. Read, Study, and Ponder After Reading This. Watch, wait and pray as well as watch." Locals were advised to look out for the proprietors of this "FLIMSY, TRANSPARENT FRAUD," for "they are SHYSTERS OF THE FIRST WATER who will defraud and disappoint the generous public. FARMERS, MECHANICS, BANKERS, and PEOPLE IN GENERAL, WATCH THEM."

Inter-Ocean's press agent took a beating in that particular sheet. "WHO IS STREBIC, Their Agent? A poor demented, shallow-brained Scab and Filthy Cur of the worst grade of humanity, who OPENLY PROCLAIMED THE ASSASSINATION OF OUR LATE HONORED PRESIDENT A JUST RETRIBUTION and upholds his murderer, Guiteau, as a saint and wants to see him honored with a MONUMENT OF GOLD! This is a fact and can be proven. Citizens, what ought to be the punishment of this HUMAN HOG? Hang him with the assasin and CAST HIS DIRTY CARCASS TO THE SWINE."

Next came a scandalous morsel involving circus partner George Batcheller and the "$10,000 Beauty." "WHO IS THE SENIOR PARTNER?" the rat sheet asked. It advised readers to ask the Philadelphia chief of police, who would tell them what happened when Batcheller went in search of the "$10,000 Beauty," "which title they stole from the Big 4 Paw Show." Batcheller met "a fair, but not unsophisticated damsel," the rat sheet claimed, who invited him to her apartment, where she somehow managed to rob him of $550. "HE SQUEALED, and arrest was the order of the night" until the damsel "handed over one-half of the spoils." According to the rat sheet, the *Philadelphia Times* found the rest of the proceedings too obscene to report. "Oh! George, where is thy Shame?" the rat sheet asked.

Only John Doris escaped insult. He was such a nice fellow that the writer couldn't seem to find words to describe him: "Who is the Junior Partner of this Tripple Handed Fraud. If you can solve it you have the prize. Look at his lithos in the windows and his pictures upon the bill-boards. He is too sweet and cunning to survive the season through. For the want of room his further history and pedigree will be continued in our next NOTICE!"

The only Inter-Ocean performer singled out in the attack was unlucky Millie-Christine, and the charge was stunning: "*The DOUBLE-HEADED DARKEY they advertise so extensively is the same they have carted around the country for years gone by, and exhibited for 10 cents, when they want 50 cents to see the dark-skinned monstrosity. A disgusting sight for ladies and children to gaze upon.*"

The sheet was unsigned but reeked of Forepaugh's street-brawler style.

Inter-Ocean's train arrived at Fort Wayne, Indiana, early on Saturday, May 20. The gaudy wagons had barely begun rolling off the flatcars when someone spotted Adam Forepaugh's latest rat sheet tacked up at the depot. "*The one great feature this concern extensively advertises is a horribly repulsive Negro monstrosity*," the newest attack on Millie-Christine began.

It is hard to guess what caused such venom against her. Perhaps

Forepaugh had tried to hire Millie-Christine for his own circus and been turned down. Or perhaps the butcher's boy experienced the same turmoil that Mark Twain once confessed he felt toward an educated black American he met in Italy. "I could not bear to be ignorant before a cultivated Negro," he wrote, "the offspring of a South Carolina slave."

Whatever sent Forepaugh into his tirade, he'd gone too far. Libel, as *Black's Law Dictionary* defines it, involves "a maliciously written or printed publication which tends to blacken a person's reputation or to expose him to public hatred, contempt, or ridicule, or to injure him in his business or profession." The newest rat sheet fit the legal definition to the letter.

On Monday, Millie-Christine sent Strebic into town with a copy of the rat sheet. He carried it to the firm of Robertson & Harper, Attorneys & Solicitors, where he was told that Millie-Christine stood a good chance of winning a libel suit against Adam Forepaugh. Strebic retained the firm and ordered it to proceed with the case.

Inter-Ocean had moved on to Illinois by the time the lawyers filed the complaint three weeks later in the United States Circuit Court, District of Indiana. In the complaint, Millie-Christine said that, by reason of her peculiar form, she was unable to perform manual labor, but that, for the same reason, the public desired to see her and converse with her. That public desire had enabled her to obtain a livelihood by exhibiting herself and to amass the means by which she hoped to become independent.

Adam Forepaugh, the complaint said, intended to exhibit his rival circus at many of the points where Millie-Christine had been advertised to appear. It alleged that on or about May 20, 1882, Forepaugh had composed and printed show bills with the malicious intent to injure her in her business of exhibiting herself for gain. Those show bills, posted in public places and delivered to many hundreds of people residing in Fort Wayne and the surrounding country, contained false and defamatory matter such as the following: *"The one great feature this concern* [Inter-Ocean] *extensively advertises is a horribly repulsive Negro monstrosity. No lady would knowingly ever look upon it, little Children cover their faces with their hands when encountering this frightful malformation, and the sooner this hideous human deformity is hid from public view the better it will be for the community. All good Christian people can but regret that this afflicted object should be hawked over the Country to satisfy the greed of a couple of side show exhibitors."*

Because the show bills had injured Millie-Christine's good name and fame, the complaint said, she demanded judgment in the sum of twenty-five thousand dollars.

Forepaugh was playing Michigan at the time Millie-Christine's lawyers filed her complaint in Fort Wayne. He'd just been hit with another twenty-five-thousand-dollar lawsuit in Detroit, where a Mr. Busch claimed that one of Forepaugh's men had struck him with a club while he was looking under the canvas, which caused him to lose one of his eyes. A United States marshal caught up with Forepaugh and handed over a writ commanding him to appear for Millie-Christine's case at the next term of court in Fort Wayne.

Meanwhile, in Philadelphia, Forepaugh's "$10,000 Beauty," Louise Montague, had raised the ante to $50,000 to settle her breach of contract and injury suits. Barnum likely had matters pending against Forepaugh, too. He usually did. Over the years, Forepaugh and Barnum sued each other so often and spent so much money sending advance men out to post rat sheets against each other—"FRAUD! FALSE-HOOD! and DOWNRIGHT DECEIT!"—that they eventually signed a routing truce. One season, Forepaugh would tour the western states while Barnum covered the east; the next season, they would trade territories.

Despite Forepaugh's effort to ruin Batcheller and Doris's star attraction, Inter-Ocean proceeded west still doing good business. "No circus has ever appeared in this city that has drawn a better class of people," said the *Chicago Times* on July 8, "and no show has ever given more general satisfaction." Millie-Christine earned special mention. "By her lady-like and intelligent manner, aside from her peculiar formation, she has made numberless admirers."

ᴥᴥᴥ

Train wrecks were a hazard of life for traveling shows. Sooner or later during the thousands of railroad miles, most circus trains suffered a catastrophe of some sort. Collisions and derailments usually happened in the middle of the night with a thunderous crash and a grinding, jolting stop, followed by human and animal screams and roaring, trumpeting, and howling in the darkness. Surviving a train wreck put lesser problems like lawsuits in perspective, at least temporarily. Millie-Christine went through the frightening experience in Texas. "A freight-train collided with Batcheller & Doris' circus-train at Mesquite last night," said a telegram datelined Dallas on October 7, 1882. "The circus-train was wrecked. Three men were injured. One will die."

There were other dangers as well. An Inter-Ocean contracting agent, Samuel P. Cox, narrowly escaped his demise during a Texas shootout. He rode an advance car into Clarksville and checked into the Donoho House for a good night's sleep. By sheer coincidence, a Clarksville black man had been accused of rape the previous day. After being thrown in jail by the marshal, the prisoner was hustled out by local citizens and lynched. The next evening—the very night Cox checked into the hotel—"the negro's brother got several colored persons together to look for the marshal to kill him," as Cox later reported. "When I arrived there to do business for the Batcheller & Doris' Circus," Cox wrote to his friends via the *Clipper*, "I was put in the room where the marshal used to sleep. . . . In the evening of Sept. 5 the negroes fired through the window of the room about five shots, which, fortunately, did not touch me, but you can rest assured I was very much frightened. You can state to my numerous friends that I am safe, and hope to be home by Dec. 1." Home was Philadelphia. Cox arrived in good shape, ahead of the rest of the circus.

Batcheller and Doris broke up their partnership at the end of the 1882 season. Batcheller put a good face on the split with a press release announcing that Inter-Ocean, after a successful thirty-five-week season, had closed December 8 in Jackson, Tennessee, "and G. H. Batcheller then retired from business, having accumulated a fortune, and sold his interest to his junior and managing partner, John B. Doris."

Truth be told, Batcheller fell far short of a fortune. One old agent who traveled the southern states that season spread word that, as far as he knew, every menagerie and circus that ventured south lost money, "and some of them heavily." Another old-timer predicted that only nine railroad shows would be on the road the coming season, against thirteen in 1882.

Doris, now the sole owner, promised that Inter-Ocean would be one of the nine. He shipped the circus directly from Tennessee to its Pennsylvania winter quarters for "the usual routine of Repairs, Painting, etc., etc.," reported the *Clipper*. "Its present owner intends enlarging it greatly the present Winter, with Open Cages, Tableaux,

Calliopes, Wardrobes, etc., and intends to keep it in the future where it has been in the past, viz., in the front rank with all tenting-amusement enterprizes."

Millie-Christine wintered at Joe Smith's villa along the south fork of the Edisto River in South Carolina. Nearby Branchville was a thriving rail junction, handy for professional travelers like Joe and Millie-Christine. The mild climate couldn't be beat.

Her libel suit against Adam Forepaugh hung in limbo. He went out to Fort Wayne in December to negotiate with her lawyers. Both sides temporarily withdrew their legal documents, perhaps hoping to settle out of court over the holidays. On January 25, Millie-Christine refiled her complaint. Through 1883, it sat stalled in Fort Wayne—continued on the court calendar when the parties failed to appear, continued again, continued yet another time. Trying to pin down roving circus people to trial appearance dates could strain the patience of any court administrator.

⤸⤸⤸

Having been re-engaged by Doris at a salary of twenty-five thousand dollars, Millie-Christine put the finishing touches on her costumes for a second circus year. Newspaper ads announced 1883 as "positively her last season" with Inter-Ocean.

Doris prepared new postcard-sized advertising fliers for Millie-Christine, copied from last year's pretty poster. On the fliers, she is depicted holding sheet music and wearing long white gloves. A surviving copy shows colors so delicate that the little flier looks hand-tinted— the stage curtains are strawberry and peach; a sky-blue gown is clasped with a pale pink bow; the fans and slippers are butter yellow.

The text on the reverse side describes "A HUMAN MIRACLE . . . most astonishing and pleasing." It speaks of "faces beaming

John Doris's full-color advertising card for Millie-Christine's 1883 Inter-Ocean circus season.

with intellectuality," of "sparkling black eyes denoting vivacity, life, animation, and genuine mirthfulness," and of mental faculties "of a superior order, and double."

Zazel, the "Human Cannon Ball," signed on again with Inter-Ocean, as did trick riders Willie Showles and Sallie Marks, Prince Satsuma, most of the leapers and jugglers from the previous season, and Johnny Patterson and his fellow clowns.

They spent their first week performing in Philadelphia, working out the kinks. "SEASON WAS BRILLIANTLY OPENED BY THE INTEROCEAN SHOW," said the *Philadelphia Times* on April 10. "A brighter, prettier or more generally pleasing street-parade than that of J. B. Doris' Interocean Circus and Menagerie yesterday was never seen in Philadelphia. The pageant moved over all the principal streets, and the sidewalks were jammed with people."

Posters promised that the parade would be "a Colossal Carnival of Grand, Gorgeous, Glittering, Colconda of Golden Chariots. . . . THREE SOLID MILES OF SUPERB SPLENDORS."

Professor Harry Armstrong's band led the parade, seated in a golden chariot called "Flying Pegasus," drawn by eight handsome silver-gray horses. The musicians played their hearts out on twenty-four gleaming new instruments from the C. G. Conn Company. Then came Semiramis on her elephant and a long procession of animal cages and gilded and mirrored wagons. Millie-Christine and other ladies of the company waved to the crowd from Mr. Doris's own painted coach. Clark's Slave Cabin Jubilee Singers, seated upon a crystal-plated chariot called "Jubilee," rode along singing plantation melodies and camp-meeting hymns. The Goddess of Liberty and her attendants waved from another wagon. On and on, they swept past. Zazel's gun appeared, drawn by four stout horses. Clowns on mules, dashing jockeys, camels, elephants.

A pachyderm with John Doris's old stage moniker put on an impromptu show. "On Broad Street an elephant named 'Hunki-dori' spied a tempting stand full of peanuts on the sidewalk," said the *Times*. "Forgetting for a moment his keeper's spear, 'Hunki' lumbered through the crowd, and with his trunk scooped half-a-bushel of the nuts into his mouth. Then he thought of the keeper and spear, and plunged back into the line of the procession."

Like a fantastic caboose, the steam calliope came last in the parade. Circus folk pronounced it "*cal*-i-ope," with the accent on the first syllable. Doris had ordered a superlative new calliope from Cincinnati. The manufacturer swore it was the largest in the world. Fortunately for the paraders, Professor Will Horn "manipulated" his wheezing "steam piano" so it deafened only those near the end of the line. "The calliope in Doris' show has, it appears, ten more whistles than any other steam chest on the road," said one listener. "It struck us in that light. We might be able to stand a few more whistles, but it is doubtful. The line has to be drawn somewhere or some circus will be coming with a calliope that may strain the municipality and fracture the verandas."

There hadn't been such a street show in years, someone said later in the summer when the show reached New Bedford, Massachusetts, "although in the past two we have seen both Barnum and Forepaugh."

John Doris was a hands-on owner. "Mr. Doris is a worker," said a Rochester, New York, paper. "Instead of riding about in a carriage with paste diamonds and fine clothes, he is at the tent, here, there and everywhere, personally attending to the details of his show."

The fast-paced show pleased Inter-Ocean customers wherever it played. "There are no tedious waits; everything moves along smoothly, and every person connected with the entertainment, from the performers to the sawdust-rakers, seems to know and understand his business," said the Rochester paper. Circus-goers appreciated Doris's new rule that candy "butchers," peanut sellers, and lemonade vendors had to do business outside the main tent. There was no more climbing over the audience's legs during the performance and blocking the view.

In June, when the circus was playing Vermont, a Yankee confidence man tried to turn a quick dollar at Inter-Ocean's expense. Millie-Christine felt the sting first. She heard rumors that her agent had arranged a new contract for her without her consent, and it made her hopping mad. Evidently, Joe was not on hand to deny the rumor. She sent off a decidedly tart announcement to the *Clipper*:

TO MY ACQUAINTANCES AND WHOM IT
MAY CONCERN.

Feeling that there is an impression prevailing that my agent has that complete control of me (that I myself am a nonenity), he having the power to direct and redirect my movements regardless of my wishes, I take this method of making it known that such is not the case. He has not now, nor ever has he had, any right to transact any business for me without first consulting me and knowing if it was agreeable, and as remuneration for his services gets a percentage on my income.

Respectfully, MILLIE CHRISTINE

John Doris cleared up the misunderstanding with a public warning in the *Clipper* the following week. An imposter was on the prowl, he said, a man posing as a business agent who offered bogus contracts with the intention of stealing an agent's percentage. Doris asked that all parties "keep a wary eye on this individual, who has no connection with this show in any way."

Inter-Ocean performers continued to enjoy good notices in every town where they "spread canvas." Doris clipped the local reviews and sent an assortment for the *Clipper*'s weekly "Circus News" column.

> "The trapeze performance of Millie Tournour is a revelation of Woman's strength and courage."

> "Zazel is a 'daisy,' pretty, lively, finely formed, . . . the very queen of performers."

> "William Showles, the daring bareback-rider, accomplishes apparent impossibilities and utterly disregards the laws of gravity. . . . We saw yesterday what we never saw before, a man throw a forward somersault and the horse going full gallop."

Millie-Christine gathered her own stack of raves.

> "We have not space to describe the really fine performances of all the different members of the company, but cannot refrain from complimenting Millie Christine."

> "One of the most astonishing things in the show is Miss Millie Christine."

> "Dr. Purday, Dr. Weaver, Dr. Pratt and others went to see the wonderful double woman . . . this afternoon. They pronounced her a remarkable being."

> "Millie Christine, The Two-headed Lady, has become quite

popular here, her intelligent, affable manner drawing all towards her."

"Millie-Christine are very much attached to each other, and
never tire of each other's company. At each performance they
appear in the ring on an improvised floor, where, besides dancing, they sing a pretty duet."

"Millie Christine and Christine Millie, the two—no, the
one young lady, who is the fortunate possessor of two heads
and four feet—was next introduced, and entertained them
with singing and dancing. This wonderful freak of nature is
well worth seeing, and makes an entire exhibition in herself
or their selves."

Johnny Patterson was still in top form. A feature writer prowl-
ing the tents one day asked the circus's press agent to introduce him
to the famous Johnny. "Patterson is a broth of a boy and genuine
Irish clown," he reported, "with a rich, tuneful brogue that is pleasant to the ear." Patterson loved working with Inter-Ocean because it
was a solid, old-fashioned circus that didn't drive the audience cross-
eyed trying to watch too many acts at once. He wouldn't travel with
a two-ring circus, Johnny told the reporter, because the attention of
the people was so divided that it made a clown's work too much like
manual labor to suit his instincts. "He says the only being he knows
who can properly appreciate a two-ringed circus is Millie Christine,
the double-headed woman."

Inter-Ocean was on the jump between New Haven and Providence when word arrived that General Tom Thumb had collapsed
and died at his Connecticut estate. He'd suffered apoplexy—a major
stroke. Tom was only forty-six. He'd lived a rich life with Lavinia—
too rich, for he'd grown as round as the billiard balls on his custom-

built table. His oldest friend, P. T. Barnum, immediately wired Tom's Lavinia. "Yourself and family have my warmest sympathies. Death is as much a part of The Divine Plan as birth," his telegram said in part. He and ten thousand other mourners attended Tom's funeral. Barnum had been in New Hampshire shortly before the sad news came. Even on vacation, he never neglected business. "I am at the top of Mount Washington," he telegraphed the New York papers. "It is the *second* Greatest Show on earth."

Inter-Ocean toured New Hampshire that same month. In Portsmouth, bareback rider Sallie Marks celebrated a special occasion. She finished her act and dashed from the ring, but before she could leave the tent, the ringmaster called her back. The "Petite Princess of the Arena," he announced to the crowd, was celebrating her birthday. The beaming Sallie accepted cheers from the audience and an armful of gifts from fellow performers. She was sweet sixteen, and if she'd never been kissed by Willie Showles, chances are it happened that very day, for sparks were flying between them, as everyone in the circus couldn't help notice.

Out west in September, Inter-Ocean entered a neck-and-neck routing race with W. W. Cole's circus. Cole pulled into Boonville, Missouri, one week ahead of Doris's train, which meant that lots of potential customers had their fill of circuses and were broke by the time Inter-Ocean arrived. To fight the competition and keep up with the times, Doris reluctantly set up a second ring. Most old-timers agreed with Johnny Patterson that it was a shame to split the audience's attention. Doris understood how they felt. He'd been a performer himself. But Inter-Ocean would be running a marathon against Cole for the rest of the season, and a double-ring show might give it an edge.

His people grumbled, but they were professionals, right down

to the sawdust rakers. They altered their acts and learned to play
two rings at the same time as smoothly as if they'd always worked
tandem. "Doris' Inter-Ocean Circus, which gave two entertainments
here on Wednesday last was as good as has visited Boonville in years,"
the *Weekly Advertiser* said. "There were two rings and two performances were kept going all the time, so that there was really more
show than the audience could well keep in sight."

The Inter-Ocean company would remember Boonville, a town
on a bluff above the Missouri River. One section of the circus train
"ditched" off the Missouri Pacific Railroad track west of town. Two
brothers who worked for the circus were badly injured in the wreck;
two workhorses were hurt, and the gorgeous bandwagon and the
"Flying Pegasus" chariot were demolished. Another Boonville occur-
rence made for a happier memory. Sallie Marks and Willie Showles
took time out for a wedding ceremony.

Doris managed to outdistance W. W. Cole as they ran their shows
through Texas in late fall. He booked Inter-Ocean into San Antonio,
Columbus, Galveston, and Houston a week or so ahead of Cole and
took the early-comer profits.

Inter-Ocean closed the season in Newport, Arkansas. The twins
said good-bye to Mr. Doris and the friends they'd lived with for the
past two years. They were leaving Inter-Ocean for good. This time,
the twins were truly going home. They had earned more than enough
to build and furnish the grand house Millie had designed. She was
the artistic one, everyone always said.

The twins would not give up touring—not as long as the public
still desired to see them and converse with them. As they had declared in their lawsuit, exhibiting themselves had always been their
livelihood, their way of becoming independent. They'd lay off for

longer intervals between jobs, however, and enjoy ordinary life at their own fine home on family land.

Joyfully, they packed their trunks and marked them care of the Whiteville, North Carolina, depot.

Chapter 18

BIGGER and BETTER. Last Year a Wonder. GRANDER and RICHER. This Year a Marvel.

Barnum & London circus ad, 1886

Clipper columns offered a handy way for roaming show people to keep track of each other's comings and goings and to keep in touch.

A *Clipper* post-office service held performers' letters until they called for them and published a weekly alphabetized column of men's and ladies' newly arrived mail. A letter for "Christeen, Millie" showed up on a late-August list, waiting to be picked up when she stopped by the office at the end of her Inter-Ocean tour.

Weekly columns noted arrivals and departures. "Deaths in the Profession" told of final journeys. Paid-advertisement pages served as weekly bulletin boards. They included personal items like "Write immediately to me at Tony Pastor's" and announcements of new business ventures. A retired fire-eater, for example—"the Original and only DIBOLO, King of Fire"—spread word about a new saloon he'd opened in Chicago. "Would be pleased to see or hear from my friends in show bis," he said. Bond & Lillard's and McBreyer Whiskeys were his specialty, he promised, and the *New York Clipper* was on file for browsing.

An intriguing personal message appeared for Joe on January 13, 1884: "MR. JOS. P. SMITH, Will you please give your Home address in this paper, and oblige a late arrival from Paris, who longs to see you." There were three dashes in place of a signature. Poor lady, assuming it was a lady. There was no answering word from Joe in the *Clipper* the next Saturday or any future Saturday.

For an entire season after they left the circus, the twins stayed out of the public eye and the *Clipper* columns. They were busy arranging their fine new house. There were fourteen rooms for Millie to decorate—or twelve or ten, depending on who was remembering—with high ceilings to stir the summer breezes, extrawide doorways, and a special storage room for their baggage and the countless gifts they'd collected during their lifetime of travel. Their furniture included a curious, curvy, oversize chair made entirely from the horns of Texas longhorn cattle, cunningly laced together with leather thongs. The wonderful settee, some people said, was a present from Buffalo Bill. Others claimed that the twins had paid five hundred dollars for it out west.

Joe spent the winter at his South Carolina villa. He was a handsome and well-bred bachelor who had hobnobbed with royalty. Naturally, he was in great demand at parties in Branchville and St. George, as well as up in Spartanburg.

As for Millie-Christine's social life, she made a point of welcoming neighbors from Welches Creek and Whiteville and visitors from afar. Anyone might drop in during the week, as long as they gave her fair warning. Sundays were reserved for people of color and friends whose only free hours fell that day. Jacob and Monemia lived next door. The McKoy brothers and sisters had built their own places close by. All the family called her by the sweet, plain name "Sister" and treated her as though she were nobody special.

In June 1884, Millie-Christine packed her travel-scarred trunks for yet another English tour. Joe notified the *Clipper* so friends and business contacts would know where to find her: "MILLIE CHRIS-TINE, two-headed girl, sailed for Europe June 17 on the steamer Wisconsin." The "Foreign News" column reported that Millie-Christine's party arrived safely in London on Saturday, June 28.

The twins appeared at Marlborough House the following Monday, greeted by the Prince of Wales and "a large assembly of Royalty," according to the *London Times*. "Piccadilly Hall was closed last night, for Millie and Chrissie were commanded to appear at Marlborough House—her third time there."

While they were in London, a mishap caused some giggles at the Metropolitan Theatre. A ballet dancer hit upon the idea of liter-ally outshining the rest of the cast by using an electric light bulb as part of her costume. "Sometimes she places it in her hair, next as a brooch, while recently she adjusted it at the bottom of her skirts," said the *Clipper*. "The carpenters and scene-shifters were not prepared for this, and when Mrs. D'Auban was making a speedy exit one of the men, imagining that her dress was on fire, pounced upon her and rolled her over and over, to the intense disgust of the lady and her husband," but to the great delight of the other dancers.

Millie-Christine may have chuckled over the story, but for the most part, laughter was scarce that season. She worried over her

Millie-Christine wearing the diamond hair clips presented by Queen Victoria
THE REGIONAL MUSEUM OF SPARTANBURG COUNTY, SPARTANBURG, SOUTH CAROLINA

longtime English companion, Blanche Brook, who fainted with dizzy spells and simply wasn't herself. Joe extended the exhibition dates, and Millie-Christine stayed on in England, waiting for Blanche to grow stronger. In early October, Joe sent an announcement to the *Clipper*: "To Acquaintances, and others who have written offering engagements to MISS MILLIE CHRISTINE . . . I take this method of answering. Will first thank them for offers, next wish them all a prosperous season, and in conclusion say that Miss Millie Christine will not accept of any engagements in America the present season."

Worry and prayers and doctors' remedies could not mend Blanche's failing heart. In October, the grieving Millie-Christine sent off an item for the *Clipper* to print under "Deaths in the Profession": "BLANCHE BROOK (for the past ten years the faithful and constant companion of Millie Christine) died suddenly of heart-disease at the home of her sister, in Manchester, Eng., Oct. 20. For several weeks previous she had been ailing and under medical treatment, but was confined neither to room nor house until three days before her death. Her loss will be deeply felt by many friends in distant lands."

Shortly after the funeral, Millie-Christine gave long-distance approval to a settlement the Fort Wayne lawyers had hammered out with Adam Forepaugh on the old libel charge. Before leaving the States, Millie-Christine had withdrawn her twenty-five-thousand-dollar lawsuit and refiled a ten-thousand-dollar claim. Whatever the amount Forepaugh finally paid her, it was enough to convince her to skip the turmoil of a trial. The damage suit was settled in United States Circuit Court, District of Indiana, "Mr. Forepaugh paying the costs and having the case withdrawn from the docket," said a December 1884 *Clipper*.

Millie-Christine lingered in England, renewing old friendships and entertaining a new generation of visitors who'd never had a chance to see her. As her departure date neared, she exhibited at a Liverpool wax museum. "Miss Christine gave her first reception on Monday afternoon at Reynolds' Exhibition, when a large number of visitors shook her by the hands, enjoyed her singing, and engaged in conversation with this wonderful two headed lady," the *Clipper* reported. "She was dressed in an exceedingly neat style, and on each bosom she wore a handsome brooch which had been given to her by the Princess of Wales." Joe later boasted to friends at home that the engagement brought Reynolds its largest house ever.

✌✌✌

Millie-Christine and Joe returned to the States a year to the day after they'd left. Her newest updated biographical *Description* proclaimed that she'd now appeared "Four Times by Command before the Royal Family."

"MISS MILLIE CHRISTINE, THE 2-HEADED NIGHTINGALE, arrived in New York from Europe on Wednesday past, June 17," said a double-column *Clipper* ad. "Anyone wishing to engage her, or them, will please address her manager, JOS. P. SMITH, at his home."

Joe also sent a personal note via a friend's confidential *Clipper* mailbox number: "J. P. sends kind regards to 142 and hopes to have a letter soon. He brought over with him this time a Marquis, a Sir and a Prince." Presumably, Joe hoped this new trio of titled gentlemen would meet with show-business success, as had Count Rosebud and Baron Littlefinger when they sailed back with him seven years earlier. The Magri brothers had brightened Millie-Christine's show for a season. Then, when she joined Inter-Ocean, they'd gone off on their own. They'd done very well for themselves, especially charming little Count Rosebud.

In fact, while Millie-Christine and Joe were away in England, they missed the count's stylish wedding to Lavinia Stratton. Luckily, there was full *Clipper* coverage to keep them informed: "Mrs. Gen. Tom Thumb became the wife of Count Rosebud (or Count Primo Magri, as his Italian title more properly is)," on April 6 at the Church of the Holy Trinity in New York. The guests—"only those were admitted who had received cards"—crowded the service. Show people like Tony Pastor, Colonel Bunnell, and Frank Uffner attended, as did Mrs. Astor and other society people. Barnum missed Lavinia's second wedding, but he sent the bride a darling brooch in the form of a bee, with an opal head, a body of two huge rubies, ruby eyes, and diamond wings.

Tiny Lucy Adams served as a bridesmaid. Lucy, a descendant of the family that produced Samuel Adams and President John Quincy Adams, sang with Lavinia's Lilliputian Opera Company. Lavinia's brother-in-law, Edward Newell—"General Grant Jr."—was best man. Newell had married Lavinia's sister Minnie; poor Minnie had perished trying to birth their full-sized baby.

Lavinia's gown was "a symphony in amethyst, with velvet frieze decollette, court train, with white lace front embroidered in pearls and peacock feathers, and with tiny shoulder-strap sleeves, with a fall of rich white lace about the neck," said the *Clipper*. Diamonds sparkled in her hair, and she carried a large bouquet of roses. Guests climbed onto the pews, the better to see the ceremony. The newlyweds then sailed off for a long honeymoon in Bologna, Italy, so Millie-Christine had no chance to congratulate her old singing partner and the new Countess Magri.

Millie-Christine also missed a funeral while she was away. The Great Zazel, "the Human Cannon Ball"—daring, beautiful Zazel—had died in March while bringing a baby into the world. She was twenty-two. "The child born to Zazel in her last hours is dead, and is buried with its mother," the *Clipper* said.

Safely home in Columbus County, the twins rested, enjoyed family life, and brought their wardrobe up to date while they waited to see what would turn up. The sisters had made their own clothes for years, both everyday dresses and fancy gowns. They'd always been smartly turned out, not counting a dowdy outfit or two right after the war. Mrs. Smith had taught them the mysteries of ruffling and smocking and sewing on yards of ribbon trim with invisible stitches. Their final fittings, though, required help. Millie tended to lean forward to avoid rubbing Chrissie's shoulder, which made for tedious alterations and refittings. An important part of Blanche Brook's duties had been as wardrobe mistress. At home now, working on new costumes, the twins' younger sister Clarah took Blanche's place. Clarah, a wizard with a needle, was willing to kneel patiently with a mouthful of pins while the twins slowly rotated so she could straighten endless skirt hems.

The circuses had already been on the road for a couple of months. Circus business in general was very bad. Small shows like Inter-Ocean were struggling to survive the 1885 season. Inter-Ocean played to very poor business at Fort Wayne in May. Everything seemed against Mr. Doris, including the weather, said a *Clipper* columnist. "A heavy rain set in about seven o'clock and continued for two hours, and very few farmers came to town on account of the threatening weather. I understand they have had very hard luck so far this season." A bill collector from Doris's printer caught up with the show in Fort Wayne and settled a claim for an overdue twenty thousand dollars by taking a chattel mortgage on the circus.

"BAD NEWS FROM THE WHITE TENTS," said a June *Clipper*.

The paper reported that two or three of the smaller shows were in trouble and that "there has been some lively scrambling for coin on more than one occasion. Now one of the big shows is about to hedge."

Adam Forepaugh tacked up a notice in his dressing tent stating that, until further notice, performers would be obliged to eat all meals except breakfast in the cook tent on the lot. That meant no more hotel dinners and suppers. Furthermore, management would no longer arrange for the luxury of hotel accommodations on Sunday layovers. Forepaugh had already slashed salaries by 25 percent.

Another show was far behind on salaries, and at least two major proprietors had taken out big loans. Hints leaked out that even Barnum & London was feeling the pinch of hard times.

❧❀❧

Of course, old P. T. Barnum always bounced back. Millie-Christine, her excited sister Clarah along as companion and helper, joined Barnum & London—"Nine Jumbo Shows United"—for the 1886 season. Barnum, now seventy-five, was happy to share the headaches of running a big road enterprise with younger partners like James Hutchinson. One of his other partners, James Bailey, had temporarily bowed out at the end of the 1885 season. Barnum friend James Cooper and one of Inter-Ocean's old competitors, W. W. Cole, were replacing Bailey on the current tour.

Barnum once said that a good showman needed plenty of soft soap. He and his partners hired publicists who produced enough bubbles to lather up the whole country. If Barnum & London faced hard times, publicist Richard F. "Tody" Hamilton would never admit it. This was the "Sixth Year of the Mighty Compact, Binding Together the Nine Giant Shows of Christendom," he proclaimed. "In the Past Without a Rival, in the Present Without an Equal, With no Probability in the Future for a Superior." At least, not until Barnum and Bailey secretly arranged a powerful new partnership the following year.

Barnum's "dear Jumbo" was with the 1886 show, but in a radically altered state. Four years earlier, Millie-Christine had missed Jumbo's arrival in New York. It was too late now for her or anyone else to see the living " Towering Monarch of His Mighty Race." An unscheduled express had plowed into Jumbo six months earlier as he was ambling to the circus train. Though the engine crushed Jumbo's mammoth skull, the resilient Barnum managed to resurrect his famous attraction. "Double-Jumbo," he called him now. Jumbo's stuffed hide and reassembled skeleton stood ready to roll in the 1886 street parades, mounted on two heavy-duty wagon beds.

As for Millie-Christine's fellow human oddities, Barnum had put out a January call for "Attractive Features of Every Kind. Novelties, Freaks, Sensations, Curiosities, Phenomena, . . . in fact, everything and anything of a remarkable character adapted to exhibition purposes. Every Artist must be First-class. Every Feature must be the Best. None others engaged." Publicist Hamilton figured that the combined height of the giants in the show "exceeds the towers of the Brooklyn Bridge" and that their total weight "would snap asunder the big cables." Chang, "the Chinese Colossus," stood at least seven foot six and stretched to a towering eight feet by wearing thick-soled wooden clogs and a high Oriental cap. At the other extreme, Lucia Zarate, a Mexican midget twenty inches tall, was a vivacious, perfectly proportioned lady said to weigh five pounds.

Tody Hamilton preached a golden rule of advertising to his copywriters: "To state a fact in ordinary language is to permit a doubt concerning the statement." The circus's publicity department pulled out all the stops for Millie-Christine: "WONDROUS MILLIE CHRISTINE,

CHARMING MILLIE CHRISTINE, BEAUTIFUL MILLIE CHRIS-TINE. The most truly remarkable human being of which there is any record. A duality of persons in one. Two living mortals combined. Two minds forming beautiful thoughts, two mouths expressing gentle sentiments and two perfect heads receiving impressions and ideas from one common heart. A veritable Female Janus, with two classic faces looking in opposite directions. Undoubtedly the most agreeable, pleasant, and wonderful of living and breathing objects. Two living branches on one stem, talking and singing simultaneously in different languages."

Barnum & London offered myriad novelties, countless attractions, elegant wardrobes, superlative aerialists, acrobats, and equestrians, a hippodrome for Roman chariot races, and four tents, the main one with three rings. Most wonderful of all, the posters announced, the dazzling show was not only entertaining, it was educational as well. "Civilization's grandest dream realized. A traveling school of universal knowledge for the people—the only public show on earth combining innocent amusement with valuable instruction. THE MUSEUM OF LIVING WONDERS AFFORDS SOUND INFORMATION. THE DOUBLE MENAGERIES TEACH NATURAL HISTORY. THE TRIPLE CIRCUS GIVES USEFUL INSTRUCTION. THE ROMAN HIPPODROME CONVEYS REAL KNOWLEDGE."

Millions of Americans agreed with poet-editor William Cullen Bryant's assessment: "Barnum's show is a place where more information can be gained in an hour than in a month from books."

Barnum & London held a rehearsal at ten o'clock in the morning on Monday, March 22, to prepare for the scheduled Saturday-night grand pyrotechnic street parade. The first performance would take place in Madison Square Garden the following Monday.

But when Saturday came, rain drenched the city. Again, rain forced postponement on Monday and Tuesday nights. "Barnum is in hard luck," said the *Clipper*. Madison Square Garden remained empty. The circus owners prayed for fair weather and shuddered to read that "the big show is getting a big black eye at the send off." Still, they held firm. Circus tradition demanded a parade before the opening performance.

But three days of bad weather shook their resolve. Rain or shine, parade or no parade, the big circus would open Thursday, April 1. The evening before, the skies cleared enough to chance a parade. The spectacle had covered about a quarter of the planned route when another rainstorm let loose. Nevertheless, the sacred procession was accomplished, and the show could go on.

The opening-day house was only fair sized but "notably fashionable in its make-up," according to the *Clipper*. At the evening show, upper-class "circus parties" filled most of the reserved seats, "contributing to the brilliancy of the occasion."

The acts, in order, were these: a pageant in the three rings and around the ellipse; a procession of freaks, Chang leading the way; performing ponies, dogs, and stallions; tumblers, jumpers, and chair balancers; bicyclists; jugglers; roller-skaters; a gladiator act; equestrian Willie Showles; performers on the double high-flying rings and flying trapeze; head balancers and contortionists; a greyhound jockey; trick pigs; an educated ape; trained doves and elephants; the Abdullah Ben Said troupe of Arab acrobats; and on and on and on.

Barnum and his three partners were in attendance on opening day. Jumbo's skeleton proved a great draw.

As the circus continued its two-week New York run, the box

office had to turn customers away. But on April 14, during the closing performance, a rampaging elephant brought the show to the brink of disaster. "Hebe became enraged and acted in so unruly a manner as to startle the other elephants," the *Clipper* reported. The alarmed beasts all dashed out of the ring, and for a moment, the audience panicked. "Fortunately the coolness of the trainers and attendants averted what might have proved a very bad stampede."

That summer, Inter-Ocean's male elephant, Hunkey Dory—who had once slipped out of line in Philadelphia to raid a peanut vendor's cart—brought John Doris both trouble and grief. Poor Hunkey broke his left foreleg when the circus was playing Tarrytown, New York. Doris sent him into the city "to be either killed or cured," said the *Clipper*. The New York vet regretfully chose the first solution. He shot his patient in Central Park, where there was room to butcher the carcass and burn the hide and bones. "The animals in Central Park began on a diet of elephant meat August 20," reported the paper. Hunkey was only about six years old. Doris valued him at five thousand dollars.

That same August week, Barnum's circus, out in Illinois, broke all attendance records when excursion trains pulled into Mendota spilling over with passengers. The afternoon performance delighted an audience of ten thousand. Eight thousand more customers came to the evening show.

A week later, crowds in Rockford also totaled eighteen thousand. One drawing card was a crack baseball team drawn from the circus. Barnum's boys played local clubs across the Midwest. In one particularly exciting game, they demolished a Terre Haute, Indiana, team by a score of 39 to 6. Advance publicity spread the word that Barnum's team was eager to cross bats with local clubs in any city where the circus stopped over on Sunday. Incidentally, added the circus correspondent, "THE CLIPPER is read every week by the boys and is received with open hands and a warm heart, welcome visitor that it is."

❦

Barnum's circus sailed for Europe at season's end, but without Millie-Christine. Instead, she stayed in the States and worked the popular dime-museum circuit.

Millie-Christine spent Thanksgiving 1887 at Frank M. Drew's Cleveland Museum and Theatre. "She sings with both mouths at the same time, and dances most beautiful on her four feet," said Drew's ads. "Refined and cultured, cheerful, happy and contented, and enjoys life as much as any among the millions of people who populate the globe. There is no other—Millie Christine stands alone, and with Christine Millie, is the greatest of all curiosities. FAIL NOT TO SEE HER."

For the double-piano part of her act, Drew later recalled, she could play a simple piece with two hands or an intricate composition with four hands.

"I contracted to bring her to Cleveland," he said. "She was to have so much a week and her hotel and traveling expenses. I took her over to the old Kennard House and the manager started an argument. He said as two mouths had to be fed I would have to pay two board bills. That opened the question, and when she left town the ticket agent compelled me to pay two railroad fares. She was an expensive proposition."

For all his good-natured griping, Drew liked Millie-Christine. "Great girl she was," he recalled fondly.

❦

On the day when John B. Doris's circus went bankrupt, Millie-Christine was packing the house at Lit's Museum in Milwaukee.

By order of the St. Louis Circuit Court, "the late Doris & Colvin's Colossal Shows" fell under the auctioneer's hammer at the St. Louis Fair Grounds on February 23, 1888. Nineteen lots of circus property went to the highest bidder—everything from a sable antelope to a yak, tent poles to railroad cars, a blacksmith's forge to tin soup plates. Among the items to be had were "1 Band Wagon (very handsome, elaborately decorated in gold and mirrors, cost $1,400); various other gold and mirrored street-parade wagons; 3 Racing Chariots (almost new) . . . Steam Calliope (26 pipes, Hobson's make, without a doubt the best ever used on the road, in first-class condition) . . . Red and black trappings and head pieces for horses, Indian blankets, etc." Trade gossip had it that John Doris dreamed of opening a museum in New York City, once he got back on his feet.

By now, every decent-sized city had one or several museums like Drew's or Lit's or Bunnell's, all of them Barnum offshoots—variety houses that charged ten cents for admission and featured special acts and human oddities. An anonymous poet, imagining Millie-Christine and all the dime-show regulars together in an empty museum after closing time, created a rollicking fantasy entitled "The Dime Show Slaughter":

> A battle was fought not long ago—
> A terrible row in a ten-cent show;
> The story, though awful, I give in detail;
> 'Twill fill you with horror, and turn you pale.
>
> The big "Injun" Chief in his feathers and paint
> Had frightened the "Midget" mite into a faint.
> The "Giant" in anger then pounded the cuss
> Who raised all the racket and caused all the fuss.

The "Skeleton" rattled his bones with fear
And said that the "Giant" had too much beer.
But woe to old Bonesie! The fair-haired "Circasian"
Gave him for his "sass" a most terrible thrashin'.

Like Jumbo in fury, the woman of fat
Upset the "Prize Beauty" and down on her sat.
The "Two-headed Lady" came nearly apart—
Each head took a different side from the start.

The riot was fearful when joined by the Band,
And all the "Attractions" were taking a hand.
The conflict it raged in a manner terrific
That never was seen on this side the Pacific.

* * * * * * * * * * * * * *

My muse is too scared to go on with the theme.
'T'was worse than a nightmare or opium dream;
So here I must pause and the curtain let fall,
As the furious Manager enters the hall.

Chapter 19

Where shall we wander at evening,
Seeking retirement's shade,
On its seclusion reposing,
Watching the daylight fade?

Songs of Miss Millie-Christine

*M*illie-Christine's father was seventy-six and anxious about passing along his precious land. Millie-Christine and Jacob McKoy believed with Abraham Lincoln that property is the sweet fruit of labor and a positive good in the world. Jacob valued Millie-Christine's gift so greatly that he worked out a plan to keep it safe in family hands after he was gone.

His last will and testament began in familiar nineteenth-century style: "Being of Sound mind and memory but considering the uncertainty of my Earthly existence . . ." It went on to divide seventy-eight acres among nine children and grandchildren already settled on the place.

First, Jacob left his son Preston half of the section where Preston's house stood. He bequeathed the other half to his granddaughter Frances. "But," said the will, "if her Father Josiah McKoy comes back and want to live with her he can live with her his life time on her half, it being a part of the tract where I now live and where my sons Preston McKoy and Josiah McKoy built and lying on the east side of the Public Cart Way that leads from Love Grove Church to Whiteville."

Second, he left Clarah the upper part of the tract she lived on, bordered on the south "by a cross fence as it now stand between my daughter Clarah McKoy and my Grand Son Coleman McKoy."

Third, he left Coleman the lower part of that tract.

Fourth, he left his son Murphy half of a fourteen-acre tract bought from neighbor Henry Chancy; the other half went to grandchildren Jacob and Paul.

Fifth, he left "my Daughter Millia Christine" the parcels of land "known as the place where I now live including my Dwelling house and other out houses."

Sixth, he left daughter Amy "a piece of land lying west of my house and known as where her house and field now is."

Seventh, he bequeathed "to my beloved wife Manemia McKoy for her use during her natural life And then to Millia Christine all my Personal Property of what Nature or kind Soever."

Eighth, Jacob spelled out his determination to keep the property intact. "My will and desire is that in giveing my Real estate to my Children and Grand Children is for them to keep it into the family and not to sell or mortgage or dispose in any manner to any other Persons except to each other and the one making such conveyances to any other person or persons than one of my heirs it shall be null and void." In case he had not made himself 100 percent clear, Jacob added, "And now to prevent misconseption, my meaning is that my heirs shall not have the right and power to convey any of my land to any person except my lawful heirs down to the third and fourth generation."

He saw the will safely witnessed, and he signed with his mark. The will was entrusted to the Columbus County clerk on May 3, 1888.

Jacob lived for three years more on his Welches Creek land, easy in his mind about his family's future.

For Millie-Christine and Clarah, part of the fun of being home was Sunday-afternoon entertaining on Millie-Christine's wide porch, after church. Relatives and neighbors gossiped, sang, told stories, and caught up with each other's lives. In between the good times at home, Millie-Christine and Clarah would pack and drive off in the two-horse surrey, heading for the depot on the way to a new engagement. "Millie Christine would like to arrange with some responsible party for a tour of the fairs," said a June 1, 1889, ad. "Address Jos. P. Smith, Edisto Villa."

That season, she signed with F. R. Blitz and his partner-wife, Aunt Lou. The Blitzes promptly scheduled all of Millie-Christine's available time for the fall state fairs and expositions and went about putting together a new act: "Wanted, FOR THE FAIRS to travel with the MILLIE CHRISTINE MUSEUM, FIRST CLASS LECTURER, who can make openings; PIANO PLAYER who has a powerful voice, with popular songs; LADY BANJO PLAYERS, who are good singers, or anything that is suitable for an inside or outside attraction." F. R.

Blitz's ad contained a special invitation to an old "blower" friend: "AMBROSE, SIDESHOW TALKER, I will give you more money than any one else will give you, for my show, at the Fairs. Telegraph me. F. R. Blitz, Atlantic City, N.J." He also needed a strong man to handle canvas. Applicants were to name their lowest acceptable salary and be ready to work on September 3.

Blitz and Millie-Christine opened at the Buffalo International Fair. Four days into the engagement, an unintended bit of high-flying excitement enlivened the fair grounds. In the midst of a parachute-jumping demonstration, the daring young chutist's balloon caught fire. "A large portion of it was ablaze as the ascent was being made," a Buffalo correspondent reported. "A jump with the parachute at the proper time saved him from severe if not fatal injury."

Blitz boasted that Millie-Christine was the only real moneymaker at the fair that season. At age thirty-eight, she was still a drawing card—and always would be. But she was no longer the featured attraction she'd once been, and the offers occasionally fell off. At those times, Joe would insert a notice in the *Clipper*. "TO MUSEUM MANAGERS," he advertised in mid-December 1890. "MILLIE CHRISTINE, The CAROLINA TWIN . . . would be pleased to hear from any who do not feel she must go on exhibition in forenoons and Sundays to be able to pay her salary." Parties wishing to engage her could reach Joe at John B. Doris's Harlem Museum, 351 Eighth Avenue, New York City. Millie-Christine again had the pleasure of working with her old Inter-Ocean friend.

During Christmas week that year, she appeared at New Haven, Connecticut, under the management of—of all people!—Frank M. Uffner. Somehow, the showman who once promoted the Double-Headed Bohemian Wonder and called Millie-Christine and Chang and Eng "repulsive" had made peace with her.

Outside a Millie-Christine fairground exhibit, 1890s
The back of the photograph is stamped by a Pennsylvania photographer.

♔

Jacob McKoy died in the spring of 1891, as his fields were sprouting a tender green haze. He had reached age seventy-nine, give or take a year or two for lack of records. Born a slave without hope for anything better, he'd lived the second half of his life as a free landowner in charge of his own affairs, famous because he'd fathered one of nature's great surprises.

P. T. Barnum died that same April. He'd made it to eighty years. In a fond gesture, the *New York Evening Sun* printed his obituary two weeks before he died, so the old showman could enjoy reading what the papers would say about his flamboyant life.

The twins celebrated their fortieth birthday in July. They marked the event with a matching pair of gold rings, each inset with two garnets. They wore the rings forever after.

Beloved friends and relatives vanished as the years spun by. Anna Swan's big body wasted away with consumption; she had died in 1888, two days short of her forty-second birthday. Mary Smith, Millie-Christine's dear "white mama," passed on in 1893 at age seventy-one. Sister Amy McKoy went in 1894. As Jacob wished, Amy left to "my Sister Millia Christine McKoy the tract of land that my Father Jacob McKoy willed to me . . . to enjoy and to hold for her use as she see fitt during her natural life." At Millie-Christine's death, Amy's land would pass to nieces Hattie and Lovittia.

Long after everyone had given up the idea that Joe would ever settle down, the forty-nine-year-old bachelor married Miss Ella McAlhany of St. George, South Carolina.

A year later, in 1896, Millie-Christine's sister Clarah scandalized Welches Creek by marrying twenty-six-year-old Lawrence Yeoman. Clarah was forty-one. She married a "soft" man, as one neighbor described him. Clarah and Lawrence later moved into Millie-Christine's roomy house.

Millie-Christine would never be a mother, but there were plenty of nieces and nephews to dote on and fuss over. Indeed, it was hard to keep track of all the McKoy and Smith babies. Mary Smith's many grandchildren (daughter Annie Smith Johnston, for instance, produced an even dozen offspring) all called her "Aunt Millie-Christine" when she visited Spartanburg.

The tight connection between Millie-Christine and the Smiths passed to new generations. "My mother knew her well," said Mrs. Dicksie Cribb, Mary and Joseph Smith's great-granddaughter, descended through Annie. "My mother told me she had often sat in her lap." Millie-Christine, Mrs. Cribb added, had to sit on a chair without arms. "My mother had her to dinner after she became famous, after she had been to Europe and met all that royalty. Mother always said she was delightful and a real joy to talk to."

The twins wove their way into Smith memories. "They were part of my family!" Mrs. Cribb's daughter once exclaimed to someone who asked if she'd ever heard of the Carolina Twins.

At home in Welches Creek, Millie-Christine was a loving aunt to every McKoy child who came along. "She was always Aunt Millie to me," great-nephew Fred McKoy said. "She named me and clothed me until I was ten years old. The first suit I ever wore, she sent me from Michigan. She was the best Christian-hearted person I ever saw. She'd spend time with everybody." Fred remembered Christmas toys from Aunt Millie, and her wonderful, big two-horse surrey. A dozen people could squeeze into it for a ride to church or the store.

Fred McKoy and all the children loved Millie-Christine's thousand and one stories. Imagine a country boy who'd gone no farther down the road than Whiteville sitting on her front steps listening to stories about circus life. "I often wish I could live the life she lived," Fred said.

A Welches Creek neighbor boy remembered the twins with equal fondness. "I sat on their laps many a day," James P. Troy recalled. "They came back to North Carolina when I was about six years old. They influenced me to try to get an education, not by telling me but by being so very intelligent themselves. They could speak seven different languages fluently. I learned a lot of words from them." Young Troy was struck by a peculiar thing that happened whenever Millie carried on a conversation with one person while Chrissie spoke with someone else. "They could talk to you for hours," he said, "and then, at a certain point, they'd both say the same thing at the same time." He remembered the pump organ in their big house, and the twins' beautiful duets. "They could sing in French, and I would enjoy that because French has a musical sound."

Troy and Fred both remembered the twins as notably religious. "They went to Christian Plain Church," said Fred. "Was a Methodist church. They would go there often for services, and St. John's, they built that themselves. They'd also go to Love Grove Church and Welches Creek Church. St. John's was Methodist, about two miles from their home."

By all accounts, the twins practiced what the pastors preached. "Once, they waited on me when I had typhoid fever and pneumonia," Fred said. "They'd walk about three-fourths of a mile just to care for me."

Millie-Christine organized a school for Welches Creek African American children in 1880. She supported it for the rest of her life, according to great-great-nephew Lloyd Inman, a present-day family descendant. "She built a church and a school for black children and gave money to Shaw University in Raleigh, Bennett College in Greensboro, Johnson C. Smith College, Henderson Institute, and Palmer Institute. But she never got, or wanted, credit for it. Every spring, a gentleman would come to Palmer Institute with money and leave it. They never knew where it came from."

Millie-Christine's body restricted her physically but also freed her. She was able to live outside ordinary social conventions, to walk her own independent path through slavery and freedom and the clampdown that followed.

"She was more than just a circus freak," descendant Inman said. "She was a talented, generous black woman who was one of the greatest black women of her time. She said that when God made her, he gave her two heads and two brains because her responsibility was so great."

Inman's mother passed along to him the family's love, pride, and respect for Aunt Millie-Christine. "She did a lot to bring blacks and whites together because she was someone everyone—black, white, or Indian—in Columbus County could be proud of," he said. "She was also one of the richest people in the county. White folks treated her like an exception, not as a black woman in the South was treated then. She got the finest rooms in hotels." Coming home from a tour, if Millie-Christine and Clarah happened to pull into Whiteville too late to drive on through to Welches Creek, they overnighted at Mrs. Howell's Hotel on the southeast corner of Courthouse Square, the best hotel in town and the favorite residence of young doctors and teachers, circuit judges, out-of-town lawyers, traveling salesmen, lecturers, and entertainers.

Crackling calamity struck the twins' fine house one terrible night in 1909. They and Clarah and her husband escaped before flames roared through the roof. Burning pine timbers crashed down and devoured all the carpets and furniture Millie had chosen. Sitting in the yard on a salvaged trunk, the twins shivered and watched the inferno devour their home. By dawn, a lifetime's worth of treasures and mementos and scrapbooks were gray ash, though someone managed to wrestle out the curious Texas Longhorn chair. Afterward, folks blamed sparks from a faulty chimney flue that Clarah's husband hadn't tended to.

The twins built a six-room cottage and moved in. They were living there when the 1910 census taker, William Dorsett, stopped by to enter them on his list of Welches Creek inhabitants. It was the first time a federal census had ever caught the twins at home. This thirteenth United States tally marked the fifth time that former slaves were named and counted as citizens.

Faced with the dilemma of listing the twins as one person or two, Dorsett decided on two. In the column headed "Name of each person whose place of abode on April 15, 1910 was in this family," he wrote, "McKoy, Millie Christian" on the first line and "Twins" on the second. He noted each as "Head of Family" and wrote "Mu" for mulatto, although he marked all the twins' relatives "B" for black. He recorded their age as fifty-nine and their marital status as single. As for their trade or profession, he wrote, "Public Exhibitor to the Public," and added the explanation, "Working on their own account." He further noted that they were able to read and write and that they owned their own home and farm, free of mortgage.

✌✌✌

Millie never recovered from the fire that destroyed the big house and all its treasures. Fred McKoy believed that exposure to the chill air that night weakened her constitution. She'd always been the delicate sister.

At first, Millie's hoarse cough could have been mistaken for a stubborn cold. Clarah may have tried the local time-tested remedy—herbs mixed with cornmeal and onions, cooked into a hot poultice, slathered on soft flannel, and laid on the chest.

But sooner or later, the family had to face the truth. Millie was wasting away with tuberculosis. "Consumption," old-timers called it. The "White Plague" had swept into the twentieth century unchecked. During the first decade, tuberculosis carried off four hundred Americans daily. Whatever name people called it, its symptoms were unmistakable. Chrissie probably suspected early on, when Millie's violent coughing fits shook them both awake at night. Millie certainly knew, tasting the blood and pus she spat into her handkerchief. Clarah, changing Millie's sweat-soaked nightdresses for fresh ones, must have worried over her ashy pallor. Christine remained healthy, though both twins now lived in the shadow of death.

Chrissie's handwriting—by long habit, she handled most correspondence—was steady and clear as ever in a letter to a niece dated April 26, 1911. "My dear Ella," she began. "We are glad your letter left all well, hope this will find each the same. You need not be ashamed about not having written. There are often things to prevent."

The twins' religious convictions deepened as Millie worsened, and niece Ella had warmed their hearts by writing to tell of her own recent conversion. "We too are so glad you can give Praises to One that is greater than all the world," Chrissie continued. As she wrote, she skipped easily between "we" and "I." "Dear aunty's and our words were strange to you in those days and hard to understand. I can of course see why you would feel lonesome. We are glad more than we can tell that you are no longer in the dark.

"It is so nice to have faith in Our Lord Jesus, the Saviour of mankind," continued Chrissie. "Yes, there is nothing like being able to feel His glorious Presence, when earthly friends are gone. Yes, we must always pray for each other. Yes, we will have trials and tribulations as long as we dwell here, but they are meant for a purpose and we will win crowns if we hold out to the end. No, we must never forget our Saviour. I will close now, hoping to hear from you again when you have time, and feel like writing. With much love to and from all I am as ever your very affectionate Aunt Chrissie-Millie."

Whiteville doctor William Crowell recommended that the twins try a rest cure at a tuberculosis sanatorium up north. They counted their dwindling money, sold some of the lovely jewelry Millie had once delighted in choosing, and left home for a stay of several months. It's unknown where they "cured." Tuberculosis patients avoided publicity. Saranac Lake, New York, would have been a good choice, for some of the specialized "cure cottages" in that village catered to circus people.

Wherever they stayed, the standard practice was to spend each day outside on an open porch in the fresh air, resting in a wide Adirondack recliner. The twins slept either on a sheltered porch or in a bedroom with wide-open windows. Millie may have breathed the fumes of tar rosin to clear her lungs, as some specialists ordered. Or she may have sipped sulfurous water from a heavy agate cup, as patients did at Saratoga Springs.

❧❧❧

Chapter 20

O angel, sweet angel, I pray thee
Let the beautiful gates ajar,
Only a little, I pray you,
Let the heavenly gates ajar.

Songs of Miss Millie-Christine

T he twins returned to Welches Creek with Millie uncured.

One Sunday during the summer of 1912, the sisters exchanged Methodist ways for Baptist. They settled themselves in a sturdy chair and let a local minister and several strong helpers plunge them under and raise them up streaming with the waters of baptism, witnessed by a large gathering of the curious.

A doleful Baptist hymn, "Come, Ye Disconsolate," which promises a heavenly remedy for earthly anguish, had become one of their favorites. "Here speaks the Comforter," they would sing, "tenderly saying, 'Earth has no sorrow that heav'n cannot cure.'"

Millie-Christine signed her last will and testament in an uncharacteristically shaky hand in September 1912. She left her real estate and personal belongings to "my beloved Sister Clarrah Yeoman to have and to hold . . . during all of her natural life." After Clarah's death, everything would pass to four nieces—one named Millia Christine, the others Flossey, Isabella, and Emma.

ᘐᘖᘗ

In the Bunkers' case, Chang had died in his sleep, alone except for his ever-present brother sleeping beside him. Eng soon followed, panicky and unattended by a physician.

By contrast, Dr. Crowell was on hand to offer what help he could to the sisters. The family sent for him early on Tuesday, October 8, 1912. Before he drove out to the house, Crowell called Johns Hopkins Medical College to ask if he should make a last-minute effort to separate them. The doctors told him what he already knew. After Millie passed away, he should comfort Christine with massive doses of morphine and let the sisters leave the world as they had entered it— together.

He called Raleigh next, according to Whiteville historian Frances Sessions, and left an urgent message for Governor William Kitchin asking official permission to speed Chrissie on her way after her sister died.

Dr. Crowell then drove out to Welches Creek. He sat with Clarah and the family as evening came on, alert to any change in Millie. It was six o'clock, getting on toward dusk. Chrissie was the one who first realized Millie was gone. "She passed away as in a dream, a peaceful dream," Chrissie told the doctor.

The news flashed over the country in an Associated Newspapers dispatch. "The death of Millie, one of the famous Millie-Christine twins," said a Cincinnati paper, "is a matter of interest to hundreds of

Cincinnatians who saw the twins when they were on exhibition at a Vine street museum years ago. . . . The dispatches from the home of the twins near Wilmington, N.C., state that Christine's death is expected to follow in a few days. Whether a heroic surgical operation would save the life of Christine is a question that has been asked by doctors."

Chrissie's strong body fought to stay alive. Some accounts say she lingered eight hours, others seventeen. Dr. Crowell's opiates soothed her as the night dragged on. She sang hymns—her voice rising and falling alone without Millie's rich contralto—and prayed for release. At long last, the governor's message arrived allowing Dr. Crowell to increase the dosage and ease Chrissie through the heavenly gates she and Millie used to sing about.

"There was a wake for Millie-Christine, about two nights, near as I can remember," Fred McKoy said. Carpenter Harley Armstrong, her neighbor, built a double coffin of cypress lumber. He attached six store-bought metal handles, three on each side, for the pallbearers to grasp.

The twins had wanted to be cremated. They'd been horrified when Dr. Pancoast shipped the Siamese Twins to Philadelphia for autopsy. Even after family members swore they would never let that happen, the sisters had cause for worry. As Millie grew sicker, rumors circulated that graverobbers were scheming to dig up the twins for a sideshow exhibit. When he learned that the sisters were fretting, Joe Smith promised he would hire a guard to stand watch day and night.

The funeral crowd filled the small Baptist church near the twins' home and overflowed into the yard. It was standing room only. They would have appreciated that.

McKoy brothers and nephews shoveled out a four-by-six-foot

hole in the family graveyard at the edge of a cornfield and braced the sides with heart-pine boards to hold back loose dirt. Water lay only five feet below ground in that part of the county. The men stopped excavating just short of that depth. After the funeral service, they lowered the cypress coffin into the swampy Columbus County land.

The grave marker was as unusual as Millie-Christine. A craftsman shaped lead sheets into two joined arches and embossed them with raised letters. One arch said, "Millie-Christine, born July 11th, 1851, Columbus County, N.C. Child or children of Jacob and Monemia McCoy. She lived a life of much comfort owing to her love of God and joy in following His commands. A real friend to the needy of both races and loved by all who knew her." Inscribed on the second arch was this: "Christine-Millie, died October 8th and 9th, 1912. Fully resigned at her home, the place of her birth and residence of her Christian parents. 'They that be planted in the house of the Lord shall flourish in the courts of our God.' Ps. 92:13." Two more lines of raised letters bridged the arches: "A soul with two thoughts. Two hearts that beat as one."

Joe's watchman and Millie-Christine's family kept an eye on the grave for nine long months. It lay peaceful and undisturbed.

Over the decades, brush and brambles conquered the old burial ground. Then a pinewoods fire raged over the site and swept away most traces.

Fred McKoy found a piece of the metal marker with part of the inscription still legible. He took it home and kept it with Millie-Christine's old hump-top trunk, where she'd sat watching the big house burn.

Much later, when Fred was an old man, someone from the Smith family offered to buy the trunk. "Oh, no," Fred told him. "That's a mark from Millie-Christine, and I can't part with it."

Epilogue

> And all that's left of the bright, bright dream,
> With its thousand brilliant phases,
> Is a handful of dust, in a coffin hid,
> A coffin under the daisies.
>
> *Songs of Miss Millie-Christine*

Millie-Christine played one last public engagement.

Fifty-seven years after her death, the Columbus County Historical Society and the North Carolina Department of Archives and History asked permission from Millie-Christine's kinfolk to open her bramble-covered grave.

On a November Saturday in 1969, Fred McKoy led historical society members and two professional preservationists to a section of Welches Creek where field met woods. Even before they set to work clearing the area, they could see the outline of a four-by-six-foot depression.

They photographed the site as they found it, then staked off a ten-by-seventeen-foot area with the depression in the center. Working that rectangular piece of ground, they slashed away underbrush, raked scrub-oak leaves aside, stripped off turf. Fifteen inches from the sunken grave, diggers found the base of the original marker and several broken and melted pieces of lead with raised letters spelling parts of Millie-Christine's epitaph.

The excavation continued. The crew members found several flower bulbs buried over the grave and set them aside for replanting. Fifty-one inches below ground level, they discovered three layers of thick cypress boards. The lowest, which had formed the casket bottom, sat on white sand. The fallen lid lay in the middle and the collapsed sideboards above that. On top of the stack, covered by water that had seeped in and preserved the boards, lay six metal casket handles.

The experts troweled and sifted and carefully gathered the few earthly remains of the twins. Nature had nearly completed its work of returning dust to dust. All that was left of the sisters was a handful of bone fragments and what appeared to be a spinal vertebra—a poignant reminder of their joined bodies.

The rest was a small collection of man-made items: a scrap of the black alpaca dress the twins were buried in; a small, white celluloid button with four holes; two sets of upper dentures made of gutta-percha (a dentist's imitation of the sisters' dazzling natural rows of pearly white teeth); and a gutta-percha hairpin. Also remaining was a gold finger ring with two garnet stones, inscribed "M. C. July 1891"; a similar gold ring, with one garnet missing, inscribed "C. M. July 1891," and another ring found positioned as if it had been worn on the same finger. This extra ring, which must have belonged to Chrissie, was a gold band inlaid with blue enamel. The letters on the outer surface spelled out "AS GOD DECREED, WE AGREED," a nearly perfect five-word summary of the twins' courageous lives.

The remnants were placed in a one-by-three-foot pine box. The next day—a wind-swept Sunday afternoon—a proud and respectful crowd of neighbors, kin, and state officials gathered at Welches Creek Community Cemetery, just down the road from the old McKoy burial ground. Fred stood foremost among the notables as they watched the burial of the box and the rescued flower bulbs in Millie-Christine's new resting place at the front corner of the cemetery. There were speeches. Someone placed a large bouquet of fresh flowers at the base of the handsome polished-granite headstone.

The wide marker lies nearly flat in the cemetery grass. The stone-cutter fashioned it higher at the back edge, so the surface slopes toward visitors and the words are easy to read. Incised letters spell out the words once embossed on the old lead marker. A carved banner links the two texts with the same old loving epitaph: "A SOUL WITH TWO THOUGHTS. TWO HEARTS THAT BEAT AS ONE."

Today, standing at the grave, you sense that Welches Creek isn't much changed from the place Millie-Christine loved. Most of the township's roads are paved now, of course. The community cemetery is new since her time, and a state historical marker has been posted beside U.S. 74-76 just east of White Marsh. "MILLE-CHRISTINE," it says, "Negro Siamese twins born near here, 1851. Exhibited in U.S. and Europe. Died in 1912. Grave is five miles N." Visitors approach the cemetery along Mille Christine Road, marked by a green sign.

In its country way, the cemetery is a welcoming place. Graves lie scattered over a rough-clipped meadow. Fresh and artificial bouquets of flowers, bright and gaudy as circus banners, cheer the graves of the recently deceased. Fred's upright headstone—"J. Fred McKoy, May 3, 1887 to Jan. 22, 1983"—stands guard some distance from Millie-Christine's more prominent location.

For the most part, Welches Creek would still feel like home to Millie-Christine and her family. A rooster crows from a nearby farm; a woodpecker drills a hollow tree. Across the dirt lane bordering Millie-Christine's corner are rows of corn and a rust-roofed tobacco barn half-hidden behind oaks and pines. Farther away, down toward the swamp, cypress trees still stand up to their knobby knees in amber water.

The little blue-enameled ring with its brave motto—"AS GOD DECREED, WE AGREED"—and the matching rings set with garnets again lie buried out of sight, as forgotten as the twins' old songs. They are lost reminders of Millie-Christine, now only "a handful of dust, in a coffin hid, a coffin under the daisies."

Acknowledgments

I met Millie-Christine McKoy at the library in Whiteville, North Carolina, in a nine-page booklet by the Columbus County Historical Society. "I often wish I could live the life she lived," said a grand-nephew in that little biography. I wondered what kind of life con-joined, enslaved female twins could possibly have lived, to make him say that. My curiosity resulted in this book.

Beginning with the State Archives in Raleigh, one source led me to another. My thanks go to all the museum archivists, librarians, county clerks, and private collectors who helped me pull together the scattered remnants of Millie-Christine's life.

Special thanks go Dicksie Cribb—Joseph P. Smith's delightful great-granddaughter—who shared her fond and extensive family lore about Millie-Christine. She took time to show me what remains of the old Smith home where Millie-Christine lived in Spartanburg, South Carolina, and Captain Bivings's great intact house, where Millie-Christine took wartime refuge.

I couldn't have done without Millie-Christine's own 1869 booklet, *History and Medical Description of the Two-Headed Girl*, and the updated souvenir biographies that followed. Another indispensable source for information on her long show-business career was the *New York Clipper* weekly newspaper, America's show-business bible during the latter half of the 1800s.

My thanks to my local library specialists, Kaye Brown and Joy Mercer, who summoned copies of the show-business booklets, countless personal reminiscences, pictures, posters, medical descriptions, advertising fliers, and playbills from long ago and far away.

I'm indebted to Bernth Lindfors, professor of English and African literature at the University of Texas in Austin, who found 1850s British newspaper stories that shed light on Millie-Christine's early misadventures and who lent pictures from his remarkable collection on show-business personalities.

Thanks to Steve Gossard for pictures from the Circus Collection at Milner Library, Illinois State University.

I was granted permission to quote from the abridged transcript of Queen Victoria's journal entry for June 24, 1871, by the Royal Archives and Her Majesty, Queen Elizabeth II.

The College of Physicians of Philadelphia sent invaluable medical records on Millie-Christine.

Thanks go to the Robert L. Parkinson Library and the Circus World Museum at Baraboo, Wisconsin, for posters and circus lore;

to Kansas circus historian Orin Copple King for information on Millie-Christine out west; and to Ted Bowman for Inter-Ocean's travel routes.

The vicious circus rat sheet preserved in the Parkinson collection seemed in a class by itself until Beverly Watkins, the archivist at Chicago's Great Lakes Region National Archives, discovered Millie-Christine's libel action against an even ruder Forepaugh rat sheet.

Merci beaucoup to Kay Hodge and Peggy Crawford, who helped me translate French accounts of Millie-Christine in Paris.

Brooklyn historian E. A. "Bud" Livingston contributed the lively 1881 newspaper interview.

Fittingly, the Columbus County Library in Whiteville, where I found the little historical-society booklet, also held local accounts of Millie-Christine's hometown life in retirement, including a treasured letter from her.

My warm appreciation to Carolyn Sakowski and her able staff at John F. Blair, Publisher, and especially to editor Steve Kirk, who worked nearly as hard as I did to make a good book of Millie-Christine's life story.

Above all, I give my heartfelt thanks to my husband, Bob, for his endless patience and unswerving enthusiasm.

Bibliography

Batcheller & Doris' Great Inter-Ocean Show. *Description and Songs of Miss Millie-Christine, the Two-Headed Nightingale.* New York: Torrey & Clark, 1882.

Benson, E. F. *Queen Victoria.* Longmans, Green and Company, 1935.

Bertillon, Dr. "Mesdemoiselles Millie et Christine." *La Nature* (January 3, 1874): 63–68.

Biographical Sketch of Millie Christine, the Carolina Twin, Surnamed the Two-Headed Nightingale and the Eighth Wonder of the World. C. 1889. This pamphlet is available at The Library Company in Philadelphia.

Biographical Sketch of Millie Christine, the Two-Headed Nightingale. 1871. This pamphlet is available at the British Library in London.

Blakely, Phyllis R. *Nova Scotia's Two Remarkable Giants.* Windsor, Nova Scotia: Lancelot Press, 1970.

Bogdan, Robert. *Freak Shows: Presenting Human Oddities for Amusement and Profit*. Chicago: University of Chicago Press, 1988.

Broca, Paul. "Communications: le résultat de son examen du monstre connu sous le nom de Millie-Christine." *Bulletin de l'Académie de médecine* (January 13, 1874): 39–44.

Buckmaster, Henrietta. *Let My People Go*. New York: Harper and Brothers, 1941.

Columbus County Historical Society. *Mille-Christine: Columbus County's Siamese Twins*. 1969.

Courtney, Ann, and Ward Little, eds. *Columbus County, North Carolina, Recollections and Records*. Columbus County Commissioners and Columbus County Public Library, 1980.

Drimmer, Frederick. *Very Special People*. New York: Amjon Publishers, 1973.

Feller, Bruce. *Under the Big Top*. New York: Scribner's, 1995.

Fiedler, Leslie. *Freaks: Myths and Images of the Secret Self*. New York: Anchor Books, 1978.

Fisher, George J. *Diploteratology*. Albany, N.Y.: Van Benthuysen's Steam Printing House, 1868. This publication is available at the library of the College of Physicians of Philadelphia.

Gallos, Philip L. *Cure Cottages of Saranac Lake: Architecture and History of a Pioneer Health Resort*. Saranac Lake, N.Y.: Historic Saranac Lake, 1985.

Gash, Leander. Papers. North Carolina Archives. Letter to Adeline Gash, February 11, 1866.

Gedda, Luigi. *Twins in History and Science*. Springfield, Ill.: Charles C. Thomas, Publisher.

"The Giants' Wedding." *Harper's Bazaar* (July 29, 1871): 477–78.

Glass, Paul, and Louis C. Singer. *Singing Soldiers: A History of the Civil War in Song*. New York: Da Capo Press, 1975.

Gould, George M., and Walter L. Pyle. *Anomalies and Curiosities of Medicine*. Philadelphia: W. B. Saunders Company, 1897.

Graham, Lloyd. "Blondin, the Hero of Niagara." *American Heritage* (August 1958): 35–37, 106–7.

Gwathmey, Emily, and Ellen Stern. *Sister Sets*. New York: William Morrow and Company, 1997.

Harris, Neil. *Humbug: The Art of P. T. Barnum*. New York: Little, Brown and Company, 1973.

Hibbert, Christopher. *Queen Victoria in Her Letters*. New York: Viking, 1985.

Huber, Leonard V. "Heyday of the Floating Palace." *American Heritage* (October 1957): 15–25, 96–98.

Hurmence, Belinda, ed. *My Folks Don't Want Me to Talk about Slavery*. Winston-Salem, N.C.: John F. Blair, Publisher, 1984.

Jackson, J. B. S. "The Carolina Sisters." *Boston Medical and Surgical Journal* (February–August 1869): 414–16.

Jennings, John J. *Theatrical and Circus Life*. St. Louis: Sun Publishing, 1883.

King, Orin Copple. "Only Big Show Coming." *Bandwagon: The Journal of the Circus Historical Society* 41 (May–June 1997): 37–42.

Kunhardt, Philip B., Jr., Philip B. Kunhardt III, and Peter W. Kunhardt. *P. T. Barnum: America's Greatest Showman*. New York: Alfred A. Knopf, 1995.

Lindfors, Bernth. "The United African Twins on Tour: A Captivity Narrative." *South African Theatre Journal* 2 (September 1988): 16–36.

Major, Ralph H. *A History of Medicine*. Vol. 2. Springfield, Ill.: Charles C. Thomas, Publisher, 1954.

McKoy, Millie-Christine. *History and Medical Description of the Two-Headed Girl*. Buffalo, N.Y.: Warren, Johnson and Company, 1869.

Medley, Mary L. *History of Anson County, North Carolina, 1750–1976*. Wadesboro, N.C.: Anson County Historical Society, 1976.

New York Clipper, May 7, 1853–October 26, 1912.

News and Observer (Raleigh), October 12–17, 1853; November 29, 1925; March 8, 1984.

Ogden, Tom. *Two Hundred Years of the American Circus*. New York: Facts on File, 1993.

Packard, Francis R. *History of Medicine in the United States.* Vol. 2. New York: Hafner Press.

Pancoast, William H. "The Carolina Twins." *Photographic Review of Medicine and Surgery* (1870–71): 43–57.

Parkinson, Tom, and Charles Philip Fox. *The Circus Moves by Rail.* Boulder, Colo.: Pruett Publishing Company, 1978.

Ramsbotham, F. H. "A Description of the United African Twins." *Medical Times and Gazette* of London (September 29, 1855): 313.

Robinson, Rebecca. "Memories of the Siamese Twins." *Kin'lin'*, Hallsboro, N.C., High School publication (1976–77): 39–41.

Robinson, Victor. *The Story of Medicine.* New York: Tudor Publishing Company, 1931.

Rothman, Sheila M. *Living in the Shadow of Death: Tuberculosis and the Social Experience of Illness in American History.* New York: Basic Books, 1994.

Shapiro, Larry, ed. *Abraham Lincoln, Mystic Chords of Memory: A Selection from Lincoln's Writings.* New York: Book-of-the-Month Club, 1984.

"Siamese Twins." *Nova* show #2205, air date February 14, 1995.

Smith, William Alexander, and W. Thomas Smith, compilers. *Family Tree Book: Genealogical and Biographical.* W. Thomas Smith, 1922.

Stem, Thad. *The Tar Heel Press.* Southport, N.C.: North Carolina Press Association, 1973.

Stowe, Harriet Beecher. *Uncle Tom's Cabin.* 1852. Reprint, New York: Bantam, 1981.

Sullivan, Cheryl C. "A Strange Kind of Bondage." *American History Illustrated* (November 1979): 48–49.

Tardieu, Dr. "Communications: le résultat de son examen du monstre connu sous le nom de Millie-Christine." *Bulletin de l'Académie de médecine* (January 13, 1874): 36–39.

Thomson, Rosemarie Garland, ed. *Freakery: Cultural Spectacles of the Extraordinary Body.* New York: New York University Press.

Thoreau, Henry D. "Quebec and Montmorency." In *Great American Travel Writings: A Journey around America.* New York: Mallard Press, 1990.

————. "A Yankee in Canada." In *The Portable Thoreau*, edited by Carl Bode. New York: Viking Penguin, 1976.

Touchatout. "Millie et Christine." *Le Trombinoscope par Touchatout* (November 1873): 117–20.

Towsen, John H. *Clowns*. New York: Hawthorn Books.

Twain, Mark. *The Autobiography of Mark Twain*. Compiled by Charles Neider. New York: Harper and Brothers, 1959.

————. *The Innocents Abroad*. 1869. Reprint, New York: New American Library, 1980.

————. *Life on the Mississippi*. 1883. Reprint, New York: Bantam, 1990.

Verrier, Dr. "Des Anomalies dans la Nature Organisée." *Gazette Obstétricale* (1874): 13–16.

Walker, Kenneth. *The Story of Medicine*. New York: Oxford University Press, 1955.

Wallace, Irving. *The Fabulous Showman*. New York: Signet Books, 1962.

Wallace, Irving, and Amy Wallace. *The Two*. New York: Bantam, 1979.

Warner, Eugene. "The Carolina Twins." *Sandlapper* (November 1969): 19–21.

Whitney, Ralph. "The Unlucky Collins Line." *American Heritage* (February 1957): 48–53, 100–102.

Wilborn, Elizabeth. "Strange Cargo: North Carolina's Unusual Twins." *North Carolina State Ports* (Summer 1967): 10–11.

Wright, Louis B. *South Carolina: A Bicentennial History*. New York: W. W. Norton, 1976.

Index